THE
MYSTIC
COOKBOOK

praise for

THE MYSTIC COOKBOOK

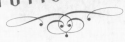

"We can connect with nature, spirit, and family through the food and the ritual behind the food we eat daily.
Read this and see how you can transform your life through the simple act of cooking and eating!"
— MARIEL HEMINGWAY, actress and author of *Mariel's Kitchen*

"This is a charming cookbook written from a quirky and original point of view. Mothers and daughters should love
it, but more important, it taps into something I have always believed—that cooking is the only remaining socially
acceptable form of alchemy." — JOANNE HARRIS, best-selling author of *Chocolat*

"Oh, what a delight of a book. Combining beauty, flavor, and spirit into a daily sacrament called cooking and eating.
Now *that* is what I call holy." — CHRISTIANE NORTHRUP, M.D., author of the *New York Times* bestseller
Women's Bodies, Women's Wisdom

"*The Mystic Cookbook* is a delicious, brilliant, and captivating book that elevates preparing and eating food to the
realm of the magical, mystical, and sacred. . . . It has forever changed the way I view, cook, and ingest food."
— ARIELLE FORD, best-selling author of *Wabi Sabi Love*

"Food isn't just nourishment, it is the thread that connects us to each other and to the earth. In *The Mystic
Cookbook*, Meadow and Denise Linn explore that thread as a source of spiritual learning and well-being. . . . It is
a tenderhearted collaboration that sustains both belly and spirit." — JOSH VIERTEL, sustainable food activist
and former president of Slow Food USA

"*The Mystic Cookbook* is a delicious feast in a deep and soulful way. Filled with recipes, rituals, and endless
reasons to fall in love with cooking and eating, you'll be nourished by a whole new spiritual relationship with food.
. . . I loved every bite of this book!" — CHERYL RICHARDSON, *New York Times* best-selling author of
The Art of Extreme Self-Care

"*The Mystic Cookbook* is absolutely enchanting. Beyond that, it's an outrageously clever way to incorporate
knowledge about nutrition, spiritual rituals, and your health. This book belongs on everyone's bookshelf."
— CAROLINE MYSS, *New York Times* best-selling author of *Defy Gravity* and *Sacred Contracts*

"In a culture that is perennially starved of the sacred, this book is a feast for the soul. . . . Denise and Meadow
give us simple recipes to transform the preparing and eating of food into a celebration of life and spirit."
— SARAH BRIGHTWOOD SZEKELY, president of La Cocina Que Canta, Rancho La Puerta's Culinary
Center and Organic Farm

"You'll not only discover amazing recipes in *The Mystic Cookbook*, but you may even find yourself."
— JAMES F. TWYMAN, author of *Love, God, and the Art of French Cooking*

"I love how Denise and Meadow have shared their culinary talents to help everyone change the way that they look
at and experience food. It's so insightful and has had a powerful impact on me." — LISA WILLIAMS, psychic,
healer, and star of two Lifetime television series

"Meadow's recipes are sure to delight the taste buds, as she and Denise weave the deep wisdom and truth of
our mystical relationship between our food and our selves. The world is hungry for such a book! Savor its magic
and try to resist the urge to gobble up its pages in one sitting." — COLETTE BARON-REID, author of the
international bestseller *The Map*

"Denise and Meadow have written a guide to achieving delicious good health that's empowering, nourishing, and
sure to inspire your journey." — TERRY WALTERS, author of *Clean Food*

"Meadow and Denise's book opens a new world on how to think, love, enjoy, and even heal yourself on a physical,
emotional, and spiritual level, with one of the most enjoyable things in life—real, delicious food!"
— LAURA LYNN KLEIN, co-founder and publisher of OrganicAuthority.com and TV host

ALSO BY DENISE LINN

ALSO BY MEADOW LINN

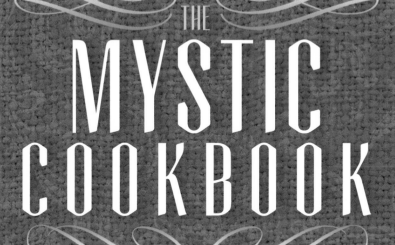

THE
MYSTIC
COOKBOOK

the secret alchemy
of food

DENISE LINN
&
MEADOW LINN

HAY HOUSE, INC.

Carlsbad, California • New York City
London • Sydney • Johannesburg
Vancouver • Hong Kong • New Delhi

Copyright © 2012 by Denise Linn and Meadow Linn

Published and distributed in the United States by: Hay House, Inc.:
www.hayhouse.com® • *Published and distributed in Australia by:* Hay House
Australia Pty. Ltd.: www.hayhouse.com.au • *Published and distributed in the
United Kingdom by:* Hay House UK, Ltd.: www.hayhouse.co.uk • *Published
and distributed in the Republic of South Africa by:* Hay House SA (Pty), Ltd.:
www.hayhouse.co.za • *Distributed in Canada by:* Raincoast: www.raincoast.com •
Published in India by: Hay House Publishers India: www.hayhouse.co.in

Project editor: Lisa Bernier

Book design: Charles McStravick

Interior photos: Malcolm Lidbury (100); David Linn (24 and 60); Denise Linn
(xxi, 44, 86, 99, 109, 126, and 151); Meadow Linn (i, viii, 18, 24, 45, 69, 78,
80–84, 86, 96, 98, 106, 108, 109, 110, 114, 124, 132, 137, 140, 144, 146,
148–151, 154, 156, 158, 160, 162, 164–166, 172, 188, 190, 192, 194, 196, 198,
200, 202, 204, 206, 208, 210, 214, 216, 218–219, 222–224, 226, 246, 247–248,
254, 256, 258, 264, and 280); Kim Christie Photography (xi and 290)

Library of Congress Cataloging-in-Publication Data

Linn, Denise.
  The mystic cookbook : the secret alchemy of food / Denise Linn and
Meadow Linn.
    p. cm.
  ISBN 978-1-4019-3722-5 (pbk.)
  1. Cooking. 2. Well-being. 3. Mysticism. 4. Gastronomy. I. Linn,
Meadow. II. Title.
  TX714.L5567 2012
  641.01'3--dc23
                                          2012015528

Tradepaper ISBN: 978-1-4019-3722-5
Digital ISBN: 978-1-4019-3723-2

15 14 13 12 4 3 2 1
1st edition, November 2012

PRINTED IN THE UNITED STATES OF AMERICA

To my wonderful
husband, David,
thank you for such
a delicious life.

Denise

For my mom, whom
I love even more
than cooking.

Meadow

CONTENTS

The Mystic Chef

PREFACE

We are currently on the verge of an evolution in our understanding of the universe. Science is beginning to assert what the ancient mystics and seers of the past have known for millennia . . . that there is an unseen, but viable life force that permeates all things, and we are not separate from this vast sea of energy.

In this book, you'll learn how to harness this pulsating power and infuse it into every dish you prepare to create transformative meals that profoundly inspire and uplift the energy of anyone who eats them. By doing so, you'll become a Mystic Chef. This hallowed culinary journey also activates the deepest spiritual wellsprings within you. We welcome you to a delicious sojourn to the soul.

I hardly remember a time when I wasn't mixing, concocting, and experimenting with food in some way. One of my earliest memories involves crawling into the upper kitchen cabinets—with the aid of a chair—and pulling down assorted ingredients to make a sweet treat. Although I've had significant experience in the kitchen over the years, I opted for a liberal arts education over culinary school, and most of what I know about cooking, I taught myself. There are many who have culinary skills that far surpass mine; however, what I have is a secret arsenal of magical tools that you, too, can learn to use.

The enjoyment people feel when eating good food isn't just from its taste and nutritive qualities or even the way it looks on the plate—though those are all very important—but also it's from its energetic properties. As food passes from farmer, to cook, to dinner plate, it continues to grow and change on a spiritual and energetic level. On numerous occasions, people have told me that something I've made is the best they've ever tasted. This often surprises me, considering how simple the ingredients usually are. One might wonder how a plain green salad or grilled-cheese sandwich can bring so much joy. However, the taste is actually more than the sum of its parts. It's not just a salad or grilled cheese that they're eating, it's also the joy and love I felt when preparing it.

Cooking is both an artistic and meditative endeavor for me. I've found that some of my best dishes are created when I work in silence and focus my whole being on the foods I'm preparing. But sometimes I laugh when I'm cooking. Sometimes I sing. Sometimes I quiet my mind. My thoughts wander and dance, and there's no sense of time. While chopping, stirring, or frying, I infuse the food with my being. Just as a painter or musician might get swept away in the colors on his canvas or the melody created from individual notes, I feel completely connected with the food as if there were no separation between its essence and my own.

Since graduating high school (many years ago), I've spent nearly every summer cooking for the wonderful people who attend my mom's residential workshops and trainings. Over the years, I've developed a steady repertoire of favorite dishes. I'm constantly changing the menu to keep things fresh and exciting, but the recipes contained within these pages are tried-and-true and are filled with light and delight. It's such a joy to be able to share with you these delicious recipes and time-honored techniques for infusing food with spirit.

From my kitchen to yours and from my heart to yours . . . with love,

Meadow Linn

Meadow loves to cook. I love to eat. We're a perfect match.

I love not only the taste and texture of food, but also the preparation and presentation of every meal. I have 12 sets of dishes. (Seriously . . . who has 12 sets of dishes?) And I have about as many napkins, placemats, and napkin rings. I look at a table setting as a kind of mini-altar, and each meal as an offering to the Creator. I have so many settings because I want every meal to have a beautiful backdrop. Just as a great painting looks even better with the right frame, so a fabulous meal shines even more with the right setting and energy. A splendid, energized meal can make me as blissful as a deep meditation.

I haven't always looked at food as a path to spiritual awareness. When I was a child, my parents were more concerned about food bacteria than gracious meals. (Both my parents had advanced degrees in food chemistry, and my mother had worked in test kitchens in various parts of the world.) Growing up, I had no idea there was a connection between what we ate and our spiritual journey on Earth.

However, after a powerful near-death experience when I was 17 years old, then a two-and-a-half-year sojourn in a Zen Buddhist monastery in my early 20s, and decades in which I studied my own Cherokee heritage and trained with native cultures throughout the world—including the Aborigines in the Outback of Australia, the Maori in New Zealand, a revered Hawaiian kahuna, and the Zulu in Africa—I realized that food is more than just nutrients; it's also swirling with life-force energy and consciousness. When we eat, we absorb that consciousness, and this makes a huge difference in our mission here on the planet. Our sustenance connects us intimately to the hills and valleys of the earth and invites the energy of the soil into our soul. It allows us to taste the wind that blew through the wheat field and ingest the sunshine that brought life to the seed. It connects us to the sentient beings who have tilled the earth, farmed the land, and harvested our food, as well as those who have transported and prepared it. It allows us a deeper understanding of what it truly means to be human and can be a gateway to Spirit.

There are many paths to the top of the mountain of spiritual awareness, and many are arduous and hard; however, you don't need to suffer to grow. Your approach to food can be a wondrous catalyst to reaching the peak where the view is rarefied and glorious. You can grow heaps and bounds amid the joy and celebration of creating magical meals.

We've written this book so you can have a delicious life, and your food can feed your soul as well as your body. We hope you enjoy the journey!

Blessings and sparkles,

Denise Linn

INTRODUCTION

Embarking on Your
Mystical Culinary Journey

 is not a cookbook in the traditional sense. It's a culinary gateway that will open your eyes to the remarkable link between physical sustenance and spiritual awakening. While there are original recipes and directions for making tantalizing meals from places as far-reaching as Mexico, Italy, Vietnam, France, North Africa, and India—as well as from mystical, legendary, and mythic realms—there is also ancient wisdom, practical advice, personal anecdotes, magical enchantments, and radiant ceremonies and rituals, which are all intended to help you live deliciously and invite Spirit into your life.

What you eat and how you eat can make an enormous difference in your spiritual path. In this book, you'll learn how to channel the sparkling life-force energy of the Universe into your food to make it both sacred and lusciously vibrant. Additionally, you'll gain little-known wisdom about how food can mystically transform your life on a cellular level. You'll experience cooking in new and exciting ways, and dine as never before. By doing the visualizations and activities in this book, you'll enter into the transcendental world of the ancients and learn how to harness the wondrous hidden dimensions of food. A dash of imagination, a sprinkle of intuition, and an ounce of intention, and your kitchen will be shimmering with magic.

Scattered throughout this book, you'll also find original recipes that I created, tested, and retested with love (and photographed). Although some contain meat, many are vegetarian. Most are dairy-free, and many are gluten-free, but my true aim is to share some of my favorite, delicious, and spirit-filled dishes. I've been cooking

for many years both for my own enjoyment and for my mom's spiritual retreats. Most recently, I've been the resident chef for her workshops held at Summerhill Ranch. My culinary interest has spanned the globe, from learning how to make spring rolls when I was in Thailand; to discovering how to combine and grind chilies for mole in Mexico; to realizing the French art of shopping at farmers' markets in Provence; to enjoying culinary forays in Bali, Italy, Spain, Germany, and England. My passion for cooking led me to graduate school in Paris to study the history of dining in France and has taken me on adventures near and far to better understand how food is savored in different cultures. During my travels, I've learned to cook and eat with passion. (Many of the tidbits I've gleaned about life, love, and eating, I share in a lifestyle column I write for a Seattle newspaper and in my food blog.) When deciding which dishes to include in *The Mystic Cookbook,* I chose recipes that you could easily use to cook up enchanted energy in your kitchen without needing an excessive amount of groceries or time to prepare them. Additionally, I wanted them to have a variety of colors, flavors, textures, and energetic vitality. I hope you enjoy them as much as we do!

Within the pages of this book, my mom shares her knowledge of spirituality, combined with insights from her decades of training in native and ancient cultures, including our own Cherokee heritage. As the result of her near-death experience, my mom became interested in realms beyond the physical plane. She made it her

life's quest to share her insights to help others lead more fulfilling lives. She has chronicled much of her awareness of metaphysical and shamanic practices into her 16 previous books, including her best-selling book, *Sacred Space*. However, she says that *The Mystic Cookbook* feels like a distillation and culmination of all the guidance she's received over the years.

We are both so excited to have the opportunity to write this book together on a subject that is so dear to our hearts. Embarking on a book as mother and daughter, however, was at first a bit daunting. We were unsure how it was all going to work. We normally have a great relationship, but we wondered what it would be like to collaborate on a book. Would we find areas of disagreement? Would our writing styles clash? There was only one way to find out . . . and that was to jump in with both feet firmly planted and see what happened. We were so delighted that we did. Even though we sometimes approach the world differently, we're both so passionate about the valuable information contained within these pages that not only did we not quibble over ideas or the content of this book, but we actually grew more alike. (I now have a penchant for wearing flannel pajamas while writing, just like my mom does!) As we spent day after day typing at our individual computers in our respective home offices, our writer's voice became similar, and we even began to finish one another's sentences. In no small way, it seemed that we had wonderful celestial guidance throughout the process, and this writing experience further strengthened our relationship.

Although no special tools, skills, or kitchen gadgets are required to embark on this mystic culinary voyage to the center of your soul to embody what we like to call "The Mystic Chef," you might want to consider having a journal to use for some of the exercises contained within these pages.

Our fervent desire is that, as a result of reading this book, a portal opens for you to embark on the sacred journey from nourishment to nirvana. May you not only create meals and dining experiences that empower all aspects of your life, but may your magical meals bring people together in a spirit of love, connection, and transformation . . . for this, after all, is the secret alchemy of food.

Meadow Linn

EATING YOUR WAY TO A DELICIOUSLY ENLIGHTENED LIFE

Simply put, food is much more than, well, just food. It's surprising, but it's true: you really can eat your way to a deliciously enlightened life! When we think of a spiritual path, we often envision meditation, yoga, fasting, chanting, or prayer. We don't usually consider our everyday meals as a potential gateway to mystical transformation. Yet the food you eat and your approach to it can be one of the most powerful pathways to spiritual renewal.

In this chapter, you'll learn how your food absorbs and transmits consciousness . . . and how the subtle energies in your meals can profoundly influence your entire life.

When you take the time to tune in and connect with the vast array of energy fields within your meal, magic happens. Suddenly you're no longer contained by the confines of your identity and your physical body. You enter into the awareness that you're not separate from the universe. Each item of food you ingest can be a key that opens doors of perception and connection. As you shift your awareness to merge with the energy of a mango grown in Hawaii, for example, you'll inhale the sunshine and ocean breezes. With each bite, you can intimately connect to the moist tropical rains and be grounded by the red, iron-rich soil in which the tree's roots grew. By melding with the consciousness of the mango, you expand your "sense of self" beyond the boundaries of time and space to encompass not just your limited surroundings (of your apartment, for example), but also it can allow you to become more of a cosmic citizen, connected with the greater universe.

INNATE CONSCIOUSNESS IN YOUR FOOD

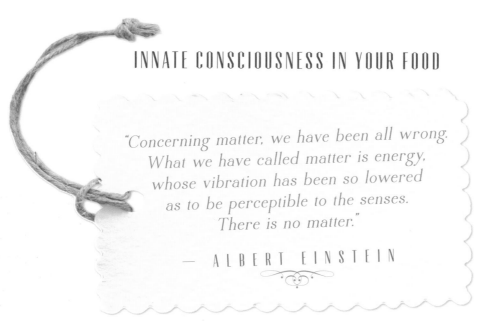

"Concerning matter, we have been all wrong. What we have called matter is energy, whose vibration has been so lowered as to be perceptible to the senses. There is no matter."

— ALBERT EINSTEIN

Tapping into the sacred power of your food starts with understanding the nature of the universe. When Einstein said that there was no matter . . . only energy vibration . . . he reflected the sentiments of metaphysicians and shamans throughout the ages, who speak about the world around us consisting of vibrating, pulsating energy fields. From both a mystical and scientific point of view, everything is made up of energy. Famed inventor and developer of the theory of electromagnetism, Nikola Tesla, said, "If you want to find the secrets of the universe, think in terms of energy, frequency and vibration."

Your food is indeed composed of undulating energy fields *that can profoundly impact your life.* Many people view their physical body as a static biological entity. However, in reality, your body is a vibrating, intelligent force field of energy that's constantly transforming and renewing itself. When the viable energies of your food interface with the energy flows of your physical form, it allows you to step into a higher level of spiritual frequency. (But only if you understand how to attune to those fields; this is one of the secret recipes for savoring your life.)

Not only does your food consist of "energy, frequency, and vibration," but its energy is also always in motion. Beneath the surface of that red apple on your kitchen counter or the buttered toast on your breakfast table exists a river of energy force fields that swirl into form, dissolve, and coalesce once again. All life is energy, and in every moment, we're immersed in a great ocean of it. It's constantly ebbing and flowing in ever-changing currents that pulsate through time and space. In every morsel of food you eat, there's an infinite, yet patterned, timeless cosmic order of waves of pulsating electrons that spiral in and out of existence, which have an effect on your body and on your life. Throughout this book, you'll

be learning how to tune in to these flows of energy within your food to harness its power for every aspect of your being.

You're Not Separate from the Food You Eat nor the World Around You

With every bite you take, it's possible to ingest the encoded information of the universe into your inner biology. Through merging with the etheric energy of your food, you can download remarkable and powerful wisdom imprinted in the food's DNA. The subtle energies in your food are a kind of

vibrational language that communicates with the core of every cell in your body. These energies stream information about the minerals in the earth where the food was grown, the amount of rainfall it received, the vitality of the vegetation that the animal ate, and every part of the natural world from which the food came, as well as who harvested, transported, and prepared it. All of this innate intelligence is transferred into your body with every bite.

The challenge is that in our Western culture, there's a belief that we're separate from the world around us. In our dash for technology, we've forgotten that we're connected with a living, pulsating universe—a universe that sings with life and resonates with Spirit. This idea that we exist independently from our environment is an illusion; for in truth, there's nothing out there that is not you. Our ancient ancestors throughout the world understood this. Their worldview was that none of us exists separate from the entirety of the world. The understanding that you're not separate from the energy of your food (or the world around you) allows you to step into the realm in which everything has consciousness, including your food. You then discover how to interface with the soul of the meals that you eat . . . which can be a profound and majestic experience.

Our Native Ancestors Believed There Was a Living Spirit in All Things, Including Food

Ancient native people believed that everything had a spirit, and they understood the importance of communicating with the life force in all things. For example, they would ask for blessings from the Spirit of the Sea before fishing, or they would ask for support from the Spirit of the Rain for their crops. Plants were honored before they were harvested. Before a hunt, hunters would give thanks to the Spirit of the Elk and ask forgiveness for the life that was taken. However, in our present times, we've traveled a long way from these earlier beliefs.

Although most people today would concede that animals have consciousness, they would be hesitant to concede that plants or inanimate objects do. However, modern researchers have done experiments that suggest that plants *can* respond to the energy fields, thoughts, and emotions of humans. Cleve Backster, a former polygraph expert with the CIA, discovered that plants could demonstrate an emotional response similar to that in humans. (Backster is the founder of the longest-running polygraph school in the world.)

He attached electrodes to the leaves of dracaena houseplants, and remarkably, like humans, the plants registered reactions to certain stimuli.

For example, when he thought about burning a leaf with a match, electronic responses were elicited in the plants. (He didn't even have to actually do it.)

Scientists are just beginning to explore bio-communication and have even shown that one-cell organisms have a kind of consciousness. However, just because modern science hasn't decreed it, it doesn't mean the mountains, clouds, rivers, and stones don't also have a form of consciousness. Our ancestors (and even some modern-day researchers) understood that we're all related, that everything is alive in one way or another, and that if you connect with the living consciousness within your food, its life force will support you. (Even if it has been picked, harvested, or gathered and doesn't seem to be "alive," there's still life force within it.) To the extent that you know this . . . and honor the living spirit within all things . . . is the extent that your food creates a powerful alchemy in your body and expands your consciousness.

THE SECRET ALCHEMY OF FOOD

In India it's said that a mother's love is transferred into her cooking. It's believed that the love she feels for her family infuses her food, and as result, her meals nourish and satisfy her children more profoundly than food cooked by anyone else. Perhaps you've even experienced this with your own family. Maybe you've "tasted" the love (or anger) in a meal prepared for you by someone else. If so, you understand that eating is more than ingesting nutrients. In the deepest sense, it's a palpable interaction with the entire universe.

When a bright orange carrot is pulled from the earth, someone might congratulate the gardener on a job well done, and when a delicious meal is served, someone might send compliments to the chef, but there's much more at play than simply the physical act of growing a vegetable or creating a feast. Have you ever

made a snowman with wet snow? You start out with a small snowball, and as you roll it, it continually picks up more and more snow until you eventually have a very large snowball. It's similar with food, but instead of snow that's being picked up along the way, it's the energy of the land where a plant was grown, the energy of the people who harvested and prepared it . . . and every part of its journey to your table.

In my early 20s, many of my friends had home gardens, and we used to do blind tastings to see if we could tell which garden a particular vegetable or herb had come from. One fellow gardener did an hour of yoga every morning. One bite of a cucumber from his garden, and I would feel instantly calm and relaxed . . . I could always guess correctly that he had grown it. Another friend was very type-A and always in a hurry. One bite of a cucumber from his garden, and I was ready to get up and go. Even though the cucumbers tasted similar, the energy of the person growing them seemed to influence the effect they had on those who ate them.

Denise

The path to higher consciousness can be delicious. When you eat food that was sown with love, grown with love, harvested with love, and prepared with love, your vibrational level skyrockets. The challenge is that for the most part, we no longer grow our own food, nor do we harvest it, and in our fast-food society, we often don't even prepare it ourselves. In many ways, your soul is deficient as a result. Throughout this book, however, we'll be offering suggestions on how you can bring back some of the love and life force found in homegrown food, even if you're purchasing a ready-made sandwich or fast-food burger.

Studies have shown that music can affect plant growth. When soothing music was played to one group of plants, they flourished. Another group of plants heard only hard rock music, and they grew weak and sickly. The plants actually had a physical response to the music, which means it's highly likely that plants also pick up on the energy and vibrations of the people who tend them, just as Backster showed in his tests. (There's even anecdotal research that suggests that putting seeds in your mouth before planting them encodes them with your DNA. Your saliva then "programs" the seed to sprout and grow in alignment with your nutritional needs.)

Have you ever noticed that homegrown fruits and vegetables taste so much better than anything you could ever purchase? This is often for the obvious reason that you're growing a more flavorful variety of tomato, for example, than what's typically grown commercially, but also couldn't it be because you grew it yourself and put so much care and attention into tending that precious fruit?

There's a growing movement to get children who are picky eaters to start gardening. Anecdotal evidence shows time and time again that children who once would never come within ten feet of a detested vegetable suddenly start eating (and loving) it when they grow it themselves. They're involved in the process, which makes the disliked item more appealing, but also on a deeper level, the vegetable actually tastes better to them, because it's infused with the child's delight and joy of watching the seeds they planted grow into strong (and delicious) food. Additionally, the plant also carries a vibrational match for the particular child who grew it, and it will have a greater positive impact on that child's health than a vegetable they didn't grow themselves.

The People Who Prepared Your Food Influence Its Vibration

Sometimes the same food can taste different depending on who cooked it or whose plate it's on. A happy cook often makes happy food. A depressed chef may make food that looks good, but you may come away feeling empty. A cook's energy seeps into whatever he or she is cooking . . . and then you absorb that energy as you're eating. In no small way, there's a powerful connection between the energy and consciousness of the people involved in preparing your food and the way your body reacts to it. Even the emotions of the laborer who picked the lettuce, the trucker who transported it, the grocer who displayed it, and the checker who put it in your shopping cart all influence the deeper energetic qualities of the food you bring home.

Just as food picks up energy and consciousness from the people who grew it, raised it, harvested it, and cooked it, it also has energetic qualities based on where it's from, how it got to your table, and how it was prepared. Although food provides us with the physical energy we need to climb mountains, concentrate on difficult tasks, and even get us out of bed in the morning, it's the intangible yet nevertheless palpable energy that can affect the way it reacts in our bodies.

The Origin

Both the country of original origin and the country where a particular food is grown can also affect the subtle energetic characteristics of your food. Have you ever noticed how lobster tastes best from a shack on the coast of Maine, raspberries are the sweetest right off the vine in the Northwest, and peanuts somehow take on a completely different meaning in the South? This has to do with the aura of a place. Plants and animals absorb the energy of their environs and transmit this to you when they're ingested. The land holds the collective memories and the energy of all that's been before. The culture, the people, the history . . . everything that's happened in that area . . . are infused into the land and all that grows or roams there, which means that when you eat raspberries from the Northwest you are, indeed, absorbing the soul of that part of the world.

Potatoes, for example, originated in South America, but today many of us of connect them more frequently with Ireland or even Idaho. A potato is a potato . . . or is it? How might a potato grown in Peru be different from a potato grown in Ireland or Idaho? Does a russet grown in your backyard taste the same as a russet grown in your uncle's garden across the country? The energy of the Irish people, their history, and the sun, fog, and wind are all a part of the potato from Ireland, just as the potato from Idaho is infused with the energy of the Native Americans who once walked the land, as well as the farmers who till the soil today. Likewise, a potato grown high in the Andes is the product of the mountains, the altitude, and the Incas. As strange as this may sound, it's true. As you bite into that potato, you absorb the energy of the Irish, Peruvians, or Idahoans; and these energies will affect you in different ways. You may feel the infectious laugh of the Irish, the rugged determination of the Peruvians, or the stoic energy of the Native Americans.

The French use the word *terroir* to describe this phenomenon. This word, unfortunately, doesn't have a good translation in English. Literally, it means "soil" or "land," but it's used to describe a concept that's much more complex. It connects palate to place. This concept is deeply ingrained in the French culture and psyche. *Terroir* is the idea that the land affects what's grown there. Food is rooted in the terrain. It's what gives the food its flavor, uniqueness, and context. For example, it's believed that the particular flavor of the cabernet grape used to make Bordeaux wines cannot be replicated elsewhere. Although cabernet grapes are grown in California, Chile, and many places in between, the idea of *terroir* is that only in the Bordeaux region will the cabernet grape taste like Bordeaux cabernet. It's believed that in each sip, you taste the *terroir,* which means the soil, stones, minerals in the earth, sun, wind, water, and all the other factors that make that region distinct. The climate, land, history, and people who have worked the soil for generations all imbue a food with energy and affect the final outcome.

The Journey

The journey your meal takes before it gets to your table can also have a profound effect on its energetic characteristics. The egg—brought home by you, and cracked into a hot frying pan for your morning breakfast—absorbs energy from the foraging hen, the woman who raised the flock, and the land that grew the grass the hen consumed. Perhaps the woman sings when she collects the eggs. Her love and dedication will infuse the eggs with her happy energy. Maybe every Saturday you go to the farmers' market to buy eggs from her and then have coffee and pastry at a nearby café. The contentment you feel every time

you think of this weekly routine will also infuse the eggs with that energy. However, an egg that was laid by a caged hen, transported in a semitruck across several states, and packaged in a warehouse before arriving at your grocery store will have a different kind of energy. Your food has had many adventures before ever reaching your dining table, and each one can impact its vibratory rate.

The energetics of your food can also be affected by how you cook them. Food cooked over a fire, for instance, will not only taste different because of the smoke but will actually have a different kind of energy. And food cooked over gas has a different energy than food cooked over an electric burner, even if there's no perceptible difference in the taste.

This is also true of the materials used to make the vessels we cook and serve our food in. Have you ever noticed how a meal prepared in cast iron somehow seems different from one made in stainless steel or nonstick Teflon, even if your mind and taste buds can't exactly explain why? Of course, some of this is because materials conduct heat differently, and some leach minerals into your food. However, the energy of iron is different from that of steel or Teflon, and each one will carry its unique energetic vibration.

Have you ever served the same food on new dishes and had a completely changed experience? A meal served in crystal is going to have a different energy than one served in earthenware, and porcelain will have a different feeling than glass. What about paper plates? Have you ever noticed how a dinner served on a paper plate never seems to taste quite as good as one on an actual plate? Porcelain and ceramic plates are solid and give a sense of stability and a feeling that this is a meal to be enjoyed and cherished.

Additionally, the use of a microwave oven can also affect the energetic characteristics of your food. A common science project for schoolchildren is to water one plant with regular tap water and another with water that's been microwaved and cooled. In nearly every experiment, the plant that receives the microwaved water becomes weak and often ends up dying. A microwave works by sending out electromagnetic radiation—low-frequency waves of electrical and magnetic energy—that reacts with the water in food. The friction creates heat, which cooks your food. Studies have shown that microwaving food can have a harmful effect on the micronutrients in your food as well as potentially create carcinogens. Although studies have been done that prove the health risks of using a microwave oven, there's still much debate about this device. Regardless, the simple mechanism by which food is cooked in a microwave—infusing it with electrical and magnetic energy to shake (and sometimes break) molecules—will affect its overall energetic characteristics. Have you ever noticed how food warmed in a microwave oven seems to lack some of the vitality of food cooked in another way? This is because the microwave is actually shifting the energy of the food.

Most of us also don't have the time, ability, or resources to grow and cook all of our own food filled with the love and energy we'd ideally want to ingest. But it's not a lost cause! In Chapter 3, you'll learn techniques to infuse your food with healing and loving energy to make it the most nutritious and physically and spiritually satisfying food you'll ever eat, no matter its origins.

YOUR SECRET BELIEFS AFFECT THE VIBRATION OF YOUR FOOD

Do you see a large banquet and think, *How opulent!* Or do you think, *How wasteful!?* Does eating in restaurants feel like a special treat or just something you do to avoid cooking? Does a decadent dessert make you want to jump up and down and celebrate, or does it make you want to run for cover and hide from the calories? Do some foods or cuisines fill you with joy and others with dread? Are you always trying the newest diet, or do you stick steadfastly to one particular way of eating? Do mealtimes make you feel joyful or tense? Does eating fill you with a feeling of burden for no apparent reason?

Your subconscious thoughts, beliefs, associations, and emotions dramatically influence the vibrational energy of what you eat, and, in turn, your food then affects you accordingly. You may think you're the sole architect of these feelings and reactions to food, but in fact, much of the way you relate to food has to do with the way you were conditioned as a child by your family, your religion, your society, your culture, and even by your ancestors. In many ways, your food associations are like family heirlooms that get passed down through the generations.

Within every grain of rice, leafy green, and piece of meat that you eat, there's a multitude of associated beliefs. Without being consciously aware of it, every time you choose to eat one thing over another, or find yourself making a judgment about a particular kind of food, you may have activated a behavioral conditioned response that is strongly rooted in your subconscious. These food associations and beliefs run so deep that they can even radiate beyond mealtimes and positively (or negatively) impact all aspects of your life.

Your beliefs about yourself based on what you eat can also affect you. For example, if your identity is as a vegan and you find that something you've eaten has an animal product in it, you might feel ill. This could be because your body isn't used to it, but it could also be because eating meat is inconsistent with your view of yourself. Or if your identity is of being a gourmet and you're given a meal of boxed macaroni and cheese, you might feel off-kilter. Perhaps you see yourself as an easygoing, meat-and-potatoes kind of person and if you're given a meal that looks more like art than grub, you might not feel very satisfied. Your identity has an indelible effect on your reaction to the foods you eat. In each of these cases, your body will not get the maximum benefit from your food. The narrower your self-view, the more confined you'll be by the food you eat. The more expanded your self-view, the more positive impact food will have on you. Your beliefs about the food you eat not only inform which foods you choose and those you avoid, but also they can determine, in part, how your body absorbs and digests what you consume.

Secret Food Beliefs from Childhood

Most of us are constantly making choices about the foods we eat and how we eat them. These decisions are based on convenience, availability, and familiarity, and also on the latest culinary and health trends. However, even as a small infant, you were most likely influenced by the food choices and preferences of your family. Research suggests that even in the womb, babies can absorb their mother's predilection for certain foods. For example, studies have shown that what a woman ate in her last trimester can actually shape some of her baby's food preferences; mothers who ate garlic, carrots, or broccoli were found to have babies who enjoyed these foods as adults.

Additionally, once a child is born and develops the ability to focus their eyes on the faces of their caregivers, they can pick up on unconscious signals about whether a food tastes good or not. In an institutional care facility for babies in Massachusetts, careful records were kept about the babies' food preferences. A psychologist at the facility noticed that the infants under four months would sometimes abruptly change their proclivities for the type of juice they drank.

After further research, the psychologist discovered that the dramatic changes in juice preference *reflected the inclination of the caretaker*. For example, a child who'd always liked orange juice would suddenly only prefer tomato juice when a caretaker who liked tomato juice took charge of the baby's care. When the caretaker changed, the babies reflected the tastes of the new caretaker. It's hypothesized that the babies picked up on subtle micro-expressions that indicated a like or dislike for the juice, and responded accordingly. From a spiritual perspective, however, it's more likely that they picked up on the energy of the caretaker and responded accordingly.

Parents and caregivers can also positively impact children's food preferences. For example, if your grandmother told you that eating kale would make you strong like a superhero, then potentially even 50 years later, every time you eat kale, you'll subconsciously activate a feeling of being stronger. In other words, your secret childhood belief about kale influences the vibrational energy of this food for you.

Your Body Hears You . . . and Believes You!

Your physical form has an innate consciousness, and in many ways, it trusts what you tell it. If you believe that a particular kind of food will energize your body, then every time you eat it, your body will find ways to use the nutrients to energize you. If you tell your body that a certain food is going to make you fat, or is going to make you feel bad in the morning, chances are it will. However, the subconscious always trumps the conscious mind. So if you consciously tell

your body, "This fourth margarita is going to heal my body," but your subconscious is yelling, "Are you out of your mind? You're going to be soooo hung over!" you're likely going to feel terrible in the morning.

Faith healings at Christian revivals in which people in wheelchairs suddenly walk and the terminally ill are miraculously cured have existed for generations. It's not necessarily that the preacher has magical powers, though some may believe he does, but it is more likely that the attendees believe so strongly that healing is possible that it does indeed happen. Time and time again, studies have shown the power of belief. Reported in *The World Journal of Surgery*, cancer researchers were testing a new chemotherapy drug. This was a blind study, which means that one group of cancer patients got the new drug and another got a placebo. The researchers didn't know who got the placebo, and all the patients believed they were getting the new drug. At the conclusion of the study, 74 percent of the patients who received the drug had lost their hair, a frequent side effect of chemotherapy. Amazingly, 31 percent of the patients taking the placebo, which was simply an injection of saltwater, also lost their hair. In other words, since the patients *believed* they were taking the drug and *believed* chemotherapy leads to hair loss, *they actually lost their hair.*

Positive beliefs usually bring about positive results, while negative beliefs, in many cases, will bring about negative results. For example, those who believe strongly that eating a raw plant-based diet will make them strong and healthy tend to have good results, and those who believe fervently that eating whole foods, including meat and dairy in the tradition of their ancestors, is the route to optimal health, often also find ways to prove themselves right. Of course, eating a balanced diet full of nutrient-rich foods is vital to health and well-being, but your thoughts can also powerfully affect the way your body metabolizes your food.

It's Not Bad, It's Not Good . . . but Thinking Makes It So

The first step to getting your food to work in your favor is being aware of your beliefs. Many beliefs run deep. Throughout our lives, we're told that there are "good" and "bad" foods, but no one seems to agree on what these foods are. Once you're aware of your food beliefs, the next step is to make the positive ones work for you and find ways to diminish the negative ones. If you sincerely—both consciously and subconsciously—believe that a food will heal you, there's a chance it will benefit your body, even if it sometimes goes against conventional wisdom.

From a spiritual perspective, food is neutral. There aren't any "good" or "bad" foods; there's only energy. It becomes bad or good by the emotions you have about it, the beliefs you assign to it, *and the way your body reacts to it*. (From a nutritional point of view, there are, of course, foods that are better suited than others for optimal health.)

As a suggestion, whenever you eat, do so with the intention that the food is going to heal and strengthen you. Tell yourself that your body will absorb exactly what it needs and will discard the rest. Your body hears you! This can feel false and forced in the beginning, but as you persist, the more positive beliefs will take shape. Of course, there's a difference between wishful thinking and firm belief. As with the example of the margarita, sometimes your desires will step in. Hard-and-fast rules about food can diminish your energy field. Here's an exercise to relinquish some of your inner food restrictions.

Letting Go of Beliefs about Food

* List the negative beliefs you hold about food and where they might have come from—family, friends, religion, heritage, or popular culture.

* Regarding each belief, ask yourself: *Is this really true?*

Take time to answer the question truthfully. For example, you might believe it's bad to cook your vegetables, and that they should always be raw. But interestingly, some studies suggest that we're more likely to become ill from the food we eat today than our grandparents were because they cooked their vegetables to oblivion, and hence killed bacteria and viruses that are sometimes carried in raw food. We aren't advocating you cook your food to mush, but if you make a hard-and-fast rule about only eating in one way and become locked in a belief system, this can potentially diminish your energy field and your body's instinctual ability to get the most nutrition from the foods you consume.

When Selecting What to Eat, Use Your Intuition

Labeling food as right or wrong can cut off the innate intuition of the body that draws us to foods it needs most at that time and repel us away from foods it doesn't need. A food that on one day makes your cells sing, on another day might make them metaphorically sing off-key. But you'll never be able to access your body's natural ability if you continue to live by rigid rules about food.

As you journey through this book and begin to activate your inner Mystic Chef, you'll understand the remarkable power of intuition to choose the right foods for you. To the extent that you can step beyond food associations, rules, and beliefs and awaken your instincts is the extent to which you'll be happier and healthier. In later chapters, you'll be introduced to ways to use your intuition in your cooking, but the following exercise is something you can do anytime to discover the right foods for you at any given moment. As you do this, however, remember to tune in to your inner knowing rather than just wishing something to be true.

Exercise

* Hold an ingredient or plate of food in your hands, close your eyes, and allow yourself to quiet your mind enough to step beyond beliefs and rules and listen to your intuition.

* Ask yourself: *Is this the right food for me at this time?*

* Notice whether your energy goes up, down, or feels neutral. Or if you're more visual, you can assign colors to your visualization.

(If the food is good for you, maybe in your visualization you see a green light. If it's neutral, perhaps you see a yellow light, and if it's not good for you, maybe you see a red light. Another way to do this is to imagine putting the food on a cosmic scale. If the scale goes to 100, this food is outstanding for you, but if it goes to 0, run, don't walk, away from this food. The 50 mark is neutral.)

PAST-LIFE MEMORIES, CELLULAR MEMORIES, AND FOOD

Being a Mystic Chef means you understand not only the innate energy swirling within your food and the power of your beliefs about what you eat, but you also understand the power of the past on your food proclivities. You recognize that powerful memories not just of today but even of the far past can be triggered by specific foods. You know that when you react strongly to a certain dish, it could be because it's connecting you to a different time and place. The foods you love, abhor, and even are allergic to can be a conduit for uncovering hidden memories from your recent past, your previous incarnations, or even your ancestral history. Acknowledging the connection between your food and your far past can be healing and empowering.

Such was the case with Jennifer, who grew up in a middle-class family in the Midwest of the United States but never felt quite at home there. When she was six years old, she had American Chinese food for the first time. One taste of Peking duck and it was like she'd come home. From then on, she took every opportunity to beg her family for Chinese food. Then as a young adult, she tasted authentic Chinese food for the first time, and vivid memories of a past life in China poured into her. She quickly realized that the Americanized Chinese cuisine she'd grown to love as a child was actually a stand-in for the food she'd eaten during the Ming Dynasty in a former life. With each glorious bite, she was flooded with memories of her happy life in China. This experience was a catalyst for Jennifer and enabled her to understand herself more fully.

The concept of reincarnation has been with us since before recorded history. It's the belief that we're made up of both a physical body and an immaterial spirit, and it's this immaterial part that survives death to be reborn into another body. A new identity develops in each life, yet there's a spiritual part of the being that remains constant through all the lives. Your past lives can have a profound influence on your relationship with food. Imagine, for example, you had a past life in which you lived in poverty and starved to death. You might find that in your current life, as a result, you overeat or you're always afraid there isn't going to be enough. Or such a past life could also be behind a starvation eating disorder.

In many ways, the decisions you made in your distant past control your current life. Because of this, you can use your knowledge of a particular past life to work through present-day issues surrounding food and health, especially compulsions and phobias around food. Perhaps you had to live on rations in a former life and so in this one, you find yourself stockpiling food. Or maybe you were a devout Hindu during another lifetime, and so in this one, you have a seemingly inexplicable aversion to eating beef, even though you were raised on a cattle ranch.

When discovering past lives, it's important to remember that your past-life experiences don't necessarily create continuing problems—it's your *reactions* to those experiences that can have lasting effects for lifetimes. For example, having eaten tainted food in a past life won't necessarily create a blockage around food in your present life. Although if you swore you'd never eat anything again that you didn't prepare yourself, then potentially in this lifetime you might have issues around other people making your food. It's possible, however, to go back through time and change the meaning of an event or even alter your memory of it, and thus create a time/space domino effect that transforms your present life.

One of the ways to discover the past lives that may be affecting you is to do a past-life regression, but another way is to look for clues.

Food Preferences and Past-Life Clues

Your childhood preferences around food and meal preparation can sometimes be indicative of past lives and can even have lasting effects into your adult life if not recognized and worked through. For example, if a child refuses to eat certain foods, and it's more intense than the average childhood food preferences, it might be a result of a past life. As a child, Sarah refused to eat anything that had beans in it. No matter how her mother disguised them, Sarah could ferret out the hated ingredient and refuse the meal. Her mother chalked it up to a childhood quirk, and it became a family joke. As an adult, however, Sarah experienced a past-life regression in which she was born a male slave in the mid-1500s on one of the large haciendas in Mexico. The only food the slave families were given was a meager portion of beans, which barely kept them alive. Her revulsion to beans was caused by the horrors of that previous life of backbreaking labor and starvation. When Sarah went back into that painful incarnation and healed it, not only did it change the restrictive pattern in her current life, but also she almost magically found that she actually enjoyed beans.

Sometimes the types of food you're attracted to as an adult can also offer past-life clues. For instance, have you always loved the taste and smell of Japanese food? Did using chopsticks come quickly and naturally to you? Of course, there are many reasons for the kinds of cuisines you enjoy, but it can also be an indication of one or more past lives in a particular region or time in history.

The way you eat your food can also offer important clues. Do you love eating with your hands more than with utensils? Do you eat like a peasant? King? Monk? Samurai? For example, James preferred to eat his meals with others. "The more, the merrier" was his motto. At these meals, he would regale the party with amusing anecdotes, stories, and tall tales of his adventures. In a past-life regression, he discovered he'd been a nobleman in Scotland, who loved nothing better than to share the bounty of his vast lands. It was a life in which he thoroughly enjoyed his role as generous host. It was deeply ingrained and carried with him into his current life. On the other hand, Claudine always wanted to eat alone and felt strangely guilty when she ate with others. She discovered a previous incarnation in India in which she was embarrassed if she had food and others didn't, so she always ate alone. As soon as Claudine explored this past life and healed it, she found great joy in sharing meals with others.

Food Allergies and Past Lives

Do you have an allergy to a particular food? Of course, allergies can occur for many reasons that have nothing to do with reincarnation, but they may also have their source in a past life. One or more lifetimes of suffering, poisoning, or accidents involving a specific food can lead to a current-life allergy, which is your body's way of protecting itself. For instance, Steve, a friend's husband, had an unusual allergy to cabbage that he traced back to a difficult life as a serf in Poland in the late 1800s. Russia had taken over, and feudal land systems prevailed widely. The aristocracy dined at sumptuous banquets, while the laboring peasants survived on cabbage and potatoes. As soon as Steve released the trauma around this past life, his allergic reaction to cabbage disappeared.

It's not uncommon for an allergy to onset at the same time as a current-life event that's similar to a past-life event in which there was a negative association with the allergen. For example, Laura became extremely allergic to walnuts at the age of 47. It was unusual to have such a severe allergy begin at a relatively late stage in life. Upon regression, it was discovered that Laura choked to death on a walnut when she was 47 in a past life. By working through this past life (and with the aid of her physician and allergist), she was able to lessen the impact of this allergy. Past-life regression can be a powerful tool in learning about the root of present-day food allergies; however, it's advised that you embark on such an undertaking under the guidance of your physician.

What Is Cellular Memory, and How Does It Affect Your Food Preferences?

Believe it or not, just as certain foods can trigger past-life memories, your cells also hold memories about every experience, emotion, sensation, taste, and smell of your life. You're influenced by these memories, even if you don't consciously know what they are. All of them are transmitted through the body by neuropeptides, which are your body's way of communicating with itself. For example, your cells can contain a positive association for oatmeal (even though you don't consciously remember the feeling of comfort it gave you when your mother made it for you as a child), and, therefore, every time you eat oatmeal, your cells sing with delight. Remarkably, your cells can even hold ancestral memories from your lineage and respond to the food that your predecessors ate.

Perhaps the best example of cellular memory is found in the many documented cases of transplant patients who display changed tastes and preferences after receiving a donor organ. Some medical research proposes that collections of cells, such as in the heart, have their own consciousness and can make functional decisions independent of the brain's cerebral cortex. For example, a 29-year-old lesbian who loved fast food received the heart of a 19-year-old vegetarian, but after the transplant, she apparently found meat distasteful and even ended up marrying a man. Another woman, Claire Sylvia, suddenly began to crave chicken nuggets, beer, and green peppers after receiving a heart and lung transplant in 1988 (none of which she ate before the transplant). She later found out that her donor had been an 18-year-old killed in a motorcycle accident, and he'd greatly enjoyed those exact foods. These are anecdotal, and there is no undisputed evidence to prove this premise, and not all transplant patients report such changes, but enough do have these experiences to give credence to the power of cellular memory.

Food and Ancestral Cellular Memories

The associations your ancestors had with food are also woven into your DNA and exist deep within your cellular memory. This is frequently seen in adopted children, who sometimes develop similar tastes and preferences for food, career, and even religion as their biological family, even if they've never met.

Perhaps your forefathers hailed from Korea, and even though you've never visited Asia and your parents don't eat traditional foods, you find yourself attracted to Korean dried fish and have an intense love of kimchi, the traditional fermented cabbage dish served with many Korean meals. This may be a coincidence, but it may also be that you feel this deep connection because it's written in your cells.

Believe it or not, it's likely that ancestral foods will react differently in your body than they would for someone without these strong cellular memories. They'll nourish your soul in a way that's deeply satisfying, and—surprisingly— they'll also more fully nourish your physical body. A study published in the *Tufts University Health and Nutrition Letter* found that iron absorption of Thai and Swedish women depended on their cultural connection to the foods they consumed. When fed traditional Thai food, the Thai women absorbed more iron than did the Swedish women, who were not particularly fond of the sweet and spicy food. When it was reversed, however, and both groups of women were fed hamburger, potatoes, and beans, the Swedes who enjoyed this type of food actually absorbed more iron. Eating is not just a clinical process by which you ingest nutrients and assimilate them; your feelings, associations, and ancestry actually affect how foods react in your body.

Your cellular memory may also influence how you feel about certain foods. If, for example, you're of Irish heritage, depending on your ancestors' experiences and how they approached their life circumstances, you may find that you either feel deeply comforted when eating potatoes, or you may feel a sense of revulsion and despair, even if you live in a different part of the world with different life circumstances.

It's not just the type of food, but also the manner in which you eat—such as enjoying eating with large boisterous groups as everyone laughs loudly, or preferring to eat in refined settings in the lap of luxury—that can give you clues to what might be encoded in your ancestral cellular memory. If you've ever had the sensation or thought that eating a particular way is how you're "supposed to eat" or that it just "feels right" to dine in that manner, then you may be experiencing cellular memory. It's as if your cells somehow guide you, and you eat in a manner that's like being on autopilot.

Spiritual Epigenetics

Furthering the idea that your cellular memory and food choices are intimately intertwined, *epigenetics* is a new science that suggests environmental conditions and the quality of food ingested can leave an imprint on the genes, and these genetic changes can pass down for generations. Depending on conditions, the *epigenome* (which is a part of the genetic makeup) doesn't necessarily change the genetic code in the DNA, but it tells your genes to switch on or off . . . and this imprint in your genes gets passed down—and is even magnified—for many generations. In other words, your genes are always listening and passing on complex information about absolutely everything that you consume, and what you eat today can impact the health and well-being of your descendants. If one generation doesn't eat well, then even if the next generation has adequate nutrition, the third or fourth generation can still be dramatically influenced by the switched-off genes. For example, if a mother smoked while pregnant, her children are 1.5 times more likely to develop asthma than children born to a mother who didn't smoke, but amazingly, if grandma smoked, the children are 1.8 times more likely to develop asthma . . . *even if their mother never smoked*. This is hard to believe, but it's true. The great thing is that if you have "sleeping genes" that were shut down by previous generations, you can switch them on again, simply by improving the quality and vibration of your food.

Spiritual epigenetics is a phrase we've coined that uses the context of this science to explain how your food can be an emissary to future generations. Even if you never meet your descendants, what you eat today affects both your biological descendants and, from a mystical perspective, your spiritual descendants. What you eat is your legacy to the future. Every bite you take is an investment in the vitality of our beautiful planet or is a debt that others in the future will need to pay. If the storyteller speaks in a strong, clear voice, the story passed down keeps its integrity. If the story is muffled or whispered, it can get lost in various interpretations over the generations. What you consume and how you do it is your epic story for the future. (See Denise's book *Four Acts of Power*, also called *Sacred Legacies*.)

Exploring Food Preferences from Past Lives and Cellular Memories

If you'd like to better understand your food preferences and how they might relate to past-life and cellular memories, make a list of your favorite and least favorite foods. Notice the emotions, thoughts, and feelings that each one elicits within you. You'll most likely be able to instantly identify a practical reason for certain preferences, but for those you can't, consider answering the following questions:

* As a child, what foods did you love? And what foods did you dislike? Are there any obvious reasons for these preferences? If not, there may be a past-life association or cellular memory.

* How do you eat your food? Do you eat quickly, almost as if it were your last meal (like someone who normally doesn't have much to eat)? Or do you eat slowly and methodically (like someone who had the luxury of picking at their food)?

* Do you like to eat a large meal early in the day (like someone who might be working long hours outdoors and needs a hearty breakfast)? Or do you like to have a late evening meal (like someone who lives in a warm climate)?

* Do you ever notice any personality change in yourself when you eat different kinds of food? For example, when you eat Italian food, do you find yourself becoming more boisterous? Or when you eat Japanese food, do you find yourself becoming more demure?

* When preparing meals, what foods do you tend to cook on a continual basis? Are there some foods that you never like to prepare? Are there particular cooking utensils that you always use?

* Are there any foods that always upset your stomach? Are there any foods that always bring on an emotional response within you—either positive or negative?

Healing Your Past-Life and Cellular Food Memories

If there's a food you detest and have a strong emotional response to—something you'd never eat voluntarily—consider doing the following. Find pictures of this food or, if possible, obtain a portion of it. Set aside some time when you'll be able to relax, undisturbed, for a few minutes. Visualize yourself journeying into the past to discover why this food is so repulsive to you. Imagine that you're traveling into your childhood, an ancestral time, or a past life. Allow your mind to go where it will. Follow these four steps.

STEP 1: RELAX. Sit or lie in a comfortable position. Close your eyes. Imagine yourself in a peaceful place in nature.

STEP 2: TRANSITION. Shift out of the imagined place in nature into a transition stage; an example might be to imagine that you're in a time machine, a time tunnel, or flowing down the river of time.

STEP 3: SEE YOUR PAST. Use your imagination to envision what events from the past might be associated with the food you dislike. (Often the images that spontaneously emerge, or that seemingly are your imagination, are giving you clues.)

STEP 4: RESOLVE ISSUES. It's in this stage that you can heal or shift any energy blockages that may surround the food you dislike. For example, Ken strongly disliked any meal with chicken, although he enjoyed other meats. Even the smell of it nauseated him. He discovered that the source of this aversion was a past life in Germany, in which his pet chicken was traumatically killed for a meal. (You might believe that the past isn't changeable, but actually in the mystical realms, all time and history are malleable, even the far past.) Ken changed his past-life trauma by understanding that there is no death, only change. By changing the memory of the original event, Ken was able to heal his aversion. (For information about past lives, see Denise's book *Past Lives, Present Miracles* and for information about cellular memories, see *Four Acts of Power*.)

Many things influence the deeper energy of your meals: from the people who grew, harvested, and prepared your food, to the inner beliefs you hold about particular foods, to your ancestral cellular memories, and even to your previous lives. Beginning to understand the layers of diverse, flowing, and interwoven energy fields in every bite you take will allow the varying vibrations of your food to sink deep into your body to be used for your highest good and open yourself up to leading an even more delicious and enlightened life. After expanding your awareness of what affects the energy of your food, the next step is discovering how the foods you eat can be used as a catalyst for spiritual breakthroughs. In the next chapter, you'll discover how to do this.

SPIRITUAL FOOD FOR SPIRITUAL BREAKTHROUGHS

*D*espite the dramatic expansion of modern technology, which defines our contemporary life at this time, there's also a powerful yearning for a direct experience of the sacred. For many there's a deep desire to connect with what's authentic and real and to reach into hallowed realms for answers to the great questions of life, such as "Who am I?" and "Why am I here?" There's a thirst for wisdom beyond ordinary reality. In this chapter, you will learn how to use food as a touchstone for clearing inner blockages and revitalizing your energy field, which can help bring about spiritual transformations.

FOODS FOR SPIRITUAL GROWTH

In order for your spirit to shine bright and bold, it's valuable to clear emotional blockages from your energy field. One of the ways to use food to do this and facilitate spiritual revelations is merely a matter of understanding the power of scent and the way the brain works. Have you ever smelled or tasted something that instantly catapulted you back to a specific time in your past? This is not unusual. Of all the senses, smell is the most powerful way to access potent and vivid memories. The scent of rosemary chicken roasting in the oven might make you think of your grandmother when you were a child. And a whiff of licorice might remind you of the day you were eating candy and your brother fell off his bike. And even if you don't consciously remember the event from your past, an emotional echo of the memory gets activated.

Smell is such a commanding memory trigger because the olfactory nerve is very close to the area of the brain that's connected with emotions and emotional memories. In fact, our memory and scent are so profoundly interwoven that when the part of the brain associated with memory is damaged, an individual will often lose the ability to identify various smells. This is because we recognize smells because we have a memory of them.

If you want to remember something, research has shown that simply by smelling a strong scent that was present at that time will help jolt your memory. Merchandisers have discovered how to use our smell-memory connection. Some even have camouflaged tubes strategically placed in their stores the weeks before Christmas, pumping out a mixture of cinnamon and pine. It turns out that for many people, these aromas activate memories of childhood holidays and get them to embrace the holiday spirit even more, and thus spend more money.

Researcher Dr. Gemma Calvert, an expert in brain imaging, had a group of volunteers inhale cinnamon and then viewed what occurred in their brains using an MRI machine. As they inhaled the scent, their brains lit up, especially the area connected with *emotional engagement*. In other words, your sense of smell activates not only your memories, but also your emotions. Interestingly, many stores have cinnamon-scented pinecones for sale right when you walk in the door.

Regarding the food that you eat, most of what you perceive as taste when you're eating is, in fact, smell (the only things we can actually *taste* are sweet, sour, salty, bitter, and umami, which is also called "savoriness" and often attributed to mushrooms, broth, and meat). Given the powerful smell/memory/emotions connection, the food you eat can actually be used for breakthroughs in your life. If you have any blockages that haven't responded to other methods, you may want to consider employing your sense of smell and taste to help clear them. Almost all blockages come from earlier times in our life in which we adopted a limiting belief about life or about what we thought we deserved. *And almost all of those earlier times have food scents associated with them.* So literally, you can use food to access and heal old memories.

Food Triggers to Clear Blockages from the Past

Maybe you have a blockage regarding abundance that you've traced to childhood programming. Perhaps as a child your mother always condemned people who had money. She'd say things like, "The Browns might be rich, but money doesn't buy happiness. We're poor, but at least we're happy." This kind of programming can go deep into a child's subconscious so that as an adult, every time you try to get ahead, subconsciously you sabotage yourself, or you find that you become very unhappy . . . because in the deeper recesses of your mind, you believe that if you're well-to-do, you won't be content. There are many ways to release this kind of blockage, but one simple way is through food. Since smell and taste are the most powerful provokers of memory, if you had peanut butter and jelly sandwiches as a child, then make this exact same meal, and as you're

eating it, inhale its scent, and go back in your memory to a time when your mother was telling you about rich people being unhappy.

Then imagine you're talking to that younger you and saying that even though your mother holds this opinion, there are lots of people who have money who are very happy. In other words, the food is a trigger for the memory to come to the surface, and then, as you're eating the food of your childhood, *you plant a new belief into your subconscious.* You might even give that younger you an affirmation, such as, *The more money I have, the more I can give, and the happier I am.* You can use this powerful method for any blockage or limitation in your life that comes from your past.

Using Food as a Trigger for Joy

Just as you can use food to help clear limitations and blockages, you can also use food to activate even more joy in your life. Try this: Go back through your life and remember times when you were really happy. What foods, meals, and scents do you associate with these times? Now create the dish or meal that you associate with one of those happy times. Maybe you remember a picnic by the lake as a child when you ate potato salad and got to fly a kite. If you can get the specific recipe, all the better, but even if you can't, simply making potato salad and taking a moment to be still and go back in your memory to that time can have a beneficial effect on your emotions. Once you get in touch with the joy you felt at that time, heighten the memory and the feeling until it completely fills you. Open your eyes and bring the feeling forward. Close your eyes and go back into the memory. Do this a few times to reinforce it, and then eat the potato salad while in present time. By doing this, you're creating a behavioral conditioned response.

As you do this with various foods from your past, you can in fact activate times when you felt powerful, loved, peaceful, joyful, confident, or whatever emotion you want to call forward.

Foods That Increase Spiritual Growth

You can also use food to activate spiritual growth. Spend time thinking about what foods and scents you might associate with spirituality and connection to Spirit. For example, when Ted was a child, his family was very devout, and at church every Sunday, they accepted Christ by taking a small piece of bread at Communion. To a very open child, each time he ate that small piece of bread, he believed he was bringing Christ more into his life. As

an adult Ted didn't eat bread because he was perpetually on a diet, but after learning about the connection between food and spiritual growth, he went out and bought a loaf of rustic Italian bread, took time to be still, slowly and ceremoniously tore off a small piece, and slowly chewed it. He said the result was remarkable; it felt like a wave of peace flowed through him. It was the beginning of a turning point in his life. After feeling so far from the Creator for so long, consciously eating the small piece of bread was a type of reset button for him. (Just eating bread in a mundane manner, however, wouldn't have changed anything. This method worked because he ate mindfully, while focused on a loving relationship with God.)

Perhaps the food you use to jump-start your spiritual path is from your childhood, or maybe even from a past life, but it can also be food that you imagine will activate your path. We knew a man who was convinced that dates were the food of the gods. He was already very spiritual and did yoga and meditated, but he said that his guru had told him that dates would shift his vibration and allow him to connect even more deeply with the Divine. And he always found this to be so. Whether this was actually true is not important. What's important is that he believed dates would open mystic portals, so indeed they did for him.

You can also program particular foods to activate spiritual awakenings. For example, choose a food or dish that you don't usually eat (so there won't be a lot of other associations for it). Before you prepare it, hold the intent of what you want this food to trigger . . . for example, perhaps a feeling of immense gratitude for life. As you prepare the food, feel thankful. Then as you eat it, eat slowly and allow the feeling you desire to flood through you. In your subconscious, there will now be a behavioral conditioned response to this particular food and to blissful gratitude. This becomes your Gratitude Food. Then every time you eat this food, thankfulness will be activated.

EAT WHAT YOU LOVE, LOVE WHAT YOU EAT

Eating fills our base need for sustenance, but at the same time, it can be a gateway for mystical transformations. Surely you're familiar with the old adages, "You are what you eat" and "Your body is your temple." But it's not just what you eat that makes a difference; it's *how* you eat that can be a pathway to enlightenment. Savoring the way you approach your food and deeply enjoying its textures, flavors, and aromas can open the door for miracles to abound.

Every day, it seems, there's a new study, newspaper article, or post on a social-media site about the "right" things to eat, but rarely do we talk about *how* to eat. To be healthy in mind, body, and spirit, it's essential to be spiritually connected to the food you eat and to enjoy the experience of eating. Understanding how to eat is just as important—sometimes even more so—as what to eat.

If while you're eating a meal you feel afraid that the food is going to clog your arteries, make it hard to fall asleep, make you feel sluggish, and so forth, you're not just ingesting nutrients, you're also ingesting fear. Do not eat fear. If you feel guilty whenever you eat a hamburger, for example, this is a kind of

"eating fear." It damages your immune system whenever you eat something while feeling even a slightly negative emotion. If you're eating a hamburger, eat it. Enjoy it. Relish it. Your body will thank you for "eating joy."

No matter what you eat—fried chicken or celery sticks—it's vital to eat what you love and love what you eat. This, of course, doesn't mean eating chocolate cake exclusively or completely avoiding vegetables or whatever it is that you're less keen on eating is wise, but it does mean that it's a good idea to enjoy whatever you eat, no matter how decadent or how healthy. Believe it or not, your body knows how you feel about your food and will metabolize it differently based on your mood and your feelings about what you're ingesting.

The Mood-Food Connection: Enjoy Your Food

Perhaps you've heard of the French Paradox? The traditional French diet is laden with butter and cream, among other rich and indulgent delights. On average, however, the French tend to be pretty healthy and die of heart attacks

at about the same rate as Americans, who are raised with a fervent belief that these foods are potentially dangerous. Although there are many possible reasons, one argument supporting this paradox is that the French *enjoy* their food. In France eating is a revered experience to be savored, whereas, many Americans are anxious about what's in their food. Researchers have found that the French people's lack of food anxiety (combined with smaller portion size) is a significant factor in their ability to consume rich foods without detrimental health risks.

Paul Rozin, a psychologist at the University of Pennsylvania, found that when asked about certain foods, the French generally use words like *celebration* to describe cake or *meal* to describe an egg. Americans, on the other hand, especially women, are more likely to use a word like *guilty* for the cake and *cholesterol* for the egg. According to Rozin, Americans think more about the nutritional components of food and how they react in the bloodstream, while the French focus more on the experience of eating. Believe it or not, the American fixation on calories, carbohydrates, and fats can actually adversely affect not only your experience of food but also how it reacts in your body.

Your mood, attitude, and emotions all affect the foods you eat. Have you ever met someone who eats ice cream for dessert nearly every night who's incredibly trim and healthy, or someone who exists primarily on whole-grain wafers and leafy greens and seems to constantly have health issues? Much of this, of course, is a result of genetics and environment, but also a lot of how your body reacts to food has to do with your relationship with what you eat and how you feel about it. Remember the example in Chapter 1 of the research done with Swedish and Thai women who absorbed more iron when eating their national cuisine? Your body gains more nutrition when your food is in alignment with your cultural and cellular programming. Interestingly, it's the same with your attitude about food.

Most of us know someone who is perpetually dieting. Do they ever lose weight? Some do, but many don't. Gnawing on things you hate but continuing to  force-feed yourself because you think they're good for you likely will not have the desired effect, because your mental state is not in alignment with the foods you're ingesting. To make a "diet" work, you must enjoy what you eat.

Nutritionist and psychologist Marc David says that if you're happy and delighted to be eating your favorite flavor of ice cream, for example, your hypothalamus will actually send happy messages to your organs. This will help you metabolize the ice cream and burn the calories more efficiently. He says that a healthy attitude toward the ice cream will actually stimulate the release of the thyroid hormone, which in turn jump-starts the digestive hormones. This means that the more you enjoy your ice cream and the less you worry about fat content, cholesterol, sugar, or whatever else it is that may cause anxiety (just as with the earlier example of the hamburger), you'll actually digest it better and make better use of the calories. Leading nutrition psychologists have found the converse to be true as well: negative thoughts and emotions can adversely affect digestion. If you're stressed when you're eating—not just about the food you're eating, but also about anything in your life—you will not adequately absorb the nutrients from the food you consume. The more you slow down, breathe deeply, and experience the pleasures of nourishing your body, the more nutrition and joy you'll gain from your food, no matter what it is. (For optimal health and well-being, enjoy your ice cream and savor every bite. However, it's also a good idea to find fruits, vegetables, and other healthful foods that bring you deep satisfaction.)

In no small way, when you eat joyfully, you bring more joy into your life. When you savor your meals, you savor your life. And when you're accepting of the food you eat, you're more accepting of yourself. As strange as it might sound, when you're filled with love, joy, contentment, or calm during your meals, the food you consume is also filled with that energy. The more you eat what you love and love what you eat, the more you harness the amazing power of the mood-food connection, which can lead to tremendous breakthroughs not just in your diet but also in your life.

TRANSFORMING YOUR LIFE: THE ALCHEMY OF COLOR

Just as scent, memory, and mood play an integral role in transforming basic sustenance into a pathway to spiritual breakthrough, the colors of the foods you eat have a compelling impact on your life. Color can dramatically affect your emotions, your demeanor, and even how much you eat. To understand how to transform your life using color alchemy, it's valuable to learn a bit about the nature of color. All the colors that you can see around you are composed of electromagnetic energies, vibrating at different frequencies. For example, according to the laws of physics, red is a slow wavelength, and violet is a very fast wavelength. Your body is also made of varying frequencies, and when you're out of balance, you'll be subconsciously drawn to colors with the vibrational color wavelengths that your body needs . . . and this includes the color of the food you eat.

In no small way, understanding the secret alchemy of color nutrition will have a profound impact on your well-being. Numerous scientific studies record the powerful effect color has on our emotions and body. For example, people who are angry or upset will calm down in a pink room. Your pulse and blood pressure will go up in a red environment and go down in a blue environment. Certain shades of both blue and yellow can affect the way neurons connect

in the brain. Some studies suggest that certain disorders, such as chronic pain, brain injury, and Parkinson's disease, can be affected in a positive way by color. To enhance your life, eat a colorful diet for both nutritional and metaphysical purposes. Color alchemy works exceedingly well if you hold the intent, as you're eating a food of a particular color, that the associated qualities of the color are being absorbed into your body.

To Activate Your Life: Eat Red

Red stimulates the physical body to respond with direct action. Eating red foods will fill you with dynamic energy and fill you with strength, courage, and steadfastness. Health, vigor, and sexuality are also closely associated with the color red. Red can assist in overcoming inertia, depression, fear, and melancholy. A red dining room will stimulate appetite, so if you're on a diet, this might not be the best color for your dining room.

Additionally, the antioxidants in red foods are thought to help protect cells from damage caused by free radicals. Strawberries, cherries, watermelon, tomatoes, raspberries, cranberries, beets, red peppers, rhubarb, watermelon, pink grapefruit, radishes, red apples, and red potatoes are all examples of invigorating red foods.

To Expand Your Joy: Eat Orange

Eating orange foods encourages optimism, expansiveness, emotional balance, confidence, change, self-motivation, enthusiasm, and a sense of

community. Orange is also a good color choice for your dining room, as it will encourage people to gather, socialize, and have fun.

Carrots, winter squash, pumpkins, sweet potatoes, oranges, nectarines, peaches, apricots, papayas, mangoes, persimmons, orange tomatoes, and cantaloupes are tasty ways to connect with the energy of orange.

To Activate Clarity: Eat Yellow

Yellow foods can also stimulate the intellect as well as communication. Yellow is associated with mental discrimination, organization, attention to detail, evaluation, active intelligence, happiness, concentration, and clarity of thought. Yellow is a color that stimulates flexibility and adaptability to change. Yellow kitchens tend to be gathering places for family and friends to chat about their day.

Plus, healing vitamin C is found in lemons and grapefruit. Summer squash, yellow peppers, sweet corn, pineapples, yellow watermelons, and other yellow fruits and vegetables fill you with glowing yellow energy; and they contain beta-carotene that promotes healthy eyes.

To Encourage Abundance: Eat Green

Green foods can stimulate feelings of love, balance, harmony, peace, hope, growth, and healing. Since green is found everywhere in nature, it's often used to symbolize the abundant, replenishing forces of the Universe. The color green reminds us that there will always be enough. Green is a good color for your kitchen or dining room, as it's both restful and energizing.

Green fruits and vegetables contain lutein, which research at Harvard has shown helps protect sight. Zucchini, kale, spinach, Swiss chard, collard greens, green peppers, celery, asparagus, peas, dandelion greens, green beans, green apples, green melons, kiwi, limes, broccoli, lettuce, cucumbers, Brussels sprouts, avocados, green grapes, and green cabbages are good choices to connect with the potent energy of green.

To Inspire Peace: Eat Blue

Blue encourages inner peace and living out ideals. Blue stimulates inspiration, creativity, spiritual understanding, faith, and devotion. Blue allows for gentleness, contentment, patience, and composure. As a suggestion, since there are very few naturally blue foods, consider drinking water from a blue drinking glass or water bottle. The water will absorb the powerful energy of blue and fill you with its life-force energy. You can also place your food in a blue glass bowl to absorb the blue energy.

To Open to Psychic Abilities: Eat Purple

Consume purple foods with intention, and you'll be tapping into your psychic awareness and intuition even more deeply. This will also help with your inner knowing, dreams, insight, and clairvoyance.

The antioxidants found in red foods that help protect cells from damage caused by free radicals are also found in purple foods. Some examples of purple foods are plums, prunes, blueberries, blackberries, figs, purple eggplants, purple grapes, purple cabbages, blue potatoes, pomegranates, acai berries, and raisins, all of which can stimulate the energy of purple.

To Invite the Creator: Eat White

White is the color that encompasses all colors. White vibrations are the fastest wavelength of the color spectrum. Its effects on your being are divine realization, humility, and creative imagination. White foods can be purifying, especially if you choose foods whose white color is naturally occurring, as in onions, cauliflower, and bananas. To connect more deeply with the Creator or with the angels, consider decorating your dining room in opulent shades of white. White is purity and perfection.

White fruits and vegetables are thought to lower cholesterol and blood pressure and help reduce stomach cancer and heart disease. Some white fruits and vegetables, such as potatoes and bananas, are also high in potassium. Other examples are onions, jicama, parsnips, cauliflower, mushrooms, ginger, and garlic.

COLOR FOOLS YOUR BRAIN:
USE THIS TO YOUR ADVANTAGE

In addition to the many ways color affects your energy, emotions, and mood, it also greatly influences the decisions you make about food. Have you ever noticed how much red there is in fast-food restaurants and large grocery-store chains? This is because red is an appetite stimulant. Blue, on the other hand, is an appetite suppressant. Dieters are often encouraged to eat on blue plates and are sometimes even told to put blue-tinted lights in their refrigerators. Green tends to be relaxing and soothing. It's thought that green can even aid in digestion. In no small way are the colors of foods a coincidence. Mint tea, for instance, is calming not just because of the mint, but also because its color is soothing.

Your brain is hardwired to experience and taste food differently based on its color. For example, *The Journal of Consumer Research* published a study on the effects of color on flavor in juice. The juice was identical in flavor, but one had been dyed a deeper shade of orange. Without fail, the participants in the study said the darker juice was sweeter. Then, when served a glass of unadulterated juice and a second glass that had sugar added to it (they were the same color this time), the study participants could not detect any noticeable difference in taste. The color of the foods you eat or drink affects the way you perceive it and, therefore, the way your body reacts to it.

We generally have an expectation that certain colors mean ripe or unripe, sour or sweet, wholesome or unhealthy, overcooked or undercooked, or spicy or mild, and even vibrant with life-force energy or lacking in life-force energy. In *Fast Food Nation*, Eric Schlosser quotes a 1970 study in which participants were invited to a steak dinner in a specially lit room. When they were nearly finished with the meal, the lights were lifted to reveal that the steak had a blue tint. Upon seeing the color, many diners complained of feeling ill (since steak isn't *supposed* to be blue), even though there was nothing actually wrong with the steak. Although seeing the blue steak made some people feel sick, the opposite can also be true. The way we perceive the color of the foods can make them seem more or less vibrant and vital, and believe it or not . . . they will be, as a result.

You can use the colors of your food as a springboard for the spiritual breakthroughs you desire in life. Using the information about the qualities associated with the individual colors, decide what area of your life you want to enhance or transform, and then use the associated colors of your food and table setting to propel you in the direction you desire. In order for this to be effective, however, you need to eat in a mindful, deliberate, focused way. For example, if you've been feeling agitated and overstimulated, drinking mint tea (green) won't necessarily be calming if you drink it rapidly with the same frenetic energy you're attempting to quell. If you sit down and slowly and deliberately eat blueberries out of a blue bowl, this can help move you into a more meditative space. Alternatively, if you've been feeling stagnant and can't seem to move forward in life, consider creating a red meal in a room with red decor. (For more information about color-themed meals to activate specific qualities or soothe certain aspects of your life, see the section on chakra meals in Chapter 6.)

Every bite of food—and the way you approach it—has the potential of triggering a shift in consciousness. From exploring the foods of your childhood to create positive behavioral conditioned responses to using color alchemy to kick-start spiritual awareness, your food can help clear blockages, while at the same time connecting you with the Divine. As you've seen in this chapter, your mood, attitude, and beliefs can all positively or negatively impact the way your body, mind, and spirit react to certain foods. This knowledge can help bring about spiritual breakthroughs and lift you to a higher level of consciousness as you learn to nourish yourself in accordance with your higher good. Additionally, you can consciously infuse your food with Spirit to create meals to bring about more joy, love, abundance, harmony, or whatever it is you desire. In the following chapter, you'll learn little-known secrets that will uplift the energy of your meals.

INFUSING FOOD WITH SPIRIT

RAISING YOUR CONSCIOUSNESS ONE BITE AT A TIME

*H*ave you ever taken a delicate bite of an exquisitely prepared meal or maybe even inhaled the fragrance of a warm cinnamon-crusted piece of coffee cake and been moved to tears? Have you ever felt the caring embrace of your favorite aunt in a casserole or had a feeling of connection to Spirit in a sip of jasmine tea? Or maybe after a long and frustrating day, you suddenly feel rejuvenated and revitalized as you begin preparing your evening meal. Perhaps it's the wine at Communion or wild blackberries picked in the woods that makes you feel close to God. At some point in your life, it's likely that a food (or the act of preparing it) has moved you in a powerful way. And if it hasn't, it's never too late. In the following pages, we share suggestions on how you can infuse your food with Spirit to bring about these kinds of experiences.

Almost always the food that fills you with joy, ignites a feeling of sacredness, or moves you in any number of ways is infused with Spirit. Food that's grown with love and gratitude will taste of love and gratitude. Food that's cooked with intention will taste of that intention. And food that's consumed with reverence will taste of reverence. With an open heart, a prayer of thanks, or a heartfelt song, a meal can transform from something ordinary into a powerful—and sometimes even spiritual—experience.

A few years ago, while visiting Rancho la Puerta, a resort and health spa in Mexico, we became so in awe of the incredible life force in the food served there that we decided to wander into their large organic garden to see if we could discover the secret. When we asked Salvador, the head gardener, how he managed to get so much taste and vitality into his vegetables, he told us that he feels a strong connection to the land of his forefathers and has a deep love for the soil. He said, "We're not growing food, we're growing love." As he tills the ground, his love for the land and the plants infuses the soil, and as a result, the fruits and vegetables he grows are full of life force. He said that those who eat his tomatoes are not just eating a tomato; they're also ingesting his love.

When you take time to infuse your food with love, whether it's in the growing, the preparing, or the eating, every morsel will vibrate with energy. With each bite you'll feel more love, happiness, and even holiness.

THE TRANSMUTATION OF FOOD INTO CONSCIOUSNESS

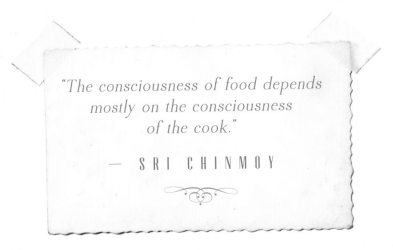

"The consciousness of food depends mostly on the consciousness of the cook."

— SRI CHINMOY

Have you ever eaten in a restaurant and although the food looked appetizing and tasted good, you noticed afterward your mood shifted? Perhaps you became irritated, angry, bored, or maybe you even felt giddy or silly. Of course, there might have been several reasons for your change in mood, but it may also have been that you were absorbing the energy of the cook. *Whatever the cook is feeling goes directly into the food.* If the cook was angry, you might have felt tinges of anger for seemingly no reason. If the chef was in love, you might have felt an unconditional love for others, again for no obvious reason.

In many spiritual traditions, the people preparing food chant and pray while cooking, because they understand that this uplifting energy is ingested by anyone who eats the meal. If you're familiar with the novel (or film) *Like Water for Chocolate,* you understand the powerful impact our thoughts and emotions can have on food. In this story by Laura Esquivel—set in an old and somewhat magical version of Mexico—days upon days are spent preparing a wedding feast. Chilies are dried and ground by hand, rose petals are carefully prepared for use in sauces, and tortillas and breads are lovingly made by hand. Throughout the preparation, the bride's sister, Tita, who's doing the cooking, is crying because her sister is marrying the man that *she* loves.

At the wedding feast, as the guests eat, they're filled with emotion. Without knowing why, they begin to weep over their plates and into their napkins. Tita's tears had infused the food with sorrow. With each bite, each of the wedding guests feels their own pain and anguish of the loves that *they've* lost. In other words, all the guests experienced the emotion that she so poignantly felt as she cooked. Although the emotions that we transmit into our food perhaps aren't quite as palpable as those experienced in this story, the feelings of a cook nevertheless influence the energy in food.

There are a number of simple things you can do to infuse your food with love, raise its vibratory rate, and transmute it into vibrant consciousness. By

using some of the following tools for food transmutation, you can increase the harmonics of the food you eat and add life-force vitality to your meals.

In between basting a roast and tossing a salad, sometimes I crank up the volume of a favorite tune and serenade the soups and stocks while I get my groove on with the vegetables and pastries. There's nothing more uplifting than singing and dancing with glee and absolute abandon while cooking. Plus, those who eat the food can feel all those good feelings.

 *Meadow*

Whenever you can, try approaching cooking with joy, laughter, and love. If you see it as a chore that you simply have to get through, the food will not be as vibrant or taste as delicious as it would if you were having fun during the

cooking process. Obviously, cooking isn't a task that everyone loves, and even for those who do, there are nights when it can feel a bit like drudgery. However, even if you're feeling tired, hungry, cranky, or just not into it, do your best to change your attitude. The more uplifted you feel, the more uplifting the food will be!

Since all food is filled with a myriad of energy fields and has a form of consciousness—even if it's different from the way we view consciousness within humans—you might want to consider turning on some music you love. Allow the sound to flow through you (and through the ingredients piled on the counter) for a few minutes before getting to work in the kitchen. The music not only influences your energy field in joyous ways, but also it aligns your rhythm with the innate rhythm of the food into one cadence. This way there will be a vibrational match. If it's a calming piece of music, take a few deep breaths and allow its tranquility to wash over you. If, however, it's a raucous piece, maybe you want to grab a broom and play some air guitar. Imagine your kitchen is Madison Square Garden, and the contents of your fridge are giving you a standing ovation. Or have a good belly laugh. When you feel the joy surging through your body, then get to work on making a love-infused meal.

As the saying goes, laughter is good medicine. This is true for food as well. The more you laugh and the more merriment you feel when cooking, the higher your spiritual consciousness will be when you consume food that's so filled with Spirit. The amazing thing about laughter is that even if you aren't feeling happy, just pretending to laugh has been shown to have a positive impact on your immune system and your entire body. So as crazy as it sounds, if you're a bit blue, acting *as if* you're happy can uplift you *and* the kitchen energy.

Infusing Food with Prayers

Studies in Japan by Dr. Masaru Emoto have shown that the molecules in water can be altered with positive intention, kind words, and prayer. Your body is made up of more than two-thirds water, and the foods you consume are also filled with water. This means that the more love, com-

passion, and prayers you put into your food, the higher its vibration and, therefore, the higher your consciousness will be when you eat it. In double-blind studies, prayers were found to increase the activity of enzymes and positively impact cells not only in the human body, but also in mice, chickens, fungi, yeast, plants, and algae. It makes sense, then, that the same principles would apply to praying over your food. By placing your hands over your meal and saying a prayer, you honor the plants, animals, farmers, and cooks responsible for putting the food on your table, as well as activate more life force in the food.

Affirmations for Uplifting the Energy of Your Meal

Another way to raise both your own consciousness and that of your food is to say affirmations while you're cooking and even right before eating. (Affirmations said with passion are more potent than those repeated by rote or in a bored manner.) Dr. Emoto also experimented with cooked rice. He placed one cup of rice in two identical, airtight jars. On one jar, he wrote, "thank you," and on the other, "you fool." He asked schoolchildren to affirm these words to each jar of rice every day for a period of 30 days. At the end of the month, the "thank you" rice was still white. But the "you fool" rice was so rotten that it was black with mold. Affirmations are an especially useful tool when you eat foods that are unhealthy, nutrient poor, or not in alignment with your views on health. Your body hears you and believes you. Here are some sample affirmations:

* *The food I consume provides me with all the nutrients I need at this time.*

* *My body has the amazing capacity to turn the food I eat into radiant vitality.*

* *The food I eat renews and revitalizes every cell in my body.*

* *This food is filled with the life force of the Creator, which surges through my entire body with each bite I take.*

Chants to Uplift the Vibratory Rate of What You Eat

Chanting has a potent effect on the body. Like everything in our bountiful universe, our body comprises vibration and energy fields. Every molecule and every cell has a frequency with its own unique energy signature, but sometimes, for one reason or another, it loses its innate, balanced signal. Chanting brings you back in alignment with the forces of the Universe. It makes no difference if the chants are Sufi, Hindu, Buddhist, Christian, Jewish, Native American, or simply created on the spot . . . chanting works!

Ancient sages understood the power of chanting to transform energy. They believed the vibration of the sounds carried a spiritual power and were an offering to God, who in turn uplifted the energy. In ashrams it's a common practice to chant during food preparation; it's believed the sound infuses every morsel of food with shimmering life force. Of all the chants, the most powerful are thought to be ones that include the name of God. Chants can purify and heal as well as lift you to a higher consciousness.

A common chant is the Sanskrit word *Om.* It's not a word as such; however, it *is* a sound, a vibration, and by Hindu tradition, the purest name of God. When you repeat the mantra *Om,* you're saying the name of God, over and over. Doing so produces positive vibrations in your life, energizes your food, and connects you to Divine source energy.

To chant *Om,* be in a relaxed state, take a deep breath, and then with each breath lasting as long as you're able, begin to tone, *Oooooooommmmmmmmm.*

Repeat this seven times in a row. Do this in the kitchen over your food and over your cooking utensils.

Here are some chanting suggestions:

* Choose a traditional chant or mantra, such as *Om* or the longer *Om mani padme hum*. Or even create your own. If you make one up, it can be with words that are meaningful to you or simply with sounds that feel right.

* Start by chanting out loud. As you chant, imagine traveling to the Source deep inside of you. Allow the sound to freely flow from that hallowed place.

* Let go of judgments about how you sound. Just imagine merging with the vibration of the sound.

* Visualize the waves of sound penetrating deep into the food you're preparing with the knowledge that you're impacting the energy of the food in a positive way.

Enchantments for Food Transmutation

An enchantment is a kind of magical spell. It may be directed to a specific food, your entire meal, or your gathering of guests. Perhaps you've read the novel *Chocolat* by Joanne Harris in which the radiant Vianne infuses her compassion and wisdom into the chocolates that she makes for her boutique in the French village of Lansquenet. However, she doesn't just make candy, she also mixes the cacao and sugar with a little Mayan magic. Hearts are opened, mysteries are revealed, and passions are ignited. This is not simply fiction—*you* can also cast a spell and invite magic in your meals.

Although enchantments using food were born in an earlier age and have all but died out, there are still remnants. For example, blowing out the candles on the birthday cake as a wish is made is an enchantment that harkens back to an earlier time.

In ancient Greece, cakes were made in the round shape of the moon to honor and invoke Artemis, the goddess of the moon. It was believed that eating a moon cake would bring the blessings of Artemis into your life. It has been suggested that candles on a cake resembled the light of the moon and that wishes traveled on the smoke to the heavens. In other traditions, a large candle would be placed in the center of a cake to represent the flame of life, thus energizing the food with life-force energy. In medieval times, people of England placed symbolic objects, such as coins or rings, in the batter of cakes. It was believed that the person who found the coin in the cake would become wealthy, and the person who found the ring would have wedded bliss. In some places, this tradition continues to this day.

With the enchantments you learn here, you won't be turning your prized pumpkin into a coach to get to the ball, as in the Cinderella fairy tale; however, you can certainly enchant a meal and gathering to uplift it to a magical and majestic level.

SPELL FOR BALANCE AND WHOLENESS: This is an enchantment that can bring more balance into every aspect of your life and the lives of those at your dining table. In the center of the table, create a symbolic medicine wheel (a Native American sacred symbol representing balance and harmony) by placing four small bowls, one at each of the cardinal directions. To represent the four elements, leave one bowl empty (air), fill one with water (water), another with a lit candle (fire), and the final one with a few stones (earth). When you've placed these items in the circle, say out loud, "I invite the Spirit of the Air, Water, Fire, and Earth to infuse this meal with balanced, healing energy. I invoke the Spirit of the Sacred Circle of all of life to bring balance and wholeness to everyone here." Then sit down to eat your meal.

SPELL FOR HEALTH: Underneath each plate, place a card on which you've written, "My body radiates vibrant health," or "This meal activates legendary healing abilities," or "This meal is filled with radiant, life-giving energy." The words will radiate through the plate up to the food. Then hold your hands over the meal and visualize energy from the heavens cascading through your hands into the food, saying out loud three times, "Vibrant health. Radiant health." Then, with the first three bites of food, say, "This meal fills my cells with effervescent light and healing energy." As you chew those first three bites, hold the intent of being dynamically healthy.

SPELL FOR LOVE: There has always been an intricate connection between food and love. In many ancient cultures, ceremonies were done during food preparation that would entice the person who ate the food to fall in love with the person who served it. We're not going to share any such spells with you, as this kind of "magic" not only is manipulative and doesn't respect free will, but also these kinds of enchantments have the possibility of boomeranging and causing harm to the person who did them. Besides, would you want someone to fall in love with you because you forced it? Love is so much more wondrous than that. You can, however, use enchantments for attracting love, enhancing the love you already have, or deepening the love you have for yourself and increasing your self-esteem.

First, set your intention and then set the stage. Decide what decorations would lend themselves to love. Then choose foods that match your intention. If you want to "spice" up your relationship, as you prepare the meal, consider adding spices to the meal, such as cayenne, cinnamon, clove, coriander, ginger, rose, and rosemary. Traditionally, these are thought to be "love spices." As you sprinkle the spices, chant these magical words three times and hold the vision of a deeper and greater love blossoming between you and your beloved.

With this food we dine

Greater love thus does shine,

As I work this magic spell

Into deeper love we dwell,

I invoke the Law of Love

Calling greater light from above

Music for Food Transmutation

One of the fastest ways to empower your food is to play music while you're preparing your meal. The vibration of the music will literally impact the vibration of the molecules of the food. Every note creates a sound wave that actually organizes and repatterns the molecules of physical objects. In other words, when various notes or tones are played, sound waves are created that can influence the molecular structure of your food. This phenomenon has been demonstrated in tests in which water, talc, or very fine-grain sand was placed on a steel plate with a sound oscillator attached to it, and various geometric forms were created in response to the sound.

Here's how it works. There are 70 different receptors on molecules, and they all react to the vibrations and frequency of various sounds; they vibrate and seemingly interact with each other in almost a kind of a dance, much like tuning forks. When you strike one tuning fork, another that's close will also start to vibrate. They'll harmonize with each other. Similarly, cells respond to the frequencies of other cells; this is called resonance. For this reason, when you play music over your food, it can have a powerful impact on your meal. It's a kind of mystical molecular gastronomy.

TO CREATE A SOOTHING ENERGY: Play classical music such as Bach or Mozart. Schubert's *Ava Maria* is excellent for soothing and yet uplifting the energy in your food. Any music that makes you feel peaceful and relaxed will infuse this feeling into your food.

TO IGNITE VITALITY AND ENERGY: Play any music that has a beat, especially if it makes you want to clap your hands or stomp your feet in rhythm. Again, notice your own feelings. Any music that feels uplifting and inspiring will infuse this kind of energy into your food.

Additionally, consider using a crystal singing bowl. This is a large bowl made of silica, which is the base component of crystal. By taking a rubber mallet gently around the surface of the bowl, a powerful tone is created. Small edible objects,

such as an apple or orange, can be placed in the center, and the vibration of the sound will profoundly affect the molecules within the fruit. Larger items will benefit from just being near the singing bowl. The best note for the singing bowl is an F sharp, as this sound relates to the heart chakra.

Ultimately, any music you love will have a potent impact on your energy and thus uplift your food. So listen to whatever makes your spirit soar.

Crystals to Activate Food Life Force

In cultures throughout the world, quartz crystals are considered to be one of the most sacred of stones. To ancient people, the clarity and transparency seemed to have a mystical quality. Native Americans considered them a means to connect with the Creator; and in cultures throughout history, they've symbolized a holy attunement and alignment with Spirit. From a scientific perspective, quartz crystals have piezoelectric qualities and have the ability to amplify energy flows (hence they were used in quartz radios to magnify the signal). So for their various qualities, they're an excellent choice for infusing your food with energy.

Whenever you use crystals to charge and energize your food, you should first cleanse them. They should be free of dirt and debris, but also you'll want to cleanse them of any residual energy they may have picked up. To do this, place them in the sunlight or moonlight, covered by a cheesecloth or loose-weave fabric to keep insects away. Or, simply hold your hands over the crystal and visualize a rainbow cascading from your hands into the crystal to energize it.

Your personal crystal will magnify your intentions, so it can be used to infuse positive thoughts, feelings, and emotions into your food. Crystals can also be added to your drinking water to supercharge it. You can even put them in the water you soak your rice in before cooking. (Just be sure to remove them before drinking your water or making the rice.) A plate of food can also be placed on a bed of small tumbled quartz. Additionally, you can hold a crystal wand or terminated crystal (faceted/pointed on one end) over your food to "beam" love, energy, and vitality into it.

Here are some quartz crystals and how they can be used. (As a suggestion, don't use any stones other than quartz crystal, as some are made of minerals that shouldn't be in contact with food.)

CLEAR QUARTZ: This is a master stone and can be used for any purpose. It's especially good for the expansion of your intentions. If you decide to dedicate one crystal solely for energizing your food, we suggest that you use clear quartz for your "Nourishment Crystal."

AMETHYST: This is excellent for its soothing energy. It will help calm your mind and bring a feeling of relaxation into the meals your create. Additionally, it facilitates meditation and opens psychic abilities. As a suggestion, to deepen the calming energy of this stone, put it in the moonlight overnight.

CITRINE: This is very effective for bringing clarity of thought to any situation. Some people also call this the "wealth stone" because of its golden color. It's a powerful means to infuse the energy of abundance into your food.

SMOKY QUARTZ: This is a wonderful stone for grounding, physical healing, and manifestation. It's also great for overcoming fear and activating courage. Use this stone to create physically empowering, grounding meals.

ROSE QUARTZ: This is the best stone to use for opening your heart and for activating even more love in your life and in your meals. It's also well known for promoting self-love.

SACRED WINE

To our far ancestors, wine was a gift from the gods. The transformation from the grapes hanging heavy on the vine to a liquid sacrament was a process that seemed mysterious and divine. From the earliest times, wine has been used for sacred purposes, and it has been considered a powerful conductor of life-force energy. There has always been an intimate connection between the cycle of the vine and the greater cycle of life . . . perhaps the dark red of the earliest wine was an echo of the color of blood, or perhaps it was the mystical way that the alcohol acts as a transporter and carrier of the energy of those who bless it. Even now, it can be more than an alcoholic beverage; it can be a purveyor of Spirit.

The history of wine seems to have followed the history of humanity. Although much of this history has been lost to us, sacred wine rituals and wine for holy purposes were undoubtedly important to many early cultures. It's believed that in the Minoan civilization, and later in the Mycenaean, wine was given as an offering to the Earth Mother goddess. In ancient Egypt, wine vessels were found in pharaohs' tombs; and devotees of Osiris, Isis, and Seti used wine in their ceremonies and in conjunction with their offerings. The cycle of life, death, and rebirth was honored with wine, and some considered wine to be the blood of the earth, so it was always revered and considered a precious gift.

In later centuries, there were spectacular festivals in Greece honoring Dionysus, the god of wine. Dionysus was associated with ecstasy, joy, inspiration, and creativity. In what is called the Dionysian Mysteries, wine was considered a sacrament and was thought to liberate an individual to return to his or her original state of divine joy and creativity. The rites of Dionysus lasted for generations and evolved over time. In some permutations, it was believed that when one drank wine, it allowed God's spirit to enter into you more freely.

Wine as a catalyst for transformative experience exists even today in the modern Catholic Church. The Eucharist includes taking a sip of wine, which is believed to be the symbolic blood of Jesus. And when we talk about wine being infused with Spirit, we can't forget that Jesus performed his first miracle by transforming water into wine at a wedding in Cana.

Infusing Wine with Spirit

One of the mystical qualities of wine is its ability to take in energy and magnify it, much more powerfully even than water. Not only will wine easily absorb the energy you infuse into it, but also it holds that energy for decades, whereas most objects infused with energy dissipate over time.

To infuse wine with blessings, before you open the bottle:

1. **Hold the bottle** in your hands to bless it. Imagine the energy of your heart is flowing into the bottle and creating a kind of metamorphosis within each atom of the wine.

2. **Give thanks** to the farmers, pickers, transporters, vintners, and merchants who brought it to your table and to those who made the bottle and label.

3. **Dedicate** your bottle of wine. You can dedicate it to joy, greater abundance, love, or anything that feels right. (You can even write your blessing on a piece of paper and place the wine on top of it. Or you can write directly on the bottle with a felt-tip pen.)

Once the bottle is open:

4. **Let it breathe in Spirit.** Once you open the bottle, invite the Spirit of Air to blend with the Spirit of the Wine to expand and enhance the flavor.

5. **Spiraling the wine.** Pour the wine into the glass so that it swirls. When you spiral the wine, it energizes and infuses it with the life force of the cosmos—just as our DNA spirals with each cell, and water spirals as a fish swims, and the moon spirals around the Earth, and the Earth around the solar system, and the solar system around the galaxy, and the galaxy around the universe. Every time you spiral wine, you not only energize the wine and release untold nuances of flavor, but also you activate energy within the wine that will in turn energize you.

6. **The ancient tradition of the toast.** To toast another with a glass of wine is to amplify the energy of the words that are said. Your toast is magnified by the sacred energy of the wine. Really feel the toast in your heart as you say it.

7. **The first sip.** Allow the first sip of the wine to cascade over your taste buds. Allow it to linger on your tongue. Invite the images of the warmth of the land where the grapes grew, the cool evening sunsets, and the great cycle of life to fill your being. If you become very still, you'll also be able to taste the soil and the vibrant energy of the devic beings who watched over the vineyards, as well as the energy of the people who pruned the vines, harvested the grapes, and especially the passion and care of the winemaker.

8. **Enjoy it.** With every sip, allow the vital energy and love of the wine to fill you. Imagine you're drinking a sacred wine for a sacred purpose.

For sacred purposes, we suggest Frey Vineyards wine. It's the first organic winery in the United States and the first Demeter biodynamic winery in the U.S. They add no sulfites to their wine, and even more important, the Frey family understands energy. Their land is infused with joy, dance, celebration, and love, unlike any other winery in the nation. For ceremonies for strong women, we recommend Calcareous wine. The woman who owns the winery is strong and clear and knows how to break through barriers. Her spirit is evident in the wine.

If you don't drink alcohol, there are still many ways to magnify intention. For example, simply pouring grape juice or pomegranate juice into wineglasses and following the previous steps will energize and sanctify your drink.

The Healing Power of Pyramids

David walked into the kitchen just as I was placing a replica of an Egyptian pyramid over a bowl of fruit. He didn't say anything, but his glance said it all. Had I gone crazy? I was just as dubious, but when I heard you could energize your food by placing it under a pyramid, I decided it was worth a try. Some things work, even if you don't believe them or understand how they work. It turns out . . . this is one of those things. Since then, I've done numerous home experiments, and inevitably, fruit from under the open-air pyramid tastes better and decays much slower than fruit left out on the counter. It still puzzles me, but I've learned that sometimes it's better to just accept.

Denise

The idea of using replica pyramids for food preservation was first postulated by a man named Antoine Bovis who, in the 1930s, while visiting the Great Pyramid in Egypt, noticed a garbage can inside the King's chamber where organic material was perfectly preserved and had no decay. Surprisingly, garbage cans outside the chamber were filled with your typical decomposing matter. He hypothesized that something about the energy of the pyramid was acting as a preservative. When he returned to France, he experimented by putting similar objects under a homemade pyramid. Surprisingly, he found that objects under the pyramid didn't age as fast as objects not under the pyramid.

Through the years, many people have done similar experiments that repeatedly chronicle the valuable effect of pyramids on food. Bill Schul and Ed Pettit, who wrote a book about the benefits of pyramid replicas, tested the theory with two identical containers of milk on a counter. They placed one inside and one outside a homemade pyramid. Seven days later, the milk outside the pyramid grew mold, whereas the milk inside only formed curds. Six weeks later, the curds had turned into yogurt.

Another experimenter, James Raymond Wolfe, put a glass of water within a pyramid for a week and a control glass outside the pyramid. His assistant filled numbered vials with the resulting water. Wolfe then watered sunflower seeds without knowing which water was which. In every instance, the seeds watered with the pyramid-charged water grew faster. Numerous experiments, with different people, also verified that seeds germinate more easily and plant growth is accelerated by pyramid power.

Additionally, blind taste tests comparing food from under a pyramid with the same food not infused with the energy of the pyramid consistently show people prefer the food that was left under the pyramid. In general, bitter and sour foods become milder. Sweet foods become sweeter; foods with high acid taste less sharp.

From Ancient Egypt to the modern life of today, anecdotal evidence suggests that the pyramid has healing properties. As long as the dimensions are right, even the smallest pyramid seems to work to preserve foods. To infuse your food with pyramid energy, consider making a pyramid with the following dimensions: 12" base, 11.4" sides, and 7.6" height. This will create a replica proportional to the Pyramid of Giza. Curiously, the material doesn't seem to be as important as the dimensions. You can use wood, copper, metal, cardboard, or even drinking straws. (However, copper-wire pyramids are usually thought to be optimal.) No definitive research has been done to validate amateur experiments, but even so, you might consider purchasing one from a local healing center or creating one for yourself to explore this secret of the ancients.

As you've seen in this chapter, there are many powerful ways to transmute food into consciousness and infuse it with Spirit. Dancing and laughing while cooking fills your food with joyful life force, and chanting over your food creates positive vibrations that connect you more deeply with the Creator. And spells, enchantments, prayers, music, and even crystals and pyramids transmit powerful love and spirit. This is vital to mystical cooking, because the more vibrant energy you beam into your food, the more you'll absorb when you eat your meal. Additionally, the act of honoring your food with an open heart allows you to step even further into the magical realms of the Mystic Chef. And now that you have your collection of mystical skills and tools to infuse your food with spirit, you're ready for the next step.

DISCOVER YOUR
INNER MYSTIC CHEF
ALCHEMICAL COOKING

In the Middle Ages, alchemists, the precursors to modern-day chemists, tried to turn the ordinary into something extraordinary. Their aim was to transform base metals into precious gold. We now know gold can't be made from iron, tin, or aluminum; however, even though they didn't succeed, these men were onto something. It *is* possible to transform something common into something special. Indeed, by taking ordinary ingredients and imbuing them with energy, food can be a conduit for a spiritual awakening and an alchemical transformation of the soul.

In this chapter, you'll gain many of the tools you'll need to become a Mystic Chef. You'll be guided through a multistep process to learn to cook using your intuition. In addition, you'll discover how to make meals that can lead to states of nirvana. You'll also be given tools to activate the powerful energy of spice alchemy. And finally, by slowing down and eating with mindful intention, you'll open your heart and connect more deeply to Spirit.

INTUITIVE COOKING:
Discovering Your Inner Chef

Have you ever listened to a piece of music and just started to sway? You weren't doing any prescribed movements or dance steps . . . you just allowed the music and rhythm to fill you, until you disappeared into the dance. It may have even felt like a holy experience. In some cultures, this type of creative dance is called "trance dance" or "ecstatic union through movement." In trance dancing, Spirit resides within you and moves through you, and you merge with the infinite Divine Source. The same principles that apply to trance dancing can apply to cooking.

Within each of us is an inner Mystic Chef. Whether you work as a professional chef, cook nightly for your family, or have the Chinese takeout restaurant on speed dial, you have the innate ability to access a deeply rooted culinary intuition that you can use to create delicious meals and infuse your food with radiant energy. Intuitive cooking isn't solely about not using recipes—most of us do that to some extent every day, whether it's frying eggs for breakfast, making a salad for lunch, or throwing together some spaghetti marinara for dinner—it's about being guided by gut instinct and intuition. It's letting go and listening to your heart (and not your head) in order to nourish your body for its highest good.

From activating your intuition when you shop; to choosing foods that resonate with your energy; to combining the colors, flavors, and harmonics of the various ingredients; to the presentation on the table, an intuitive meal can nourish the spirit as well as the body. To cook intuitively, you need a dash of free spirit, a tablespoon

of imagination, and a shake of courage, but the effort can produce food that carries amazing, beneficial healing energy. This kind of cooking can feed your soul.

A cookbook that encourages you to cook intuitively may seem like a bit of an oxymoron, but it's our belief that anyone can learn to cook transformative meals by following the whispers of their heart. This section is designed to help you access your Mystic Chef, and in the following pages, you'll be taken through a step-by-step process—starting with meeting your Kitchen Angel and finishing by tapping into your culinary intuition—to discover your inner chef.

CALLING ON YOUR KITCHEN ANGEL

I have a Kitchen Angel . . . a real one. She guides me through the preparation of each meal from beginning to end. Sometimes I'll mix a number of unlikely flavors together, and people look at me like I'm crazy, but usually it works out. With the help of my wonderful Kitchen Angel (as well as lots of practice, including many failures as well as successes), I use my intuition and throw this and that into the pot, until I create something that dazzles my taste buds but also enthralls my eyes and nose and fills me with a deep sense of nourishment. Believe it or not, she also helps me stretch time, when my time in the kitchen is limited.

⚶ *Meadow*

One of the first steps in activating your inner Mystic Chef is welcoming your Kitchen Angel into your life. You'll notice an immediate difference in the quality of the food you prepare. This sparkling being can be a great ally for cooking with your intuition and infusing your food with Spirit, be it a simple sandwich, five-course banquet, or an experimental hodgepodge of ingredients. The following meditation can help invite an angel into your kitchen. Sometimes your Kitchen Angel arrives from the heavens, and sometimes it's a beloved family member or ancestor from the spirit world who loves cooking and wants to support you in your culinary ventures.

Meditation:
Connecting with Your Kitchen Angel

1. Close your eyes. Take three deep and full breaths.

2. Imagine you're in the majestic kitchen of your dreams; perhaps it's made of crystal and marble, it has top-of-the-line appliances, or maybe its floors are a beautiful tile mosaic. While standing in this glorious kitchen, imagine your eyes are closed, and you're inhaling the fragrant aroma of food cooking on the stove.

3. Open your eyes. Standing before you in this magnificent space is your Kitchen Angel. Your spiritual culinary guide may appear in a variety of forms, such as a celestial angel with wings, a shimmering light, or a robust chef with a twinkle in his eye.

4. Ask your Kitchen Angel for guidance in your cooking. You may want to call upon your angel to assist with the melding of flavors, the timing of the meal, or the activation of energy in your food. As a suggestion, spend a few moments in gratitude. Thank your Kitchen Angel for the help that you'll receive.

5. Take a few more deep breaths. Slowly open your eyes. Now you're ready to embark on the preparation of a meal filled with Spirit and unrivaled taste. Believe that your angel is present . . . and so it will be. It's that simple.

Build Your Culinary Intuition by . . .
Understanding Basic Cooking Principles

In order to discover your inner Mystic Chef and ignite the hidden alchemist within you, it's helpful to have a base knowledge of cooking principles and flavor combinations, and cookbooks can help with that. You wouldn't sit down at a piano and expect to be able to play a jazz riff if you'd never played the piano, nor would you be able to reap a bountiful harvest in your vegetable garden if you didn't understand that a seed needs water, sunshine, and nutrients to grow strong and healthy. Henri Matisse and Pablo Picasso, early 20th-century modern artists known for their use of color and abstract patterns, studied classical painting and were able to paint lifelike images. It was only after they'd mastered the basics that they began to do abstract artwork. It's very much the same with cooking. Build a strong foundation and then use your intuition and imagination to create something magnificent and uniquely yours. Approach cooking in the same way that an alchemist might have approached the potions in his lab. Through experimentation based on knowledge, you'll be able to create delectable, mouthwatering feasts.

Build Your Culinary Intuition by . . .
Following Recipes

Practice. Practice. Practice. To activate your culinary intuition and do recipe-less cooking, it's helpful to first practice your skills by preparing time-honored, tried-and-true dishes. Go through a few of your favorite cookbooks (or try some from this book), and pick out the tastiest looking dishes, and then make them following the directions given. This will help you build your foundation.

When using a cookbook, since you're working toward strengthening your culinary intuition, even though you're following instructions, take time to reflect on each step and each ingredient. Think about why it might be important. You don't need to be a perfectionist; as your inner chef emerges, feel free to find ways to embellish your dishes and infuse them with your own creativity.

Build Your Culinary Intuition by . . .
Eating

One of the best ways to heighten your understanding of flavors, spices, textures, visuals, and scents is—believe it or not—to eat. *Pay attention when you're eating.* That may sound elementary, but it's truly the best way to learn about the mystic alchemy of food and cooking. Go out to eat. Go to gourmet restaurants, but also try foods from different cultures at small "hole-in-the-wall" joints. Chew slowly. Try to parse out the herbs and spices and other components of the dish. Ask the other people dining with you if they can discern specific ingredients or particular feelings and emotions in the food. The more you eat different kinds of food made by different kinds of people, and the more attention you pay to the way those dishes were prepared, the more your inner Mystic Chef will be awakened.

Build Your Culinary Intuition by . . .
Knowing Your Ingredients

Know your ingredients. How often do you race into a grocery store, run from aisle to aisle, grabbing the same few things you always get, and then hit the checkout without ever really spending any time taking in your surroundings?

Someday, when you have a spare afternoon, spend an hour wandering the aisles of your local supermarket. Examine the produce section. Are there fruits and vegetables you've never seen before? Ask the produce manager to tell you about them. Where are they from? Who grew them? What do they taste like? Maybe take some home to try. Explore the dry goods, frozen items, and ethnic sections. As a suggestion, buy a few new items each time you go shopping to see what different foods you can add to your cooking repertoire. This will enrich your diet and give you a greater sense of all that's available. Additionally, this can assist you in tuning in to a variety of different food energies and vibrations.

Build Your Culinary Intuition by . . .
Taking Cooking Lessons

As another step in your intuitive cooking apprenticeship, you may want to consider taking a few cooking lessons. Learn how to shop for quality ingredients, the proper way to hold a knife, how to chop without cutting your fingers, and how to turn a few humble items into an amazing feast. Mastering these skills will encourage the awakening of your own culinary genius. Plus, they can be a fun way to make cooking a communal experience.

Build Your Culinary Intuition by . . .
Experimenting

The most important step in discovering your inner chef is experimentation. *Be willing to fail.* Try different combinations and see what happens. Experiment with cooking at different temperatures and for different amounts of time. Test out new flavors, spices, ingredients, and combinations. You may also want to experiment with infusing different thoughts, feelings, and emotions into your food. Spend an afternoon being a mad scientist. Practice the ancient art of alchemy and see what happens. The final product might be inedible or incredible, but you won't know until you try.

Building Your Culinary Intuition by . . .
Meditating and Tuning In

Intuitive cooking requires a bit of courage and a lot of imagination. Once you've built your foundation, you're ready to leap into the fun and exciting world of intuitive cooking. In addition to the practical side, there are also spiritual ways to prepare for this kind of cooking. Start by quieting your mind, and then either ask your Kitchen Angel for guidance or tune in to your inner knowing. As you shop or peruse your kitchen pantry, imagine that the ingredients are telling you how they want to be combined and prepared. This simple exercise often produces powerful results.

Additionally, you might want to consider visualizations to spice up your intuitive meals. Top-ranked athletes employ creative visualization to improve their skill, and so can you to deepen your ability to create mystic alchemy in your food. The key to visualization is to not just visualize a scenario, but also to actually *feel* as if it's really so. Here are some exercises you might want to do to help activate your intuitive cooking skills. (They really work!)

* Visualize you're in a cooking competition. The pressure is on, but the depth of your skill is so vast that you've created an amazing dish in minutes. Imagine the audience applauding you for this feat.

* Imagine your inner chef creating a sacred meal for the temple priestesses. Every step and every piece of food is filled with higher vibrational energy. Imagine the priestesses' auras becoming even more sparkling and vibrant as they eat the meal you've made.

* Visualize everyone you've ever loved or cared for is at a gathering, and you're preparing food that has an energy that brings people together. Imagine everyone sitting down together. Perhaps you even see their eyes glistening, because the food tastes so incredible and is so moving.

Dowsing, Pendulums, and Your Food

Dowsing can be another powerful tool to help you build your culinary intuition and access your inner Mystic Chef. Although this ancient practice is most notably used for finding underground water, believe it or not, it can be a gateway to your own inner knowing about the foods that will combine well to make amazing meals and the foods that will best serve your body's nutritional needs.

Dowsing is the practice of using a divining rod or pendulum to locate or learn more about underground water, gemstones, metals, and other unseen items. Often the rod or pendulum will seem to move of its own accord in response to the dowser's (the person holding the rod or pendulum) intention. The art of dowsing has been around for thousands of years. Prehistoric rock paintings in Algeria depict early dowsers, and research has uncovered evidence that ancient Chinese and Egyptians also used dowsing. And

even today, people who would never buy a New Age book or use a crystal for healing will still hire the local "water witch" to pinpoint where to drill for water, and thus save a lot of money on drilling dry wells.

Even if there's no clear explanation why it works, dowsing does indeed work, and you can learn to dowse your food. Anyone can, because dowsing taps into your intuition. The traditional way to dowse your food is to hold a pendulum (or a string with a small stone or crystal hanging on it) over the item of food. Hold it lightly between your thumb and forefinger. Ask the question: "Is this food beneficial for me at this time?" or, "Is this a useful ingredient for this particular meal?" And allow the pendulum to move, spiral, or swing. Usually an up and down is a yes, and a side to side is a no. Or spiraling clockwise is a yes and counterclockwise is a no.

You can also use your pendulum to energize your food. Simply holding it over your food and allowing it to spiral freely helps activate latent codes of harmonics within the meal. You'll notice a difference in the way it tastes. It can take a bit of practice to avoid the temptation to control the movement of the pendulum, but after you learn, it's easy to use. You can use dowsing pendulums when shopping, eating out, or with the food in your home. It can help you tap into your innate knowing and choose the best foods for your mystic meals.

NOURISHMENT TO NIRVANA

I had a friend, many years ago, who lived in India as a devotee of a world-renowned guru. He wore a ring that he said the guru had manifested for him out of the air. As much as I want to believe in amazing miracles, I still have a strong skeptical side, so when he told me this, I murmured, "Maybe it was sleight of hand, like a really good magician?"

He replied, "Denise, it really just appeared. I was standing right next to him, and I saw it appear in his hand."

It was hard to accept that this was true, but I knew my friend was honest and forthright. If he said the guru manifested his ring, then I believed him. While at the ashram in India, he'd fallen in love with the cuisine, so I decided to create a special meal for him at my home. (This was before I married my husband.) I invited some girlfriends to help me with the preparation. To get into the mood, we all wore saris and chanted Sanskrit mantras while we chopped vegetables and cooked. We wanted to infuse the food with love. We also decorated the living room in Indian style, with saris that we draped over the furniture to create the feeling of a candlelit tent in the Raja's forest. Incense floated lightly in the air, the gentle drone of Ravi Shankar ragas played on the record player, and the aromas and spices of the Punjab filled the space with a devotional energy.

We imagined we were like Hindu gopi serving girls, in utter and unwavering dedication to the Divine, as we brought out course after course of chapattis, curried vegetables, and dal. There was magic in the air. You could feel it. The evening transcended—beyond our desire to create a special meal—into a feeling that a universal devotion for the Divine was flowing through us.

At one point an ecstatic look came over our friend, and he declared he was having a spiritual experience. "I can actually see through the walls! I can really see through walls!" he said in awe. "This kind of mystical thing never happened to me before, even when I was with my guru! This is even more incredible than seeing a ring appear in front of me." The meal was intoxicating, and we hadn't even had any alcohol or mind-altering substances. It was an evening that none of us will ever forget. And it made me realize the potential spiritual power of a meal made with blessings and love.

Spiritual Cooking

It's not uncommon to hear that eating can be a spiritual experience; however, the act of cooking can be filled with just as much spirit, if not more so. Sri Chinmoy, an Indian spiritual teacher, said, "Because food is life and life is God, both food and God are one," and you can be especially aware of this when preparing a meal. Cooking a meal in a mindful way—no matter your religious background and beliefs—can be a spiritual practice.

With your inner Mystic Chef and culinary intuition activated, you're ready to embark on a mystical journey to the center of your soul. In no small way, this form of spiritual cooking will take you from nourishment to nirvana.

Creating Vibrational Harmony with Communal Cooking

In ancient and nature traditions, cooking was often a communal venture. It was a time when the women shared stories, sang songs, told jokes, and supported each other through the challenges of the day. In the deepest sense, the feeling of connection they felt while they were cooking imbued the food with "community energy," which in turn created even more of a feeling of community for those eating.

Faith suppers, also known as potlucks, are gatherings where people contribute either a dish to the menu or an ingredient to the pot. The name comes from the fact that you have "faith" that everyone will contribute something. In the early days, Irish women congregated to cook the evening meal with the ingredients of the day as they only had one pot among them. It was truly a sharing of gifts and creating of synergy, as the individuals came together to create sustenance for each other. Ingesting the combined energies of everyone in the town in one meal, in fact, helped bond people together in even more harmony.

In today's world we usually cook alone, and cooking is seen by many as a chore or duty rather than a strengthening of community and a way to infuse food with Spirit. In a strange way, perhaps those in today's world who watch television while cooking are subconsciously invoking cellular memories of cooking in groups. Although it's not often possible to cook with others, making a conscious effort to periodically do so will activate cellular memories of ancestral times and will fill the food with the combined energy of your friends and family.

Instead of inviting friends over for a meal that's already prepared, as a suggestion, consider asking them to participate in the creation of a meal in which the creativity and kinship is as potent and meaningful as the actual meal itself. When this is done, the joy you feel while cooking will infuse the food with all of those good feelings.

Cooking When You Are on Your Moon Cycle

In ancestral times, when women gathered together, a vibrational harmony often occurred and their moon cycles aligned. In many traditions, the women would go to a special structure called a "moon lodge," or into a hut or tent (sometimes called the "red tent") to replenish their energy together. It was considered a woman's sacred time.

In many cultures, during a woman's monthly menstrual cycle, she wasn't supposed to prepare food. While the women of childbearing age would be in the moon lodge, the older women and young girls would do the cooking. (Food prepared by women on their menses was thought to be lacking in energy and vitality.) For most of the month, a woman would give energy to the food, but her menses was the time to turn within to reconnect with her spiritual source and revitalize her own inner stores.

Some social scientists have erroneously thought that cultures in which the women didn't do food preparation during their menses were the result of a male-originated dominance. They shared a belief that "banishing" women to the moon lodge was a kind of a punishment; however, the time that these ancient women spent in solidarity and community was anything but a punishment. It was a time-honored way of cherishing the cyclic nature of women's energy and enabling them to renew their energy.

In today's world, we don't have traditions in place to honor a woman's monthly cycle. And in many cases, it's just not possible to do so. Few employers would be willing to allow their female employees days off every month for their moon-time. There are things, however, that you can still do to honor this sacred occurrence. As a suggestion, if you're on your menses, this would be a great time to order pizza or get takeout and use the extra time to nourish yourself and replenish your energy. The more we can honor the natural cycles of life, the more in balance we'll be.

COOKING AS A SPIRITUAL CALLING

For the last 30 years, I've hired many chefs to cook at my seminars, and although my all-time favorite person to work with has always been Meadow, there have been times when she was at school or traveling. These cooks have come in many forms: an Australian chef from the Outback, who held up a cleaver and threatened anyone who would dare say anything about his food; a macrobiotic chef from Sweden; traditional cooks from Mexico; a Rastafarian; several chefs who trained at Le Cordon Bleu; a chef who had prepared a meal for the queen of England; a fire dancer who cooked in her off-season; a chef from the Caribbean, who always danced exuberantly while he cooked . . . and everything in between. Over time, I began to notice a correlation between the meals that seminar participants raved about and the chefs who cooked them.

Some of the chefs looked at cooking as a mundane task, and they did a tolerable job of putting ingredients together in a way that looked and tasted good. Although participants were satisfied with the meals, they didn't talk about transcendent food experiences. However, the chefs who cooked with passion or looked at cooking as a spiritual calling infused a kind of magic into the food. Even ordinary, simple ingredients seemed to shimmer with vitality when the chef was inspired and saw his or her profession as elevated and hallowed.

On the deepest level, your soul knows what will serve and support your spiritual evolution, and for some people, cooking can fulfill a yearning that religion and even spiritual practice doesn't seem to fill. Of course, it's more than all right to cook because your family needs to eat or because you're hungry. These meals can be warm, loving, and fulfilling. But what we're talking about are the kind of cooking experiences where it seems time stands still and the cadence of the chopping, dicing, and stirring feels like a ceremonial dance of the gods. There are many reasons why people will be drawn to being a chef, but most certainly one of the reasons is because their soul is nudging them to it.

The kind of cook who's drawn to cooking as a path to the Divine will often have an innate understanding of the flows of energy. When preparing meals for small children, she might intuitively imbue an innocent or playful energy into the food. Or if he's cooking for young adults, he might subconsciously infuse the food with a powerful and vibrant energy. If someone is flighty, the spiritual chef might intuitively make a meal that has a grounding energy. Or if someone is stagnant and stuck in his or her life, the spiritually inspired chef might intuitively create a meal that's filled with uplifting and motivating energy. The ability to prepare food with the energy that's needed might not be something that the spiritual chef does consciously; yet, there's an innate knowing of what is needed for each person and for each meal.

The true gift of cooking as a spiritual calling is that the sustenance that's provided for others ultimately cycles back to the giver. What you give out with a pure heart comes back tenfold. Food prepared in this way transmits energy from the chef to the food and from the food to the person who eats it. In turn, this energy radiates out from that person in gratitude and ultimately returns to the cook, magnified.

Just as a musician dissolves into a song or an artist loses track of himself as he paints, such as Michelangelo getting so drawn into his painting that he'd forget to eat or change his clothes, the spiritual chef seems to disappear or dissolve into the act of preparing and cooking food. It's as if part of your spirit is sprinkled in each meal. There are moments when the boundaries between you and the food dissolve, and you become the food and the food becomes you.

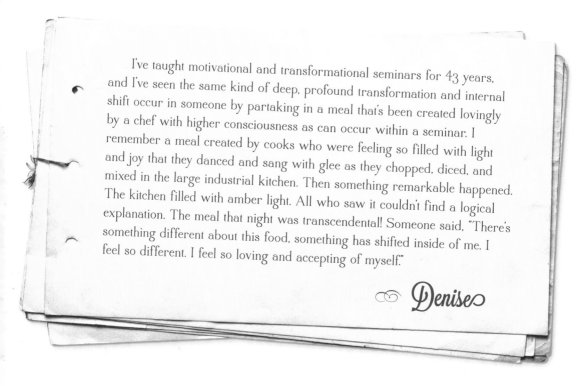

I've taught motivational and transformational seminars for 43 years, and I've seen the same kind of deep, profound transformation and internal shift occur in someone by partaking in a meal that's been created lovingly by a chef with higher consciousness as can occur within a seminar. I remember a meal created by cooks who were feeling so filled with light and joy that they danced and sang with glee as they chopped, diced, and mixed in the large industrial kitchen. Then something remarkable happened. The kitchen filled with amber light. All who saw it couldn't find a logical explanation. The meal that night was transcendental! Someone said, "There's something different about this food, something has shifted inside of me. I feel so different. I feel so loving and accepting of myself."

Denise

How to Tell If Cooking Is a Spiritual Calling for You

* You love cooking even if you have no one to cook for, and it gives you joy to eat what you've prepared.

* You find there's a feeling of being "home" that occurs while you're in the kitchen.

* While cooking, you find that time drifts away, and you lose sense of the passage of time.

* Your energy is higher and clearer when you finish than when you started.

* You seem to become *one* with the food, blending with all the flavors, aromas, textures, colors; it's like the food speaks to you!

* You notice that everything in the kitchen is glowing as you cook, including yourself.

What You Can Do If You Want Cooking to Be Your Spiritual Calling

Perhaps you answered the questions above and found that you answered *no* to most of them, but you'd like cooking to be a spiritual calling. Here are some things you can do:

VISUALIZE: Imagine yourself in your kitchen and feeling so connected to every aspect of the environment. See yourself having fun and feeling deeply relaxed and happy.

PUT OUT THE CALL: Call to those in the spirit world who had cooking as their spiritual calling during their lives on the earth plane. Ask them to assist you in your quest to be this special kind of chef. How do you do this? It's

simple . . . just ask. For example, you might say, "I humbly call upon those in the spirit world who have a passion for cooking to come forward to support me in the journey ahead." You may immediately feel a whoosh of energy, but sometimes it's just a slow awareness that those in the realm of spirit are supporting you. When you speak from the heart, those in spirit hear you and respond.

YOU CAN LOVE TO COOK BUT NOT HAVE A CALLING AS A CHEF: That's totally all right! You might enjoy the texture and taste of preparing a delicious meal and might even enjoy the loving comments you receive, but at the same time, you may feel that this isn't your calling, just as someone may love to paint but not necessarily feel the calling to be a painter. How you use your amazing talents is up to you. It's your gift to share as you please, and in doing so, you'll touch the hearts of others along the way.

THE MYSTICAL SPICE OF LIFE

Do you want to have a spicy, passionate, mystical life? You might consider spicing up your life with . . . well, spices. Herbs and spices throughout the ages have taken on nearly mythical proportions. The heady aromas of cinnamon, cloves, nutmeg, and ginger are enough to make anyone dream of far-off lands, magic carpet rides, and Grandma's apple pie. Even though in our current times spices are simply flavorings, as you step into the realm of the Mystic Chef, you can tune in to a spice to invoke its secret alchemical power. In ancient times, it was believed that each one had a hidden mystical quality that could be ignited by those who knew how to communicate with it. Activate this potent energy, and your life will be filled with delicious spice alchemy. Your cooking will go from delicious to transformative.

Our Growing Appetite for Herbs and Spices

Spices first became popular in the Western world during the Crusades. Paradise was believed to reside in the East, so naturally since many spices also came from the East, it was thought they grew in the Promised Land and carried the magic of that mysterious land. For example, allspice was considered a lucky spice, and its mystical power was used to ignite abundance. It was also burned as an incense to attract prosperity. And bay leaves were used by ancient Greeks to increase psychic powers. However, the magical allure of spices is not limited to the far past; Tulsi (also known as Holy Basil) is one of the most sacred plants in India. In present day, it's thought to open the heart center and thus bestow love and devotion.

Spice Alchemy

Spice alchemy is a powerful combination of belief, spirit, and substance. A sprinkle of this and a hint of that can completely transform something ordinary into something extraordinary. Imagine mulled cider without cinnamon or eggnog without nutmeg. What about molasses cookies without ginger and cloves or potatoes without cracked black pepper? Not to mention Indian curries without turmeric, coriander, and cardamom; Mexican food without cumin and ground chilies; or Italian sausage without fennel and dried herbs. Nearly everything we eat has some form of herbs and spices in it, from the salt and pepper that's sprinkled over a simple steak to the more exotic combinations used in soups, stocks, and curries. Imagine how much more potent those foods would be if you activate the secret life force within the spices before using them.

Herbs and spices are one of your most powerful allies in the kitchen. When creating spice alchemy, be like the ancient alchemists and play around with the spices in your cupboard to see what exciting blends and flavors you can create. Take a moment to tune in to the mystical qualities of each spice. Imagine that you're "asking" the spice what quality it's bringing into your home, and then invite it to activate that quality in the food you're preparing. *This is the secret that turns a spice into something much more than just a flavoring.*

It can be as simple as holding the spice in your hand and tuning in to the energy it will bring to your meal. Then visualize energy flowing from your hands into the spices, thus activating the mystical energy within them. Turn plain chicken breast into a tasty meal with a handful of energized fresh herbs or a blend of aromatic spices. Voilà, "Cosmic Chicken"! To create "Divine Dal," add a spoonful of curry powder and a dash of grated ginger (that you have charged with energy) to lentils, and the rich and delicious staple of Indian cuisine comes alive. With a sprinkle of blessing-infused cinnamon and nutmeg, suddenly plain oatmeal transforms into "Blessing Oatmeal."

Getting to Know Your Spices

One of the best ways to understand the powerful alchemy of your spices is to smell them. Unscrew the caps on your spice jars, close your eyes, and inhale deeply. What do you smell? Perhaps when you sniff the jar of cinnamon, you just smell cinnamon, but it's likely that its heady scent will fill your mind with images of applesauce, warm coffee cake, blueberry pie, Mexican hot chocolate, Indian rice dishes, or any other assortment of foods and memories that its smell evokes for you. Or perhaps images of camel caravans of antiquity or carting bags of spices across the golden desert swirl in your mind.

Go through each of your spices and familiarize yourself not just with their scents but also with the thoughts, feelings, and memories that they elicit from you. For instance, oregano might make you recall happy feelings of summers during your childhood spent playing in a neighbor's garden, and perhaps dill makes you feel comforted since it was your dad's favorite herb. Consider doing this once with your eyes closed to see if you can correctly identify the herbs and spices, and then do it with your eyes open. You may even want to take notes on the memories that each smell brings forth. When you cook with these spices, you can imbue your culinary creations not only with the flavors of the spices and their innate mystical energy, but also with the power of your memories. This is the secret alchemy of infusing your food with spice energy.

You might consider making a spice "dictionary" in your journal. Record what spice scents you like, what memories and emotions each one recalls, and what mystical powers you've discovered when you've tuned in to each one.

Herbs and Spices to Magically Invite the World into Your Kitchen

Learning to harness the secret alchemy of spices can transport you across oceans, over mountains, and through time to connect with different cultures and periods in history, which can lead to greater depths of understanding and powerful transformation. For instance, when combined together, mint, basil, and cilantro are the "holy trinity" of Thai and Vietnamese cuisine. Add those three herbs to any salad or stir-fry, and suddenly you you're in a longboat on the Mekong. Mix fresh mint with carrots, and you're in an opulent palace in Casablanca. Cilantro, cumin, and chili can transport you to Mexican jungles and beaches of bright blue water. And ginger, cumin, turmeric, cardamom, and coriander invite images of Hindu gods and goddesses. One taste of basil and oregano and you're in an Italian seaside village, and the wafting aroma of rosemary and thyme sends you on an odyssey to the South of France.

As a suggestion, spend time learning about the herbs and spices used in different kinds of cuisine. This will be beneficial as you tap into your inner spice alchemist. Mix, match, add, dash, and concoct your way to a spice-filled life!

VISUALIZATION: Imagine you're entering a mystical spice shop. The energy is palpable and magical. Every spice jar is labeled. You can consult with the mysterious and wise shopkeeper at the counter or choose the spices you desire to make a blend for your life. Before you go to sleep, imagine that a sachet of these spices is beneath your pillow so you absorb the energy during the night.

SAIGON SALAD

Herbs and spices have an amazing ability to transport you to
far-off lands without ever leaving the comfort of your own home.
The fresh herbs and vegetables in this salad are so light and refreshing.
This is a dish you're going to return to again and again.

SERVES 4 – 6

SALAD

1 lb. carrots, peeled and
grated

1 English (hothouse)
cucumber, grated

½ lb. (8 oz.) green beans,
trimmed and cut at a sharp
angle into thin 2-inch strips

1 red bell pepper, cut into
thin 2-inch strips

1 jalapeño, very thinly sliced
(optional)

1 cup each of chopped basil,
mint, and cilantro

½ cup chopped dry-roasted
peanuts

½ cup fried shallots*

DRESSING

¼ cup sugar

¼ cup warm water

¼ cup fish sauce**

¼ cup fresh lime juice
(from 2 to 3 limes)

Grate the cucumber, and peel and grate the
carrots, either with a box grater or a food
processor fitted with a grating disc. (Luckily,
English cucumbers don't need to be peeled!)
Combine in a large bowl. Trim the green beans
and cut at a sharp angle to create long, thin strips.
Slice the red pepper and jalapeño. Combine with
the carrots and cucumber. Chop the herbs and
toss with the vegetables.

To make the dressing, combine the sugar and
warm water in a small bowl. Stir to dissolve the
sugar. Whisk in the fish sauce and lime juice.
Drizzle the dressing over the vegetables and toss.
Just before serving, sprinkle the peanuts and fried
shallot on top of the salad.

* Fried shallots (sometimes also labeled as
"fried onion") can be found online and at Asian
markets. Although the fried shallots add a
distinctly Vietnamese flavor to this salad, it will
still be delicious if you can't find them.

** Fish sauce is the predominant flavoring
in Southeast Asian cooking. It can be
purchased in Asian markets, well-stocked
supermarkets, and natural food stores.

CASABLANCA CARROTS

This salad is extremely simple to make,
yet the flavors are bold and delicious.
My mom, who doesn't much care for carrot salads,
absolutely adores this one.
. . . I think it's the powerful energy of the mint.

SERVES 4

1 lb. carrots, peeled and grated

½ cup chopped fresh mint

3 Tbsp. fresh lemon juice (or to taste)

3 Tbsp. extra-virgin olive oil

salt (to taste)

Peel and grate the carrots, either with a box grater or a food processor fitted with a grating disc. Remove the mint leaves from the stalk and chop the leaves. Combine the carrots with the mint in a large bowl.

In a small bowl, whisk the lemon juice with the olive oil and salt. Toss the salad with the dressing and enjoy.

BLESSING OATMEAL

My first job was cooking for my mom's
retreats the summer after I graduated from high school.
I shared the kitchen with a professional cook from South Africa,
who taught me how to make spiced oatmeal. The fresh ginger warms
you from the inside, and the other spices work together to create
a type of spice alchemy that makes this oatmeal irresistible.

SERVES 4 – 6

4 cups water

2 cups old-fashioned
rolled oats

½ an apple, peeled, cored,
and chopped

¾ tsp. freshly grated ginger

½ tsp. cinnamon

¼ tsp. freshly grated nutmeg

¼ tsp. ground cloves

pinch of salt

¼ cup dried cranberries
or raisins

These directions make oatmeal with a creamy
consistency. If you prefer it less creamy, bring the
water and apple to a boil before adding the oats.

In a medium-sized pot, combine the water, oats,
and apple. On medium-high, bring the mixture
to a gentle boil and then reduce the heat to low.
Meanwhile, add the spices and salt to the pot,
stirring frequently. Add the dried cranberries and
continue to cook until the apples are soft and the
water is fully absorbed, about 10–15 minutes. Stir
frequently. Oatmeal has a tendency to stick to the
bottom of the pot.

Serve with butter, chopped nuts, grated coconut,
honey, and a drizzle of milk or coconut milk.

Leftover oatmeal can easily be reheated.
Add water to the cold oatmeal, stir, and heat
on the stove on low, stirring frequently. It will
be even creamier the second time around!

SECKEL PEARS IN MULLED RED WINE

Seckel pears are only available for a short time in the autumn.
They're small and sweet. They look elegant when poached in red wine
and served with a scoop of vanilla ice cream. Whenever I eat these,
I have visions of medieval kings and noblemen dining on something very similar.
This is a delicious dessert for practicing mystic spice alchemy.

SERVES 4 – 6

1½ cups sugar

1 bottle (750 ml.) of
full-bodied red wine

2 cinnamon sticks, broken
in half

3 star anise pods

5 whole cloves

4 approx. 3-inch long strips
of orange peel, bitter white
pith scraped or cut off

12 Seckel pears, ripe but
not overly soft

In a medium-sized pot (3 qt.) over medium heat, combine the sugar and wine. (If the pot is any larger, the wine won't adequately cover the pears.) Stir until the sugar dissolves completely. Add the cinnamon, star anise, cloves, and orange peel. Bring to a simmer, stirring occasionally.

Meanwhile, peel the pears. Be sure to leave the stem intact for the prettiest presentation. Add the pears to the simmering wine. Adjust the temperature as needed so that the pears poach in liquid that's just barely simmering with only occasional bubbles. (Don't boil!) Poach until the pears are soft and tender, about 1½ hours. If the wine doesn't fully cover the pears, use a spoon to baste them from time to time, and gently turn them over. This will ensure even cooking and color distribution.

Serve warm (but not hot) with vanilla ice cream. Yum!

The leftover syrup can be frozen to make a delicious slushy or use it as a base for festive cocktails.

EAT SLOW, CONNECT TO SOUL

> *"There is more to life
> than increasing its speed."*
>
> — MAHATMA GANDHI

I've always eaten rapidly. I trace it back to my childhood. There were times when we didn't have enough food, and the child who ate the fastest got the food. I had three siblings, and although I was the oldest, I was the smallest, and mealtimes always seemed like survival of the fittest. Even though we're grown-up and have plenty of food, my siblings and I have a fallback tendency to eat quickly. For me, learning to eat slowly continues to take real discipline. But it's well worth the reward, because when I do, life seems more luminous and the voice of Spirit is clearer.

Many years ago I had an experience in France that worked like a wonderful reset button for me. I'd fallen into the American tradition of eating on the fly in front of my computer or television. This didn't seem out of the ordinary, because everyone I knew (with the exception of Meadow) did the same thing. The first few days of eating in the restaurants in France were agonizing for me. Every course took so long.

"When's the food coming?" I'd ask. Meadow would say, "Mom, just slow down. Enjoy the experience." But I'd keep saying, "What's taking so long?" And then after we'd eaten, I'd lament, "Where's the bill?" Meadow had spent enough time in France to understand the languid tempo of French dining, but it was really hard for me.

It took about three days of anxious eating to just surrender to the slower pace. When I finally did, it was amazing. I found that I was more present with my family. I heard our conversations more intimately. The colors of the food were more vivid. I tasted the complex overtones and nuances of each dish. I enjoyed the atmosphere of the restaurant. There was radiance around the entire dining experience that never occurred when I raced through my meal. I immersed myself so much in the experience that when we returned home, I found the rapid pace of dining in the United States jarring and had a hard time adjusting.

Slowing down is the final step in connecting with your inner Mystic Chef and engaging the ancient art of alchemical spiritual cooking. By slowing down, you open your heart so that Spirit may work through you to infuse everything you touch with potent life-force energy. Once the groceries have been purchased, the vegetables washed, and the dinner cooked to perfection, consider putting just as much thought and intention into eating the meal as you did in preparing it. This is the sign of a true Mystic Chef.

You incarnated onto this planet with a mission. There is indeed a reason you're here, and part of your journey while you're in this physical realm is to experience life to the fullest and to listen to the messages of your soul. In the

dizzying pace of life, sometimes this can be a challenge. The average number of rings on a phone—before someone gets impatient and hangs up—is three rings! It's less than eight seconds before someone gets restless and moves on to the next thing. All the so-called timesaving devices—such as dishwashers, cars, cell phones, e-mail, and instant messaging—in fact, have not saved us time for leisure and relaxation; they've only sped up our frenetic pace. As the speed of life increases, we inevitably eat faster and faster. We dine on microwaved frozen pizza while sitting in front of a computer, driving a car, or talking on the phone. As a consequence, we don't taste our food, and more important, we don't taste and savor our life. This approach to food diminishes our ability to fulfill our purpose to the deepest extent.

To connect even more intimately with your purpose in being here on Earth, as a suggestion, spend time living in an unhurried manner. As you slow down, remarkable insights will wash over you. You'll be at the right place at the right time more often, and you'll also be in alignment with your soul purpose more often. When you cook or eat slowly and methodically, you're living in the present moment, rather than thinking about the things you've done in the past or the things you should be doing in the future. It's in these times when you're truly experiencing "now" that you're most open to hearing the truth of your soul.

Additionally, eating rapidly activates cellular memories of fight or flight, because in ancient times, when one was under attack or fleeing from danger, it was necessary to eat quickly and on the road. This kind of rapid eating actives a subconscious, physiological stress response; your heartbeat increases, blood pressure rises, adrenaline and cortisol are released into the circulation system, and your blood flows away from your brain and stomach and into your legs and arms for a fight-or-flight response. Tellingly, your digestive system shuts down, as you need energy for fleeing rather than digesting your food, when you are running from an angry horde. Munching quickly on the fly lessens your ability to absorb nutrients from your food while at the same time packing on weight, because in a stressful situation, with enemy tribes in pursuit, you need to store calories (as subconsciously, you never know when your next meal will be).

For a study at the University of Rhode Island, a group of women was allowed to eat as much as they wanted at two different and separate meals. During the first meal, they were told to eat quickly using large utensils. The second time they were instructed to use small utensils, take small bites, and put the fork down between bites. The first meal took 9 minutes to eat, and the second took 29 minutes. Remarkably, the women consumed 10 percent fewer calories at the second meal *and said they felt fuller!* This means that simply by eating slower, you could potentially lose over 20 pounds a year without suffering through a diet or trying to starve yourself.

The simple act of slowing down signals the body not to be in fight-or-flight mode, so food is digested more fully. Maybe you've heard of someone who was on vacation say they ate so much more than usual but didn't gain a pound or, in fact, lost weight. This was likely due, in part, to the fact that they were relaxed and eating at a slower pace, so their food was digested rather than stored as fat. Eating rapidly also shortens your breath (Ever notice how hard it is to breathe after a Thanksgiving meal?), which causes less oxygen and creates more fat accumulation.

When you breathe deeply, you actually burn food more effectively and enjoy it more, too.

When people join us for trainings at Summerhill Ranch, they inevitably say they've never eaten so much. However, with only one exception, almost everyone loses weight or at least maintains their weight. We surmise this is in part because our meals are celebrations, and we eat in a very relaxed environment. Many people also say that the dining experience at Summerhill Ranch—combined with the Soul Journeys they do in class—led to spiritual transformation. Remarkable things can happen simply by slowing your pace, breathing deeply, and eating mindfully.

It's Not Enough for Your Mouth to Know You've Eaten; Your Brain Needs to Know, Too!

My husband, David, said, "You just had lunch and now you're eating again?" I replied, "I know, but I didn't taste lunch because I was working on the computer. I don't really remember my meal, so I'm eating again."

~ Denise ~

Have you ever eaten a big meal and still felt hungry? If the answer is yes, it might be because your brain didn't fully experience the taste and satisfaction of eating, so it didn't recognize that you'd actually eaten. Thus, it will continue to send you hunger signals. It says, "Duh! I don't remember eating, so I must not have. Feed me, feed me!"

It takes about 20 minutes for your brain to catch up to your stomach to give you the signal that you're "full," so why not take the time and make it a pleasurable journey. Here's how:

Slow Down/Open to Spirit

1. Look at the presentation of the meal. Embrace the colors, textures, and aromas. Relish all of it!

2. Take time to be grateful to the Creator and to those who grew the food, picked it, transported it, sold it, and prepared it. Every meal has a story to tell.

3. Take the first bite. Put down your fork and slowly chew, savoring the nuances of flavor the way that you would savor a fine wine.

4. Only after you've swallowed the first bite, take another. Be present and focused. Taste and smell the food.

5. Remember to breathe deeply and relax as you eat.

6. Allow more time for eating.

7. As often as you can, eat without reading, watching television, working on the computer, texting, talking on the phone, or

e-mailing. (We know it might sound really hard to do, but it's all part of the process of opening yourself to Spirit.)

8. After the meal, spend a few moments being still before jumping up to do the dishes or put the food away. Quiet your mind, open your heart, and listen to the whispers of your soul.

Mindful Eating: Being Present

I have a chipped front tooth that's a permanent reminder to eat more slowly and mindfully. I was not a particularly relaxed adolescent. I would lie in bed for hours, unable to fall asleep, thinking about the homework assignments I had to do while at the same time, rewriting the ones I'd already completed. Mornings were busy as I raced to and fro, getting ready for school, and often I'd end up eating my breakfast in the car while my mom drove me to the bus stop. One time, I was so harried that I started to chew before removing the fork from my mouth. Dentists have tried to repair my tooth but have been unsuccessful thus far at finding a lasting fix. Although I'm not particularly keen on the chip, I'm grateful to have the reminder to slow down and be more mindful of how I eat.

 Meadow

Mindful eating is the next step beyond slowing down. To eat mindfully is to eat with intention. It means to be not only thoughtful and cognizant of where your food came from, how it came to be on your plate, how it smells, how it tastes, how it looks, and how it feels on your tongue, but also to eat without judgment, to be free from limiting thoughts about yourself and the quality, nutritional value, or provenance of the food you ingest. If you find yourself judging the food you eat (or judging yourself for eating it), recognize the thoughts and then move on. Little will be gained from denying those thoughts or from judging yourself for having them. Just let them be . . . and then be present with the food on your plate, the people at your table, and your environment. Indulge in the experience of eating. Embrace every aspect.

Exercise:
Be Present with Your Morning Beverage

Many of us stumble out of bed bleary-eyed and head straight to the kitchen for a cup of tea or coffee. Have you ever looked at your empty mug and not remembered having drunk that first cup? Life can be hectic, and many of us are trying to do several things at once. As a suggestion, try being really present with your morning tea or coffee.

If you can, choose one day a week to be still while you have your coffee or tea. Allow yourself to feel the warmth of the mug between your palms. Watch the steam rising off the top. Does it rise straight up, or does it twist and move like dancing sprites? Notice how your palms feel after holding the warm mug. If you put cream in your coffee, what does it look like as you pour it in? Take a sip. What do you smell as you bring the mug toward your nose? What do you taste? How does it feel as you swallow it? Imagine you can follow it all the way down into your cells.

Take a few deep breaths. Listen to the morning sounds. Are there birds chirping? What about other outside noises? Cars? Trash collection? Be present with your coffee (or tea) and be present with this moment. What do you feel?

This entire experience probably only added five or ten minutes to your day, but do you feel a difference in your body? You may find that just taking these few moments to be present with your morning beverage has a calming effect on your body, and you may also find that it was much more flavorful because you took time to taste and experience it.

Using Food to Dictate Destiny

The way you eat your food can also help dictate your destiny. What you eat and how you eat can make an enormous difference in the way you pursue your destiny. If you desire to be more passionate in your future, eat and drink with mindful, wild, passionate abandon. Immerse yourself in the experience. Eat with your fingers. Never mind getting food on your face, lick your fingers and smack your lips. Revel in

the moment, and in no small way, this sends a message to your subconscious that this is who you are.

If you yearn to be disciplined and organized in life, then use your mealtimes to reinforce this. Take care with each and every bite. Be deliberate in the way you eat.

If you want to be clear and focused, choose foods that give you this feeling. Perhaps when you think of the word *clear,* you think of soup broth. For the word *focused,* you might think of finely julienned vegetables. If you eat these foods with the intention of becoming clearer and more focused in your life, so it will be.

Being a Mystic Chef is being willing to experiment, using your intuition to create energy-filled meals, and allowing Divine energy to infuse all aspects of your shopping, cooking, and eating. Just as employing the ancient art of kitchen alchemy and eating mindfully can connect you more deeply with Spirit, similarly, by creating sacred space within your kitchen and dining room, magic can occur. For instance, a Mystic Chef could imbue a meal with the most potent life force, but if the energy in the kitchen is stagnant or the dining room lacks that special sparkle, the meal might not be quite as radiant as it could be. In this chapter we entered the realm of the chef, but in the following chapter, we'll be voyaging through time to learn ancient techniques to energize the kitchen, dining room, and all those who enter those hallowed spaces.

SACRED SPACE

ENERGIZING YOUR DINING EXPERIENCE

You can have the most exquisite bouquet of freshly picked flowers that seem to shimmer with color, but if the vase is dull and dingy, it can decrease their beauty. This is also true in cooking. Even if your cooking is stellar, a kitchen or dining space that doesn't sparkle with energy will diminish the overall experience of the meal. True mystical cooking not only includes understanding the subtle energies within each part of the meal you prepare, but also it includes a wise comprehension of the energy of the rooms where you cook and dine, and the people with whom you share your meals. To elevate your dining experience from the

mundane act of fueling your body to a delicious moment of enlightenment, it's beneficial to spend time creating sacred space in your kitchen and dining room. As a result, your meals will be filled with magic.

In this chapter, you'll learn techniques for clearing, cleansing, and activating the life-force energy in your kitchen and dining room by employing the mystical arts of clutter clearing, space clearing, and feng shui. You'll also learn how to make and use a kitchen altar, pair your meals with just the right music, and be a mystical host employing the sacred art of hospitality.

KITCHEN AS SACRED SPACE

Your kitchen's energy field can function as a beacon of light that radiates outward in concentric circles, filling your home and also flowing out into the greater universe. By using the tools presented here, your kitchen will become a collecting point, as well as a transmitting point, for sparkling energy.

In earlier times, the kitchen was considered the heart of the home because it was where the family gathered to keep warm and share meals. It represented sustenance and community. In ancient cultures, altars were often assembled in the kitchen, as it was the sacred place where one communed with the Divine. Even though, for the most part, in our modern culture we've forgotten the

mystical power of the kitchen, we can still invite the wisdom of past times into our lives by transforming it into sacred space. The ideal sacred kitchen is clean and full of free-flowing *chi* (life-force) energy. There should be excellent lighting and, if possible, natural sunlight. You should feel uplifted simply by stepping into this room. Surfaces should be clear of clutter to allow for ease in preparing meals. Beautiful ceramic dishes, baskets of fruit, old wooden spoons (wooden spoons hold the energy and history of those who have used them in the past), or anything that feels soulful can give a feeling of celebrating Earth's abundance. The energy of the kitchen will dramatically affect your mood, which in turn spectacularly affects the energy in your food. In the following pages, you'll be taken through a multifaceted process to create sacred space in your kitchen and invite Divine energy into all the food prepared there.

The Kitchen Altar

Imagine you're traveling to an ancient land. It's early morning and you slowly arise. Sun is streaming through a crack in the mud and straw wall. Your family is still sleeping, and you're alone in the stillness of a new day. Before you begin the preparation of the morning meal, you step into the kitchen and light a single candle at the family altar, giving thanks to the Creator and asking for blessings for your family and for the day ahead. You pray that the food prepared that day will be filled with energy and life force. From these moments before the kitchen altar, you gain the strength that you need for the day.

In today's world, many people think altars are only found in churches. Yet for thousands of years, people created them in their dwellings. The home altar was a reminder of the profound mysteries of creation that brought meaning into ordinary moments of life and served as a focal point for communing with spiritual realms. Although the tradition of building altars in the kitchen still exists in some cultures, most people in the West grow up without any kind of home altar, let alone a kitchen altar. However, even today, when the mystical side of life has largely been neglected or ignored, the ancient custom of making altars has persisted in some interesting, if largely unconscious, ways that range from the gathering of photos on a piano (which in some ways can be likened to an ancestor altar) to a gathering of objects on a kitchen windowsill (which can be likened to the kitchen altars of antiquity).

To create sacred space within your kitchen, you might consider having an altar in your kitchen. It need not be complicated or elaborate. Simply lighting a candle, making an offering, or saying a few words of gratitude while focusing on the altar can dramatically affect your energy and that of the food.

Kitchen Altar Placement

Your kitchen altar can be anywhere that feels right. In ancient times, the home altar was often placed close to the hearth, which was considered to be the heart of the home—the modern equivalent would be your stove. However, it can also be placed on your refrigerator, a countertop, a shelf, a window ledge, or a table. Don't worry if it's somewhere that gets spattered by mixing or cooking liquids; you can look at this as a kind of blessing. If you absolutely have no space, you can create a vertical altar such as a collage or poster on the wall. You can also place the altar inside a cupboard that you can open while cooking and then close. Another idea is to find a small portable cupboard to hang on the wall. Or, you could get a small birdhouse to decorate as your kitchen altar.

What Do You Put on Your Kitchen Altar?

Anything that makes your heart sing is appropriate on your altar. There are no rules about what you should place on it. Put items that give you joy and the feeling of being nurtured and nourished.

Here are some things to consider:

BEHIND THE ALTAR: On the back of the altar or in your designated cupboard shrine, you may want to place a photo or drawing that represents the kind of energy you want to invite into your food. It could be a symbol, such as a heart; a painting of a cornucopia of fruit; or a beautiful photo of nature, such as an apple tree filled with plump red apples.

ALTAR CLOTH: Traditionally, altars have a cloth on which to place the objects. Anything from a fabric remnant to a cloth napkin or scarf can work as an altar cloth. Pay attention to the color, for every color invites a different kind of energy. (Refer back to Chapter 2 for a refresher on the alchemy of color.)

CANDLES: Having a candle on an altar is a subliminal reminder of the hearths of antiquity. It can activate ancestral memories of sitting around the fire with friends and family. Your altar candle need not be large; it can even be a votive. As a suggestion, light your candle with a blessing before you begin to prepare your meal, and then blow it out when you're complete. Some people like to have a food-scented candle, such as vanilla, rosemary, or cloves. (Remember to extinguish your candle when it's unattended.)

EDIBLES: In many cultures it's traditional to put items of food on the kitchen altar, such as bread, fruit (oranges are common), grains, or rice. It's important to remove perishable items when they're no longer fresh.

OBJECTS: Anything that brings you joy and activates a feeling of the nurturing energy of the kitchen can be placed on the altar, such as quartz crystals, pinecones, flowers, figurines, kitchen utensils (you can paint or carve symbols on the handle), or photos of your family and loved ones who are in spirit.

HONORING THE SEASONS: It's traditional to pay homage to the passage of the seasons on a kitchen altar. For example, in the autumn, you could place corn, squash, or an apple, and in the spring, you could place cherry blossoms or even an egg.

BLESSINGS: Once you've assembled your altar, take a moment to bless it. It can be as simple as closing your eyes and asking that the Divine be present in your kitchen.

KITCHEN GODDESS: Many traditions honor a goddess of the hearth and harvest. If you decide that you want to follow this time-honored tradition, you may want to choose a goddess that resonates with you and dedicate a part of your altar to her. Here are some goddesses to consider:

∗ *Tcheft:* Egyptian goddess of food (an incarnation of Isis)

∗ *Hestia:* Greek goddess of the hearth

∗ *Demeter:* Greek goddess of the harvest

∗ *Annapurna:* Hindu goddess of food and cooking (also the sustainer of prosperity)

∗ *Edesia:* Roman goddess of food, who also presides over banquets

∗ *Inari:* Japanese goddess/god of food

∗ *Hina-puku-'ai:* Hawaiian goddess of food plants

KITCHEN GOD: Of course, you might also want to consider honoring the gods of cooking. For example, Dionysus (Bacchus in Roman mythology) was the god of food, wine, dance, theater, and the ecstatic pleasures of eating. Additionally, many Chinese make offerings, such as oranges, sticky cakes, or spirits and wine, to the kitchen god, Zaoshen, whom they believe can grace a home with bounty, prosperity, and beneficial food. In Hong Kong, salted fish is placed on the kitchen god altar in hopes of abundance and full larders.

KITCHEN WITCH: A kitchen witch is a kind of homemade doll that resembles an older woman/crone. Typically, it's hung in the kitchen for good luck. It's thought that this tradition originated in Norway and the other Scandinavian countries, and then spread. The will of a John Crudgington of Shropshire, England, dated 1599, includes among his household possessions, "one witche in the kytchyn."

THE SECRET ALCHEMY OF
CLUTTER CLEARING AND CLEANSING THE KITCHEN

In addition to creating a kitchen altar, consider getting rid of any clutter in your kitchen to make room for the vibrant, sacred energy you're inviting into your cooking space. Clutter clearing is a kind of modern-day alchemy. It's one of the fastest ways to completely transform your life and often works in seemingly magical and mystical ways. Your health improves, your abundance increases, and your relationships deepen by clearing clutter, especially when in your kitchen.

Confronting the clutter in your cooking space frees up energy. When you practice letting go of things that no longer suit you, you open a space for what is exactly right for you now. If, out of fear, you hold on to what you have, then you're not open to receiving the gifts from the Universe that are coming your way. When you unclutter your kitchen, you unclutter your life and your soul. This doesn't mean you need to get rid of everything from your past, or that you shouldn't be prepared for the future. It just means there should be plenty of space and energy available for the here and now.

What Is Clutter?

If you don't use an item or don't love it, it's most likely clutter. It's an accumulation of things that impede the flow of energy in your home. The reason clutter can be a problem is that it's often tied to identity. It can make a statement about who you are and can represent aspects of your life. But sometimes to grow and change, you need to release this old vision of self.

Examples of kitchen clutter:

* Cans of food that have sat on your shelves for years

* Pans, pots, dishes, utensils, or serving dishes you never use

* Appliances that have been broken for a long time or have parts missing or you don't use

* Cookbooks you never open

* Items under the sink that are never used

* Condiments in the refrigerator or cupboard that haven't been used in over a year

* Items in the freezer that are over a year old

* Collections of recipes for dishes you'll never get around to cooking

* Stacks of expired coupons

Try this useful phrase when deciding whether or not something is clutter: *Use it, love it, or get rid of it!*

Why People Keep Clutter

One of the most common reasons people keep clutter is fear of the future. Although you might not need a particular item (and haven't needed it for years), you might be afraid to get rid of it because a need for it might arise in the future. *By thinking this way, you create your own need and stop trusting that the Universe will provide for you.* This belief becomes self-perpetuating, because fear about what is to come tends to create a fearful future.

What you expect in life often becomes reality. Believe that all your needs will be met, and they usually will be. A person who expects to have a bad day is usually not disappointed, while someone anticipating a good day is usually rewarded. If you're holding on to that industrial-size can of jalapeños (that you've had in your cupboard for ten years) because someday you might need it, get rid of it! Trust that you'll have exactly what you need. No matter what your reason for keeping clutter, it clogs the energy in your home, your body, and your life.

THE FENG SHUI OF YOUR MYSTIC KITCHEN

Feng shui is the ancient practice of positioning furniture and objects within a home to allow for maximum flow of life-force energy (called *chi* in China), which in turn leads to increased harmony and well-being. Various forms of feng shui are found in cultures throughout the world. Believe it or not, following some simple feng shui principles in your kitchen can greatly enhance both the way you feel and the meals you create. The better the kitchen feng shui is, the more energy you'll have while preparing a meal and the more energy your meals will absorb. (See Denise's books *Sacred Space* and *Feng Shui for the Soul*.)

From a feng shui perspective, the kitchen is one of the most important rooms in the home. The kitchen is the metaphor for what nurtures and nourishes you. When the kitchen energies are balanced, harmony radiates into all aspects of life. Following a few simple feng shui "rules" can help elevate this life-force energy in your home. However, some feng shui tenets can be confusing, especially as the experts and books don't always agree with each other. So how do you know if you have good feng shui in your kitchen?

If It Feels Good, It's Good Feng Shui

If it feels good, it's most likely good feng shui . . . and if it feels bad, it's probably bad feng shui. If your kitchen feels great to you every time you enter it, and if your abundance is flowing (in feng shui, the kitchen has a direct relationship with one's prosperity), then you have good feng shui. Don't change a thing. However, if it doesn't feel fantastic to you every time you step into your kitchen (or if you're having financial challenges), then you might consider making some feng shui changes, which are further explained in the following pages.

Only make a feng shui change if it feels good to you. Some suggestions are common sense, some come from traditional feng shui cures, and some are under the category of superstition, *so look at any feng shui suggestions with discernment.* However, feel free to experiment. Even if a change seems unconventional, you might consider trying it for a while, and if things improve, keep the change; and if they don't improve, disregard it.

The Importance of Your Stove

In feng shui, the stove is the most important element of the kitchen. Since food is cooked there, it represents life force and nourishment, but also it's an energy generator. In traditional Chinese feng shui, both the stove and the food cooked on it are connected to finances and abundance. In fact, the stove is considered to have greater impact on wealth than any other aspect of the home. Additionally, the stove is thought to affect your vitality, physical health, marriage, family harmony, personal protection from legal entanglements, and many other areas of life. So pay very careful attention to your stove.

* Make sure your stove is clean and isn't surrounded by clutter. Feng shui tenets declare that a dirty stove depletes energy and clogs finances. The burners are most important, and periodically cleaning the oven and broiler is also recommended.

* Use all the burners. Only using one or two burners can suggest not making full potential of the abundance available to you.

* Burners represent prosperity, so to symbolically double the burners, consider putting a mirror behind the stove to make it look like there are more.

* If any burners don't work, get them fixed. Additionally, fix anything on the stove that doesn't work, such as the oven light, fan, clock, oven hinges, or defective knobs.

* Don't leave empty pans on your stove. This is thought to symbolize lack.

* In Tibetan feng shui, the most important burner is the one on the far left as this symbolizes prosperity. Make sure you use this burner occasionally.

* Ideally, the stove shouldn't be right next to the refrigerator. (If it is, then put something made of wood, or a photo of trees, on the refrigerator to mitigate this inauspicious placement.) The cooling aspect of the refrigerator symbolically dampens the warming aspect of the stove. However, the fire energy becomes stronger when wood is added.

* When standing at the stove, the cook should be able to see the doorway. (In other words, you shouldn't have your back to the door.) If not, then a mirror positioned so the cook can see the

door (or at least whoever is behind him or her) is advantageous. The mirror should be as large as possible for the greatest effect. This feng shui advice is based on the fact that some people have a subconscious uneasiness when they can't see who's coming behind them. Curiously, this human trait exists even when people are alone.

＊ You shouldn't be able to see the stove from the front door. This is considered very inauspicious. If so, hang a wind chime, curtain, round-cut crystal, or a mobile between the door and the stove.

＊ The stove shouldn't be directly under a window; energy is dissipated, and this can create potential loss of energy for family members. Against a solid wall is better. If it's under a window, hanging a faceted crystal sphere in the window or placing plants on the window ledge (even beautiful silk plants if real plants don't work) will help soften the effect of this.

Good Kitchen Feng Shui

＊ Keep counters as clutter free as possible.

＊ There shouldn't be any obstacles to movement in the kitchen. The cook should be able to maneuver quickly and easily throughout the kitchen.

＊ Generally bright, vibrant light is much better than dim light, and halogen or incandescent light is better than fluorescent.

＊ Toilets are considered inauspicious and shouldn't be facing the kitchen. (If so, place a curtain or beaded curtain in front of the door and keep the door closed.)

＊ In traditional feng shui, an aquarium shouldn't be in the kitchen because the water element symbolically puts out the fire element, and the fire energy of the stove is thought to activate abundance and health.

＊ Knives shouldn't be left out on the counter, especially if they face toward anyone entering the kitchen. Put them away. (However, knives kept in a butcher block is okay, if it feels good to you.)

＊ If there are multiple doors into a kitchen, if the kitchen is a passage between rooms, or if it's an open kitchen, the *chi* may be too fast. It may be hard to hold on to money, or there may be discord among family members. As a suggestion, place wind chimes, mobiles, or faceted crystals in the doorways. Visualize peace and prosperity as you place these objects.

The most important key to great feng shui is your intuition. It's always the best, no matter what the feng shui "rules" are. As a suggestion, close your eyes, relax, and imagine that you're walking around your kitchen. Notice what feels wonderful and brings your energy up and what brings your energy down. Then use that information to make any necessary changes.

SPACE CLEARING YOUR KITCHEN

Now that you have your kitchen altar, your kitchen is clutter free, and your kitchen feels warm and inviting as a result of enhancing its feng shui, you're ready to fill this space with magical, uplifting, and sparkling energy.

For thousands of years, in ancient civilizations and native cultures throughout the world, sacred ceremonies were performed to instill beneficial energy into living spaces. People have been doing these clearing ceremonies for a very simple reason—they work! The methods and tools varied from one group to another, but the intent was the same—to create greater harmony. Native Americans used drums, rattles, and burning herbs in their rituals. The Chinese used gongs, chanting, and incense. In medieval

Europe, salt and prayers cleared energy. In the Middle East, smoldering resins, such as frankincense and myrrh, were used to invite blessings into a home.

Although many of these traditions have withered, arising from the deep wisdom of the earth, like a new sprout from the root of a venerable tree, comes the awakening of *space clearing* (a term coined by Denise). Antiquated ceremonies that brought vitality generations ago are once again being used.

To understand how space clearing works, it's valuable to take time to start sensing energy. We all have this ability. Have you ever walked into an empty room where you immediately felt the atmosphere was laced with tension? Although you might have no idea what took place there prior to your arrival, you could feel that it surely wasn't

pleasant. By contrast, other places seem to emanate joy and a peaceful sense of well-being. The differences between rooms that feel great and ones that seem depressing can be explained, at least in part, by the fact that some environments are simply more beautiful or physically inviting than others. However, there's a deeper truth underlying these explanations that has to do with energy. Some environments exude an energy that's nurturing, while other spaces can deplete you and even cause you to be depressed, irritated, or angry.

When we enter a space, we not only react to the style of the furnishings and colors we find there, but also we perceive the energy surrounding us. Positive energy makes us feel good. Negative energy brings us down. Space clearing offers a simple and highly effective way to turn the latter into the former. It can turn a depressing place into a haven of beauty, harmony, and effervescent joy. To create a mystical, magical, even legendary meal, it's valuable to space clear your kitchen and dining area.

The Four Steps of Space Clearing Your Kitchen

Space clearing involves a four-step process. Each step is integrally linked to each of the others, and together they create a kind of magic.

I. PREPARATION. Getting ready for a space clearing involves preparing yourself and the space you plan to clear. To prepare your kitchen, do a thorough cleaning. Wash the dishes, put away the groceries, and scrub the counters. It's also a good idea to do some clutter clearing. Doing a clearing in

a space that hasn't first been cleaned and de-cluttered is like dressing in formal wear for a special evening without bothering to first bathe and wash your hair. The results just won't feel the same.

To prepare yourself, take some time to "tune in." The more focused you become about what you envision, the more powerful the transformation of your environment.

Decide what "tools" you want for the clearing. You can use burning sage, a drum, or a bell; or simply clapping your hands with the intention of clearing the space can make a difference. After your space is tidied and your tools are prepped, take the time to cleanse yourself with a purifying salt bath or shower.

2. PURIFICATION. As you stand at your kitchen altar, take slow, deep breaths to center yourself. Imagine that you're grounded into the earth and at the same time connected to the heavens. With focused concentration, begin at the entrance and ring a bell, listening carefully to the sound. It should sound crisp and clear. If it doesn't, continue until it does. This change in tone indicates that you've cleared the energy in that area. Continue around the circumference of the room, ringing until you return to the place where you began. Then move your bell in a figure eight to seal the room.

3. BLESSING. Complete your space-clearing ceremony by returning to the kitchen altar to say prayers and ask for blessings for the food that's prepared and the people cooking and eating it. A typical blessing might be: "May the Creator within all things bring blessings and peace for all of the members of this household. May all the meals prepared here be filled with joy, laughter, and love. So be it."

4. PRESERVATION. The final step in space clearing is to preserve the new and radiant energy that you've called into the kitchen. Doing this keeps it alive. Just as plants and other living beings need to be carefully tended in order to thrive, energy also needs to be renewed in order for it to maintain its healing power. A preservation method might be to write a powerful word or symbol on a stone in waterproof ink to place on your altar. Alternatively, you can paint or write your prayers on a piece of paper, which you bury in the soil of a plant. Each time the plant is watered, the words or symbol will be energized.

Simply tending to your kitchen altar is another wonderful method of preservation. As you spend time at your altar, your thoughts and intentions will once again connect you to the energy of your kitchen and revitalize its power. You'll have a kitchen that's filled with love, joy, and sacred space. (For more information, see Denise's books *Sacred Space, Space Clearing,* or *Space Clearing A–Z.*)

THE MYSTIC DINING ROOM

Just as your kitchen can be a beacon of light where powerful energy and nourishing meals are created, your dining area can be a sacred gathering point that speaks of community and connection to greater forces. It can be a place where family members and friends listen to each other and voice opinions about the news of the day. Sitting around a table, bearing witness to the communication of another over a meal lovingly prepared, is indeed a spiritual odyssey.

Dining Room Feng Shui

In traditional feng shui, the dining room represents your prosperity, family, friends, and career. Ideally, the dining room should be off the kitchen or near the kitchen. Since the kitchen represents your finances and the dining room your prosperity, when the two are near each other, this energy is magnified. Large dining rooms are thought to assist finances and careers. However, if you have a small dining room, you can put mirrors on the walls to visually increase the size of the room. The larger the mirror the better, but be sure the reflections never cut off the heads of your dining companions. Ideally, no one at the table should be sitting underneath a beam, as this is thought to depress finances and career. Use colors in the dining area that are warm and inviting. You want the energy in this part of the home to feel like a place that invites communication and community.

Bowls of Fruit for Prosperity

Food on your dining table represents wealth. So as a suggestion, display a decorative bowl of fruit or a container of anything that feels abundant, such as a vase with a large bouquet of flowers. This is preferable to a bare table. In Asia, a bowl of oranges, tangerines, or mandarins is especially auspicious to invite abundance into a home. Photos or paintings of fruit or flowers are also thought to promote prosperity.

Shape of Table

The shape of the table makes a difference in feng shui. A round table is thought to inspire creativity, action, and energy. It's great for getting ideas flowing. Also the round shape is thought to be "good luck from heaven." Additionally, conversation often flows more freely at a round table. However, square and rectangular tables are equally lucky because they're good for consolidating energy and stability, and becoming more grounded.

Dining Room Altar

Just as you created a kitchen altar, you might want to consider an altar or a dedication in your dining area. In China, Fuk Luk Sau, the gods of health, wealth, and longevity are often placed on a high side table in the dining area to ensure that the family is always healthy, has plenty to eat, and is prosperous. They can often be purchased at Chinese supermarkets. However, any kind of buffet table or altar decorated with items that represent fulfillment is a great idea for your dining room.

Where You Sit at the Table

In feng shui, every chair at the dining table has a different energy, and it's valuable to understand how the energy of placement can make a difference in the family dynamic. Traditionally, the parents should have more "commanding positions," which would mean that if there's a choice between a chair with its back to a door or one with its back to a wall, the parent (or a guest of honor) should sit in the chair with the back to the wall. In feng shui, this is called "having the mountain at your back," which means extra stability in your life.

Space Clearing the Dining Area

After the kitchen, the dining room is the most important space for your magical meals. It doesn't matter whether you have a formal dining area with seating for 12 or a small table for 2 in the kitchen. The principles are the same. As with the kitchen, start with clutter clearing. Then give it all a good cleaning. If you have plates and serving platters in a hutch or buffet in the dining room, you might even consider cleaning those, too. Even though you can't see them, they can still affect the energy. Make sure everything is sparkling! You might even want to tape some affirmations under the table. Create handwritten ones like, *Whoever sits at this table is blessed beyond measure,* or *All that is eaten at this table brings incredible nourishment and fulfillment.*

To space clear the dining room, use the same four-step process as for space clearing your kitchen. Consider using orange water (water that you've soaked orange peels in), and sprinkle lightly throughout the room with the intent of clearing the energy in your dining room. Alternatively, use a few drops of essential oils of orange or citrus mixed with water to spritz the space.

Take a bell and ring it above each seat, blessing and clearing the room for the next person who will sit there. Silently bring the bell to the center of the table after each ring to unite the energy of the table to all the chairs. At the end of the ceremony, do a figure-eight ring with the bell to "seal" the energy.

Table Setting as Mini-Altars

Of course, you probably don't want to do this for every meal, but occasionally it's valuable to take time to create table settings that frame and enhance the energy of the meal. Create beautiful, fun, whimsical, humorous, elegant, or mystical place settings using different tablecloths, placemats, chargers, plates, napkins, and napkin rings. You may also want to think of ways to turn your centerpiece into a form of a dining altar. Since every color has a different and powerful vibration, consider contrasting colors, prints, and solids. You may also want to combine and layer textures, styles, and shapes. These mini-altars are not only pleasing to the eye, but also they can elevate the entire dining experience.

As you set the table, do so with intention and love. It's as if the table itself becomes an altar, and everything becomes luminous and radiant. You'll be able to feel it, and so will your guests! You might consider putting an affirmation card under each plate to further energize the table setting. Everyone always seems to receive the perfect message. When your table setting is complete, take a moment to bless it. You might put your hands facing outward and imagine that Spirit is flowing through you, through your hands, and into the table and all who come to it.

THE ANCIENT WISDOM OF GIVING GRACE

"What's wrong?" I asked.

Between tears, the cook explained that when everyone came to the meals she'd prepared, they just dove in without actually seeing the food or feeling the care she'd put into it.

"It's like their minds are elsewhere," she explained. "They're thinking about something that happened during the day, or they're planning something for the future. They aren't aware of how much love I put into their meal."

I'd been leading retreat courses in California, and for each course I hired a cook. This particular chef was excellent. She'd trained at Le Cordon Bleu, but she also followed spiritual practices and took great care in the energy she put into the food. She was right. My Cherokee ancestors would have never eaten a meal without taking the time beforehand to give thanks.

At the beginning of the next meal, I said, "Tonight we're going to give grace. Could everyone please hold hands?" People looked surprised. They were hungry and ready to start piling food on their plates. With slight hesitation, everyone reached out to the person next to them and gently bowed their heads. With the words of the chef still residing within me, I spoke slowly and from my heart.

"We're gathered in gratitude for all the blessings that have been bestowed upon us this day. To the Creator for this bounty before us, we give thanks. We give thanks to the farmers who grew this food, harvested it, and brought it to market. We bless those who transported this food, sometimes very far distances. We bless those who unpacked and displayed this food in the market. We bless our wonderful chef, who bought the food, prepared it with love, and blessed it. Amen."

There was silence. No one spoke. Then someone looked up and simply said, "Thank you." And then, another, "Thank you," and then another. It was a simple prayer, but something shifted. As people served themselves more consciously, there was a feeling of reverence in the air. For the first time in almost a week, people saw the blessings of the meal before them. They tasted the love in the food. They felt the sanctity of sharing a meal with like-minded people. Privately, many came up to me to say that the food tasted completely different that night . . . and more important, they felt completely different. This is the power of giving grace.

What Is the Giving of Grace?

Grace is the name given to prayers of gratitude said before a meal, and the "giving of grace" before a meal is our earliest form of worship. Almost every culture in the world throughout history has specific ceremonies to give thanks before eating. In our frenetic world, the simple experience of "breaking bread" with a glad and generous heart can profoundly restore a feeling of humanity and deepen our connection to our spiritual roots. Sharing a meal—and partaking in the time-honored tradition of being thankful beforehand—brings families together and respects our connection to the Creator. In the deepest sense, prayers said before meals can be a powerful pathway to self-awareness and even spiritual transcendence.

These are some of the reasons that grace is said:

THANKING THE CREATOR FOR ALL BLESSINGS BESTOWED: This kind of grace is a reminder of the spiritual nature of life, and it transforms mealtime from just nurturing the body to also nurturing the soul. Additionally, it can open a mystic portal that invites spiritual beings and angels to be present during the meal.

THANKING THE PLANTS AND ANIMALS THAT GAVE THEIR LIFE FOR THE MEAL: In native cultures, the giving of grace honors the plant or animal for the gift of its life. It's a sacred act to honor the life that was given to strengthen your life.

THANKING THE PEOPLE WHO WORKED TO BRING THE MEAL TO THE PLATE: From the farmers to the cooks, and all the people in between, every meal was the labor of many people, and there's value in recounting this. A Chinese proverb gives us this reminder: "When eating bamboo shoots, remember the man who planted them."

INFUSING THE FOOD WITH ENERGY: Saying grace releases and activates the Divine essence in every molecule of food. Just as words and energy can change the molecular structure of water, so heartfelt blessings can uplift the energy of a meal.

CREATING COMMUNITY FOR THOSE WHO ARE GATHERED: The simple act of stopping for a moment to say grace in no small way unites the people present and deepens a sense of community and togetherness.

Saying Grace Activates a Spiritual Connection to the Mystery of Life

A blessing said in a routine way, or without awareness, or one that just gives lip service to the meal does little to energize the food or connect you with your spiritual source. For example, rapidly saying the ubiquitous phrase, "Good bread, good meat, good God, let's eat," can deny the true meaning of giving grace. However, whether you're religious or not, taking a moment to honor the bounty before you—simply and from the heart—is a holy act and can elevate a meal from the mundane to the hallowed.

When you give blessings that flow from your soul, mystic portals open and spiritual helpers, angels, ancestors, and guides arrive to bless the meal. You'll feel the difference as they arrive. You'll know that you've activated Spirit because the food will taste incredible, the colors will feel more luminous, the conversation will flow, creativity will blossom, and there will be radiance to the evening. Everyone will glow . . . because, indeed, Spirit is present.

How Do You Give Grace?

To embrace the time-honored tradition of giving grace, take a moment of silence in humility and thankfulness to your spiritual source. Be present. Be grateful. Speak from the heart. There doesn't need to be a formula or a set of rules. Express what's authentic and real. A short, heartfelt prayer can be much more powerful than one that has lots of flowery words and drones on and on. Grace can be shared with bowed heads, by holding hands, or by simply taking a moment to be present in silence before a meal.

In Reverence

Blessed are Thou, Divine Being,

To You who created this beautiful and majestic Universe,

We are so thankful.

We give immense thanks for the blessings we continue to receive.

And we ask for blessings for those that are not present.

Amen.

GRATITUDE GRANOLA

One morning I awoke feeling really grateful for the blessings in my life, but a growling stomach interrupted my "attitude of gratitude." As it had been awhile since I'd been to the grocery store, my refrigerator and cupboards were rather bare. I considered eating a frozen pizza but then discovered a jar of old-fashioned oats sitting on the counter. Continuing in my attitude of gratitude, I said to myself, *I am grateful for the oats on my counter and the nuts and dried fruit in the cupboard.* With that in mind, I decided to make a batch of homemade granola, and thus, Gratitude Granola was born.

MAKES ABOUT 18 CUPS

5 cups old-fashioned rolled oats

pinch of salt

2 tsp. cinnamon

½ tsp. freshly ground nutmeg

2 to 3 cups raw seeds and raw chopped nuts (pre-roasted nuts and seeds will burn); suggestions: walnuts, pecans, almonds, cashews, hazelnuts, sunflower seeds, pumpkin seeds, sesame seeds, and flax seeds are all delicious options

½ cup shredded unsweetened coconut (optional)

⅔ cup honey or maple syrup

½ cup coconut oil, vegetable oil, or canola oil

2 cups dried fruit (must be added after cooking because it will burn otherwise); suggestions: raisins, golden raisins, cranberries, cherries, blueberries, strawberries, chopped apricots, chopped peaches, crystallized ginger, chopped mango, chopped papaya, or chopped pineapple

Preheat oven to 325°F.

In a large bowl combine the oats, salt, cinnamon, nutmeg, nuts, and shredded coconut. In a smaller bowl combine the oil and honey. Mix the liquid ingredients with the dry and stir to combine. If you're using coconut oil in its solid state, you may need to use your clean hands to mix it all together. The oats should be uniformly damp and taste delicious when sampled. If they're too dry, add more oil and/or honey. If not delicious enough, adjust ingredients until it passes your inspection. This is part of what makes making granola so much fun!

Spread the raw granola evenly between two large baking sheets and put them into the oven on the lower-middle and upper-middle racks. Stir frequently, and halfway through the baking time, rotate from top to bottom. Bake until crisp and golden, about 30–40 minutes. The oats will become crisper as they cool. Stir in dried fruit. Cool completely before storing in an airtight container.

THE TRANSCENDENTAL POWER OF MUSIC

*"If music
be the food of love,
then play on."*

— WILLIAM SHAKESPEARE

I remember once, many years ago, going to a well-reviewed restaurant on the East Coast. I don't remember the food, the waitstaff, or the decor . . . what I do remember is that there wasn't any music. Nothing. It was silent. It seemed so unusual to eat in a restaurant that was completely quiet. Perhaps to some it was a relief to eat in utter silence, but to me it felt uncomfortable and even awkward. All the diners talked to each other in a whisper. I tried hard to be quiet, too, but I was fully aware of every clink of my fork on the plate, and I was self-conscious every time I put my glass on the table. Perhaps some people went to the restaurant for just this experience, but I found starkness in that meal that would have been soothed and softened by the simple addition of music.

Those who work in restaurants understand the power of music to enhance the dining experience. I'll never forget sitting in a small coffee shop in Seattle. I was cradling a large, steaming cappuccino in my hands when they began to play the soundtrack to the movie *The Mission*. Suddenly I felt like I was soaring into the heavens. The clouds outside the window seemed luminous and radiant. The smell of cappuccino and this music are forever interwoven in my mind. Another time, I was with Meadow and David in Thailand. We'd found a small open-air café. In the early morning heat and dust, with chickens running in the street and horns honking, the music of Jack Johnson wafted through the air. It seemed so strange to be hearing an American musician so far from home, but the music formed a perfect backdrop for the meal . . . one I'll never forget.

Musical Pairing

You've heard of pairing wine with food, but perhaps even more important is pairing music with your meals. As we saw in Chapter 3, music's harmony and vibration can affect the molecules in plants and infuse food with energy, joy, and vitality when played while you're cooking. However, your dining experience can also be greatly enhanced by the mystical alchemy of music. By choosing tunes that match and enhance the vibration of the food, you can create magical meals that transcend the simple act of eating. However, if you choose music that's at cross-purposes with your meal, you can diminish the energy and experience. For example, if you're dining on delicate whitefish with a caper sauce, softly nuanced chardonnay, and a lightly tossed salad of wild greens but listening to heavy metal, you might miss the grace of the meal because it's overpowered by the energy of the music. However, if you play Franz Schubert or smooth jazz, the music might deeply enhance the energy of this entire meal. The colors will be more radiant, the flavors enhanced, and most important, your body will absorb all the energy from the food, because the vibration of the music matches the harmonics of the meal.

On the other hand, if you have a fabulous handmade pizza with fire-roasted tomatoes, layers of imported cheeses, and a few feisty chili peppers on top, served with a hearty zinfandel, ambient music might underplay the robust flavors. But if you listen to flamenco guitar, a passionate opera, or even rock-and-roll or country music with a strong beat, the flavors and textures of the meal may be enhanced.

More and more, restaurateurs are realizing the value of pairing music with food. For example, Thomas Keller, one of America's foremost chefs, has hired consulting firms to find the perfect music for his food. These consultants talk about not only pairing music with the food but also pairing with the space the music is played in. Not only will one piece of music sound different in a large room with many diners compared to a small, intimate room with a fireplace and seating for two, but it will also *feel* different.

For our retreats at Summerhill Ranch, we carefully pair our meals with the music. Sometimes in a very obvious way, if we're having a Mexican-themed meal, we play Mexican music. We start off with something perky, like mariachi, and then as the meal progresses, wind down to more relaxed Mexican music. If it's an Indian meal, we use sitar music but also sometimes Bollywood, depending on the food and the night. Sometimes, however, the music choice is subtler. We may choose something perky to lift the mood or something more relaxing to have a calming effect. Additionally, Meadow usually tells a story to set the scene for each meal (see Chapter 7). For example, if it's a French meal, she might have everyone imagine they're on the Côte d'Azur, sitting on a cliff watching the sunset over the ocean. She talks about the smell of the sea, the sound of musicians playing in the distance, and the waiter pouring the wine. Meadow creates the ambiance of the French café, then we add the music, and suddenly everyone is transported in their mind to the South of France.

Experiment with different types of music with your meal to see how they affect your dining experience. You may be surprised by what you discover.

THE SACRED ART OF HOSPITALITY

When I was teaching in New Zealand, I was honored with an invitation to visit a Maori marae, which is a sacred communal gathering place. When I arrived, I was greeted by a group of Maoris (the native people of New Zealand) dressed in feathered regalia. They walked toward me, singing as they approached. The welcoming ceremony was long and elaborate and was followed by a feast in which members of the marae introduced themselves. Each person told of their lineage and ancestors. It gave me the feeling that each was a young sprout on a very old root. This was the beginning of a wonderful friendship. Whenever I visited, I was greeted with songs and ceremony and tables heavily laden with food. This experience of edible hospitality was heartwarming and sacred.

Denise

Reaching back into antiquity, in religions as varied as Christianity, Hinduism, Buddhism, Islam, and Judaism, the art of hospitality has always been interwoven with spiritual states of grace. Employing the qualities of generosity, graciousness, and reverence, hospitality is much more than being kind to houseguests. It's a gateway to a deeper understanding of the Divine. It's a spiritual power that binds families together and makes friends out of enemies. It's a practice that can indeed profoundly deepen your connection with the Creator and enhance your dining experience.

The art of gracious invitation is in our collective ancestry and resides in our ancestral soul. In the 6th century, Saint Benedict wrote: "Receive all guests as Christ." In India, hospitality is based on the principle *Atithi Devo Bhava*, meaning "the guest is God."

In ancient Greece there were rules of conduct regarding hospitality, especially during the times when it was believed the gods walked among humanity. One never knew if a stranger was a god in disguise, so all strangers were to be treated kindly. In ancient mythology, hospitality was so revered that when it wasn't offered, it was the one offense that even a god could be punished for.

At its core, hospitality is a transformative practice. It can change you, and it can heal you. When you extend a generous welcome to another, you're also activating positive qualities within yourself. As you accept others with grace, so you accept yourself. It ignites within you a way of being in the world with opening, welcoming hands rather than clenched fists.

Hospitality as a Spiritual Practice

When someone sits at your table and joins you for a meal, take the time to go deeper than pleasantries. By doing this, you'll traverse into the realm of what's authentic and real, and this can create bonds of lasting friendship. Engaging in deep, heartfelt conversation while enjoying a meal can lead to powerful communion.

WELCOMING: When your guests arrive, take time to warmly welcome them. (Have you ever been so exhausted from cleaning to get ready for guests, that by the time they arrived you were too tired to enjoy their company?) Honestly, most people care less about how perfect your home is and more about how welcomed and invited they feel. Shift gears from housecleaning and preparing, and allow yourself time to be fully present with each guest. Tune in. What is each person feeling? Let each person know how delighted you are that they're joining you. Be genuine and be present.

THE OFFERING OF SUSTENANCE: After taking coats, offering your guests drinks and appetizers is an icebreaker whose roots go far back in time. In almost every ancient and native culture, the first thing that any host does is provide food and drink. This simple gesture is the host's way of saying, "I'm glad you're here. Welcome to my home."

THE FINE ART OF INTRODUCTION: If your guests don't know each other, make it a point to introduce them, and if possible, find common interests to give the conversation a place to start.

Some questions to ask yourself:

* *How can I create an environment that makes my guests feel even more at ease?*

* *How can I create an environment that puts me even more at ease?* (The more at ease you are, the more comfortable your guests will be.)

* *What might hinder me from being more present with each individual?*

* *How might I release any blockages to being open and gracious with each guest?*

* *What's the greatest thing I can do to create an inviting, warm, and welcoming space for visitors?*

* *When have I felt incredibly welcomed in someone else's home? What did they do or say that made me feel this way?*

* *What are my ultimate desires when I have someone over for a meal?* (Deeper relationship? Networking? Fun?) *How can I best achieve these results?*

Genuine Hospitality Versus the Appearance of It

Perhaps you've met people who, on the surface, seem giving and generous. Yet when you get to know them, there seems to be a crack in the veneer. They're being kind, but with the expectation of receiving something in return. Or perhaps they desperately want you to like them, or maybe they see you as a way to get ahead. This is not true hospitality.

Hospitality isn't so much about what you do but about the attitude you have for your guests. If they feel accepted and cherished, you'll create splendid meals that no one will ever forget. Remember this: The instant you judge someone, you lose the ability to influence them. When your guests feel accepted, they will feel safe . . . and safe space is sacred space. If your guests feel totally safe in your presence and don't feel the need to try to be something they aren't, you indeed will have created sacred space. Your guests will know if you judge them, and this will diminish the radiance of your meal, no matter how much work you put into it.

A warm reception is authentic, and even vulnerable. It's about being present with others in a trusting, open, and honest way. It's not just about going through the motions. If the table is set perfectly, the candles are flickering, and the food is absolute perfection, but if the sacred art of hospitality is not employed with an open heart, the meal may feel somehow flat and lackluster. Be aware of your own needs and your guests' needs . . . and do whatever you can to attend to both. Be open to new perceptions and ideas that your guests might have. You don't need to agree with their every word, but there's value in hearing and understanding their points of view. You may even learn things from each other you never thought possible.

Sacred Hospitality for Family

Learning how to provide holy hospitality for your family can transform your relationship with yourself, others, and even with the Creator. We learn most from our families, and they fill the deep crevices of our lives; however, sometimes they're our harshest critics. There are times it can feel easier to extend a warm, openhearted welcome to friends (or even strangers) than to family members. Embarking on the path of sacred hospitality with family can be powerful and transformative . . . although not always easy.

If Uncle George always raids the refrigerator before dinner without asking, and your niece always brings her purse dog and places it on the table for meals, it might make you want to pull out your hair. Families often do things that a friend would never dream of, but if you find it a challenge to be a sacred hostess to extended family, then look at it as a venerated quest. Like the hero who has to slay the dragon to achieve knighthood, look at each family member as an opportunity to grow more deeply and become even more loving. We're not saying that you have to have your extended family over for dinner or that you shouldn't have healthy boundaries . . . it's great if you do. But if they're in your home, as a suggestion, activate the sacred art of hospitality and treat it as a spiritual practice. It may help to visualize boundaries ahead of time and know how you'll deal with them appropriately, peacefully, and with all the grace you can muster.

One act of family hospitality is to collect the best recipes from Grandma or Grandpa, Mom or Dad, or aunts and uncles, and then occasionally prepare them when family comes over for a meal. In this way, everyone is connected by the past meals you've shared together. These recipes can even be printed and bundled to share with one another. Additionally, you can use favorite recipes to remember family members who are no longer living. These recipes can be used in a similar way to collecting old family photographs or heirlooms to pass down, so there's some tangible reminder of the relatives who have passed on.

Sacred Hospitality to Self

Meadow inspires me in so many ways, but perhaps the thing that I admire most is that, in the depth of her being, she understands the art of sacred hospitality to one's self. Almost every meal she prepares is something that could be served at a luscious dinner party. The meals she cooks for herself are like a special guest will be arriving at any minute. Often I've stopped by her home to drop something off, and the candles are lit, the music is on, the wine is poured, and Meadow is sitting before a four-course meal that's stunningly beautiful and aromatic. She's always been like this. Even before she could barely speak, she'd be upset if David and I would eat in front of the television instead of at the table, and she'd insist that the food be artfully displayed on the plate.

ᴂ Denise

Hospitality toward ourselves is something that very few practice; it's a Divine spiritual path that ignites the energy of invitation, graciousness, and openness in your heart. It's often easier to be the gracious, loving, and kind host for others than it is for yourself.

As a suggestion, imagine the person you revere the most, either someone who's alive or maybe someone from history. Imagine that you're going to prepare a meal for this person. Now ask yourself, if you're willing to create this meal for them, couldn't you make it for yourself? Of course, you don't need to treat yourself this way every night, but once in a while, take the time and care to be your own honored guest.

SMOKED SALMON CROSTINI

I often shy away from making appetizers, as they generally seem to be overly time-consuming, especially when a cheese and cracker plate or a few crudités tend to be just as popular. This recipe, however, is not overly complicated. It's well worth the effort and will be a hit at your next party (or make them just for yourself!). These are so pretty and so tasty . . . I can't think of a better way to demonstrate true hospitality.

MAKES ABOUT 3 DOZEN

1 baguette, cut into ¼-inch thick slices (cut at an angle to increase the surface area)

¼ cup extra-virgin olive oil

1 8-oz. pkg. cream cheese

1 8-oz. pkg. of smoked wild salmon

¼ cup capers

¼ cup minced red onion

zest of 2 lemons

Preheat oven to 350°F.

Using a sharp bread knife, slice the bread at an angle into ¼-inch thick slices.

To prepare the crostini, put the bread slices into a large bowl and drizzle the olive oil over them. Toss the bread with the olive oil until evenly coated. If you want to be more precise about this, you could "paint" the olive oil on each side of the bread with a pastry brush. I find, however, that although tossing the bread and oil in a bowl isn't refined or precise, it gets the job done, and fast.

Divide the bread slices between two baking sheets and toast in the oven until golden brown, about 10–15 minutes. Halfway through, rotate from top to bottom, and using tongs, turn over each slice of bread. Remove from the oven and cool slightly.

When the crostini are cool enough to handle, spread them with a thin layer of cream cheese and place a slice of smoked salmon on top. Top with the capers, red onion, and lemon zest. I like to prepare them assembly-line style. I coat each crostini with cream cheese before moving on to the smoked salmon, then capers, followed by onion, and finally lemon.

When you practice the sacred art of hospitality, pair your meals with music whose vibration magnifies its energy, and cook and dine in spaces that have been lovingly energized using the ancient mystical arts of feng shui and space clearing, your meals will be filled with magic, and the gateway to true mystical cooking will begin to reveal itself to you. Your Mystic Chef journey has nearly reached its apogee. You're now ready to start cooking up magic!

COOKING UP MAGIC!

*L*et's *cook up some magic!* In the previous chapters, we've learned how to harness the life-force energy in our food, cook with Spirit, and create sacred space in our kitchen and dining areas. Now it's time to put all of this to use and whip up some spirit-filled meals that are not only flavorful but are also a gateway to eating your way to a deliciously enlightened life.

Magic is everywhere. It's in the air we breathe and in the food we eat. It's simply a matter of being open to it. In this chapter you'll create a meal to activate abundance, dedicate a dinner to the four elements, invite the fairies to join you for a picnic, and plan a meal to voyage into your far past. Join us on this journey to create magical feasts. Turn the mundane into the transformative, and awaken the Mystic Chef within you.

MYSTICAL APRON

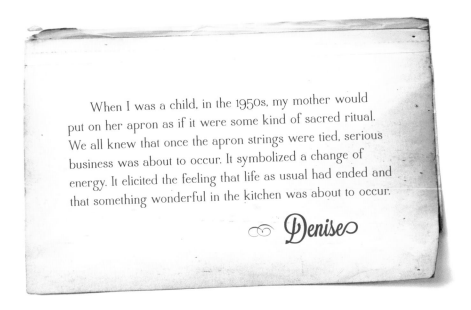

When I was a child, in the 1950s, my mother would put on her apron as if it were some kind of sacred ritual. We all knew that once the apron strings were tied, serious business was about to occur. It symbolized a change of energy. It elicited the feeling that life as usual had ended and that something wonderful in the kitchen was about to occur.

Denise

The first step in cooking up magic is procuring a Mystical Apron. Superman has his cape, but the Mystic Chef has her apron! They're practical, yes. They keep flying bits of food and spilled sauces from soiling clothes, but also they signify a ceremonial shift of energy. Similar to a high priest donning hallowed robes before a ceremony, an apron can be an enchanted vestment. It is your magic charm, and cooking with love is your superpower. Each one has its own unique energy. Simply slipping on a flowery pink one with lace invites feelings of springtime and new beginnings. But throwing on a denim apron speaks of getting down to business and having fun while doing it. Even if you prefer to cook without the use of an apron, you might consider having a Mystical Apron that you keep in a place of honor in your kitchen.

If you can sew, you might want to make your own apron and fill it with love as you do so. Play music that inspires you as you sew, and chant or sing to further energize it. If you don't have the time or ability, buy one that has the look and feel of the energy you want in the kitchen, or you can buy a plain one and decorate it. Here are some things to consider when creating or choosing your apron:

INTENT: What is your intent for the energy in the kitchen? How do you want people to feel after ingesting the food you prepare?

COLOR: Every color has a different vibration and a different energy (see Chapter 2). What color most represents your intention? For a fiery, passionate feeling, consider red or orange. For a cheerful energy of communication and courage, choose yellow. For a soothing and peaceful feeling, choose blue. For health and vitality, consider a bright green apron.

SYMBOLS: Do you have any symbols or shapes that have potent meaning for you? Maybe you want your food to be imbued with love, so you choose to decorate with the heart symbol. Use fabric paint or indelible markers. Or you can use beads or buttons.

DECORATIONS: Sew on anything that embellishes your overall intent: beads, buttons, ribbon, lace . . . even parts of old necklaces. Whatever you put on your Mystical Apron, do it with intention, prayers, and love.

WORDS: There's power in words. If certan words hold special meaning for you, consider writing them on the apron. You might use ones like *joy, love,* or *gratitude.*

GODDESSES/GODS/ANGELS: You might also want to invite the energy of a particular deity into your kitchen, so consider ways to activate their energy on your apron with color, symbols, abstract design, or words. Perhaps you want to invite the energy of Aphrodite (for love), Ganesh (for breaking through obstacles and for abundance), or Archangel Michael (for protection).

MAGICAL POCKET: Every Mystical Apron should have a secret magical pocket. In this pocket, you can put a small crystal or talisman dedicated to magic in the kitchen. Of course, when you wash the apron, you can remove it, but while you wear it, the energy will instill radiance and vibrancy in the meals you prepare.

If you're a wild and bold cook and seem to always have food splattered all over your apron, you might consider having a heavy-duty working apron and another apron for serving. Each can be individually decorated and filled with beautiful energy and love. You may also choose to have a number of aprons for different occasions.

SUPERHERO PANCAKES

Pancakes are generally something we save for lazy Sunday mornings and share with friends and family, but a Mystic Chef can make them a treat to be enjoyed any day—alone or with others. As a kid, when we had pancakes, my mom wore her apron like a cape and told me they were superhero food. They freeze well and can be warmed in the toaster whenever you have a craving for a pancake. This way you can treat yourself anytime. Throw on a Magic Apron cape and make something special. You deserve it!

These pancakes are gluten- and dairy-free, but they're tasty enough to go head-to-head with traditional pancakes. They're full of flavor and have a great texture. They're well worth the extra few minutes it takes to make them.

MAKES ABOUT 5 (4-INCH) PANCAKES

1 Tbsp. coconut oil (plus more for cooking the pancakes)

1 cup almond milk

1 tsp. lemon juice

¼ cup wild rice flour, milled in a coffee or spice grinder

¾ cup brown rice flour

¼ cup potato starch (not flour)

½ tsp. baking powder

2 Tbsp. sugar

¼ tsp. sea salt

1 egg, lightly beaten

To keep this recipe dairy-free, use a non-dairy spread on the pancakes.

If it's in its solid state, melt the coconut oil in a small pan, or to save on cleanup, melt it right in the pan or griddle that you'll use for the pancakes.

Using a liquid measuring cup, measure the almond milk. Add the lemon juice and stir. Allow it to curdle (it will act like buttermilk in the pancakes). Set aside.

Using a clean coffee grinder or spice grinder, mill the wild rice until it's the consistency of flour. (The wild rice adds a delicious nuttiness to the pancakes.)

In a medium bowl, combine the brown rice flour, wild rice flour, potato starch, baking powder, sugar, and sea salt. (When measuring gluten-free flours, to get the most accurate measurements, it's best to scoop the flour from the bag with a spoon rather than dipping in the measuring cup.)

Combine the melted coconut oil with the almond-milk mixture in the measuring cup. Stir in the egg. Pour this liquid mixture into the dry ingredients and stir to combine. Since there's no gluten, you don't have to worry about overmixing the batter!

Melt a bit of coconut oil in a medium-hot pan or griddle. Using a ladle or small cup, pour enough batter onto the griddle to make a four- or five-inch pancake. Cook until the bottom is golden brown and the top is covered in bubbles, flip, and cook for a few minutes more on the other side. Repeat the process until you've used all the batter. Enjoy with maple syrup.

LAW OF ATTRACTION MEALS:
Invite Abundance

As a Mystic Chef, you can use mealtimes to manifest your deepest desires. Simply by applying the law of attraction, you can create transformational meals that shift the energy of circumstances or events in your life. Here's how it works: Begin by creating the *feeling* that achieving your dreams would give you. For example, if you want to be more abundant, create a meal that *feels* abundant. During the meal, not only will you feel prosperous, but also you'll be ingesting the energy of wealth while you eat. This energy of prosperity then goes into your cells . . . which *magnifies the law of attraction tenfold.*

The following is an example of how to use the law of attraction for an Abundance Meal, but you can also use this for Healing Meals, Meals for Love, Forgiveness Meals, New Home Meals, or anything that you desire to manifest in your life.

Meal to Attract Abundance

If you're struggling financially, or if you'd just like to step your abundance up a notch (or a few notches), you might consider creating a meal dedicated to manifesting abundance.

Before embarking on the preparation of this magical meal, take time to set your intention. Consider placing an object on your kitchen altar that represents abundance. For example, in some cultures, oranges represent wealth, so you could

place an orange on your altar with the intention that the energy of abundance fills your life.

While creating a meal dedicated to prosperity, imagine that every action in the kitchen has a mystical purpose. For example, as you chop vegetables, affirm that you're cutting away anything in your life that doesn't support your abundance. As you stir the soup, affirm that prosperity is spiraling into your life. *Do everything with intention.* After the meal is prepared, hold your hands over it, and imagine that the wealth of the universe is flowing through your hands and into every molecule of food.

To affirm abundance, use the finest ingredients available. In many cases, believe it or not, it's more abundant to have fewer items but have them be of the highest quality. However, sometimes a kingly feast with piles of fruit and lavish dishes will create a feeling of opulence. Choose whatever feels the most abundant to you.

I am in
the flow.

Create a table setting that feels prosperous and fulfilling. Use tablecloths that feel sumptuous. Gold, green, and purple are traditional colors related to abundance. This is absolutely the time to bring out the "good" china and silver. You may also want to use candelabras to enhance the feeling of grandeur. Aim for a rich, luxurious, and expansive mood.

Before you eat, say a prayer of thanksgiving for the bounty you already have. Be open to even more pouring into your life. As you eat, with each mouthful, imagine that you're ingesting powerful vibrations of wealth and abundance. Visualize them surging into every cell in your body and programming your subconscious mind for inner and outer riches.

Allow the meal to proceed at a relaxed and leisurely pace; you also have an abundance of time to enjoy the company of those you care about . . . even if you're dining alone!

ELEMENTAL MEALS:
Activate the Spirit of Air, Water, Fire, and Earth

Everything on the planet is affected by the four elements. Without them, there wouldn't be the solid ground beneath our feet, the air we breathe, the water we drink, and the fire that keeps us warm. We depend on the elements for survival; however, for harmonious balance, our soul must also be in alignment with the deeper energy of the elements. Air traditionally represents the mental part of ourselves, water our emotional self, fire our spiritual and creative side, and earth our physical body. As a Mystic Chef, you can activate the four elements in your meals to enhance any aspect of your life.

If, for instance, you're feeling that your emotions are a bit off-kilter, you may want to prepare a meal that focuses on the element of water. Or perhaps you have a big project due at work, and you want to activate your creativity; you might then choose to create a meal devoted to the element of fire. If you want to bring balance to all areas of your life, create a meal in which each course is dedicated to one of the four elements. These meals can be powerful, so be aware of the emotions, images, and memories that arise.

And as you cook, you may want to repeat the following affirmation: *I am connected to all things, and all things are connected in and through me. I am in harmony with air, water, fire, and earth. We are one.*

Air Element Meal: Activate Clarity and Mental Capacities

To prepare for a meal devoted to the element of air, begin by focusing on the air around you. Take deep breaths. By doing so, you're igniting the Spirit of Air that dwells within and around you. Then set your intention for activating clarity and mental capacities.

Air is light and transient, so you may want to serve salads and other light and easily digested foods. However, you may want to take a more literal approach and focus the menu on foods that actually come from the air. Alternatively, you could choose foods that make you think of the air, such as wheat, since we often picture wheat fields gently rolling in the wind. To further activate your mental capacities, you may want to take a cerebral approach to the preparation of this meal. Japanese food, for example, seems to embody the precise nature of the air element.

When setting the mood for your air meal, consider dining outdoors in order to feel the air around you. In the background, play classical music with wind instruments or maybe ambient flute music. The air element is often aligned with the colors yellow and white, so you may want to consider using these soft tones to decorate your table. It doesn't matter what you choose as long as it feels congruent with your feeling and understanding of the element of air.

Water Meal: Soothe and Balance Emotions

A meal dedicated to the Spirit of Water can be a powerful tool in clearing, cleansing, and balancing your emotional self. To prepare for this meal, as a suggestion, spend some time being aware of the element of water. Notice the water around you and within you. When you take a bath or shower, acknowledge the cleansing aspect of water. Make your intention clear, and then plan the meal accordingly.

Choose a menu that will best support your intention. As with the air meal, you may want to take a literal approach and plan a meal inspired by foods that come from water, such as fish, shellfish, seaweed, or even rice and cranberries. Perhaps, however, you prefer to have water be a main component of your meal. This could mean serving soup or other liquids. Another approach would be to choose foods that give a feeling of purification or emotional balance, such as cucumber or watermelon because of their high water content.

When thinking of locations, consider the element of water. Perhaps you choose to have this meal by the physical embodiment of water—a lake, stream, river, or ocean—or maybe you prefer to find a location that speaks to your emotional or sentimental self. Consider foods and decorations in shades of blue and green, colors that are often associated with the element of water. You could also have ambient music playing with the sounds of the sea, a rainstorm, a flowing creek, or music from operas or soundtracks that evoke emotions.

Fire Meal: Activate Creativity

As you put together your fire meal, focus on the fire and light around and within you. Fire dwells within you as your life force. As you prepare this meal, focus your intention on activating your creativity and igniting your spirituality, and so it shall be.

This would be a good meal to cook over a campfire or on a barbecue. You might also consider red and orange foods, such as tomatoes, red meat, berries, red apples, oranges, carrots, and beets. The word *fiery* is often used to describe chili peppers, and even nasturtium flowers and other greens can have a bit of a fiery edge to them. Use your intuition. If it feels fire-like, then it's a good choice.

What music gets you "fired up"? While you prepare the meal, crank the stereo to full blast and dance around the kitchen and shout out the lyrics to the Pointer Sisters' song, "Fire" or maybe the Doors' "Light My Fire." If you're in a quieter mood, you could play the sounds of a crackling campfire in the background. Whatever you choose to do, have fun and welcome the energy of fire into your life.

Earth Meal: Ground Yourself

An earth meal can serve to ground you and increase your connection to Mother Earth. As you prepare for your earth element meal, spend some time focusing on your physical environment. Get a sense of the solid, physical nature of your body. Take time to notice how you relate to the physical universe around you.

This meal might comprise foods that come directly from the earth, such as potatoes, carrots, and beets, but maybe you prefer foods that seem "earthy," such as dark leafy greens and whole grains. An earth meal is solid, down-to-earth, wholesome, and nourishing. Choose foods that give you that feeling. For your decor, you may want to consider a color palette of earth tones, such as rich dark browns.

This would be a good meal to eat barefoot outdoors under an oak tree or perhaps on a mountaintop. You might consider serving your meal on handmade, earthenware platters and plates. The grounding energy of the earth, however, can find you wherever you are, whether it's barefoot with toes in the sand or at home on the couch. Foods infused with the Spirit of Earth can be some of the heartiest and most filling for mind, body, and spirit.

CIRCLE OF LIFE MEALS:
Ingest the Energy of the Seasons

Our Cherokee ancestors called the sacred circle of life the *medicine wheel*. The medicine wheel expresses a powerful understanding of the forces around us and represents the cyclical nature of the seasons. It's a symbolic representation of the balance of the universe, in which everything created has its appropriate place. It honors every aspect of being . . . our body, our spirit, and our heart.

In the medicine wheel, every season is filled with its own majesty that brings wholeness to life. However, most of us are no longer connected to the seasons as our ancestors were. We wake up in our heated and air-conditioned homes, drive to work in our climate-controlled cars, and arrive at our offices in tall buildings that loom high above the earth. Generations ago, our bodies used to be more in harmony with the natural flow of the year. For most of us now, seasonal activities such as chopping firewood to keep warm in the winter, sowing seeds in spring to ensure a bountiful summer garden, and harvesting crops in the fall are not essential parts of our lives.

In many ways, our lives are much easier than they were for our great-grandparents. We live in a time of plenty, but by not participating in the seasons on a soul level, we're bereft of the natural waxing and waning of life. However, by eating in alignment with the individual energy of each season, you can connect more deeply with these powerful natural energies . . . and as a result, you'll notice the creases in life begin to smooth. Each season has a unique energy, and as a Mystic Chef, you can call upon the energy of the seasons to initiate shimmering life-force energy.

Encoded in our brains—whether we're aware of it or not—are feelings and emotions associated with specific times of year *that you can activate simply by the meals you eat!* If, for instance, you're ready for a new beginning in your life, you may want to eat the luscious greens of spring to initiate a potent energy of new beginnings. Or if you want to expand your horizons and reach new vistas, plan a summer meal using fresh and colorful produce. By eating an autumn meal, you'll ignite the energy of prosperity and bounty. And if you're feeling a need to nurture yourself, eat the energy of winter (maybe a hearty bowl of stew), and subliminally, you'll feel more cherished. Although it's beneficial to eat these meals during the season they occur—because of our behavioral conditioned response and because of the variety of food we have year-round—you can cook a seasonal meal any time of the year.

For New Beginnings: Eat Spring

Spring is the time to plant seeds. The seeds you plant—with care and nurturing—will grow tall and strong, and their bounty you'll reap in the time ahead. What ideas, projects, actions are taking form? What are your goals for this day, month, year, or decade? A meal dedicated to the energy of spring can be especially potent if you're starting a new business, working on new projects, or embarking on a new relationship.

To activate the energy of new beginnings, choose foods that connect you with the energy of springtime. Spring foods are often tender, young, and green. Microgreens, asparagus, spring onions, leeks, peas, snap peas, artichokes, ramps, fiddleheads, wild greens (like miner's lettuce and dandelions), and edible flowers (like violets, roses, and Johnny-jump-ups) are all filled with the vitality of spring. There are also fresh eggs, spring lamb, and delicious dairy full of the flavor of spring clover and tender young grass. Treat yourself to a spring-inspired meal and soak up this time of new beginnings.

Affirmation: *As I eat "Spring," new energy is activating inside of me. This is a time of new beginnings in my life.*

EGG SALAD TARTINE

I love egg salad and will happily eat it all the time,
but there's something that seems particularly spring-like about eggs with a thin slice
of radish, especially since the egg is a symbol of renewal in many cultures.

A tartine is a French open-faced sandwich, usually served on rustic
whole-wheat sourdough called *pain Poilâne*. However, you can use
any good French or Italian bread for these sandwiches.

MAKES ABOUT 4 TARTINES

4 large slices of rustic whole-wheat bread or other high-quality artisan bread, lightly toasted

6 hardboiled eggs, peeled and mashed

2 tsp. Dijon mustard

3 Tbsp. mayonnaise

2 tsp. minced red onion

1 stalk celery, minced

1 Tbsp. capers

salt and pepper

2–4 radishes, thinly sliced (you could also use cucumber)

It seems everyone has a theory on the best way to boil eggs and the most efficient method for peeling them. I, however, don't have any hard-and-fast rules. I'm usually doing too many things at one time to pay much attention to how long I boil my eggs. Unfortunately, an overcooked egg will develop a green tint on the outside of the yolk. This doesn't bother me, but if it bothers you, you may want to be more precise about your cooking times.

Place all six eggs in a medium saucepan and cover with at least an inch of cool water. Put on the stove and bring to a boil; 10–15 minutes of boiling is a good rule of thumb. Immediately plunge the eggs in cool water to stop the cooking and prevent the aforementioned discoloration.

While the eggs are cooking, mince the onion and celery.

Generally, the fresher the egg the harder it will be to peel, and unfortunately, there really isn't any getting around this. I've found that it's easier to peel a wet egg than a dry one egg, and for some reason, starting on the bulbous bottom seems to help, too.

In a medium bowl, mash the eggs. Add the mustard and mayonnaise, and stir to combine. Mix in the onion, celery, and capers. Add salt and pepper to taste. Serve on lightly toasted bread, and top with thinly sliced radishes.

LEAFY GREENS BIRD NESTS

This is a quintessential spring dish. Eggs traditionally represent new life,
and leafy greens are the most tender in the spring. Rainbow chard sautéed with fresh spring
leeks creates the perfect nest to cradle your symbolic new beginnings and new endeavors.

Don't have any leeks or rainbow chard?
This recipe can also be made with kale, spinach, chopped cooked broccoli,
sliced roasted potatoes, grated potato, or any other vegetable that suits your fancy.
With a few added ingredients, this can transform into a quick and delicious dinner.
Add chopped garlic and thinly sliced sun-dried tomatoes while sautéing, and then just before
serving, top the eggs with a dollop of Chimichurri Pesto and grated Parmesan cheese.

MAKES 2 HEARTY SERVINGS

2 Tbsp. olive oil

1 cup sliced leeks
(from about 1 leek)

dash of sea salt

1 bunch of rainbow chard,
chopped (leaves and stems)

4 eggs

Wash the leeks, making sure to get all the dirt hiding in the crevices. Slice the white and tender part of the leek.

In a large cast iron skillet (or other heavy-bottomed frying pan), heat the olive oil over medium heat. Add the leeks and a dash of sea salt. Sauté the leeks until soft and slightly caramelized. This should take about 10 minutes.

While the leeks cook, wash and chop the rainbow chard. It's okay if the chard is a bit damp, as this will actually help facilitate the cooking; however, be very careful chopping it. The only time I've seriously cut myself was cutting wet chard.

When the leeks are soft, add the chard to the pan, and increase the heat to medium-high. Don't worry if the pan seems to be overflowing with leafy greens. They'll cook down. To speed up things, you can cover the pan and steam the chard for a few minutes, if you desire. Continue to sauté the greens until they're tender, about 5–10 minutes.

Reduce heat to medium/medium-low and make four wells (nests) in the greens. Crack an egg into each of the wells. Cover with a lid, and cook until the egg whites are cooked through and the yolks are set.

CHIMICHURRI PESTO

*When I think of spring, fresh herbs and tender young greens
immediately come to mind. The bright green of this pesto evokes the feeling
of new beginnings and fills me with joy and delight for things to come.
This sauce is good on pasta, but where it really shines is as an accompaniment
to steak or grilled fish. It's also delicious tossed with potatoes. Or, put a dollop
on the eggs in Leafy Greens Bird Nests for a delicious spring-inspired meal.*

MAKES ABOUT 2 CUPS

½ cup raw walnuts

4 cloves of garlic

1 small bunch (about 1 oz.) Italian parsley

1 large bunch (about 4 oz.) fresh basil, stems removed

1 cup extra-virgin olive oil

salt (to taste)

Place all the ingredients in a food processor fitted with a steel blade. Do 30 to 40 one-second pulses until the ingredients come together in a uniform sauce but still retain some texture. Allow the pesto to rest for approximately 15 to 30 minutes to let the flavors marry. It may taste a bit piquant at first, but after marinating, the flavors will combine to make a sauce you'll want to eat by the spoonful.

To Expand Your Horizons: Eat Summer

Imagine standing on top of a mountain in Big Sky country and looking at the vistas that seemingly spread forever. Or picture yourself standing in the middle of a gently rolling prairie and looking far into the distance. This is what it's like to eat summer. This is a time to expand your horizons and open yourself to new possibilities. Fields are fecund, trees have a bountiful canopy, and gardens are lush. Summer is the time to spread your arms wide open, feel the wind in your hair, and breathe in all that's possible. Eating a meal to reap the energy of summer can be especially powerful when you want to pull forth a feeling of expansiveness into your life.

To widen your perspective, choose foods that you associate with summer. Think of times when you felt open and expansive. What were your favorite foods then? To ignite this energy within you, ingest the summer with an open, receptive heart. Fruits and vegetables are at the peak of freshness in the warmer months. Absorb the energy of summer with an heirloom tomato salad with fresh basil, stuffed summer squash, or a colorful fruit salad served in a watermelon bowl.

Affirmation: *As I eat "Summer," my inner and outer horizons are expanding. All things are possible.*

FATHER'S DAY SALMON

This dish is great any time of year, but in my family, it's a go-to on Father's Day, since the recipe has been passed down from one fisherman father to another. Years ago, my dad started baking salmon with aioli after having halibut prepared similarly by my grandfather. Wild salmon is in season and at its peak of freshness in the summer months. Ignite the energy of summer with some delicious baked salmon!

SERVES 4

1¼ pound wild salmon fillet (plan on about 5 oz. per person)

½ of a small yellow onion, sliced into thin half-moons

1 lemon, sliced into thin rounds

DILL AIOLI:

½ cup mayonnaise

2 tsp. lemon juice

1 garlic clove, crushed

2 tsp. dried dill

pinch of salt

Preheat the oven to 350°F.

In a small bowl, mix the mayonnaise, lemon juice, garlic, dill, and salt to make the aioli. I usually can't help but dip in my fingers, potatoes, or whatever is available. Yum!

Layer two sheets of aluminum foil lengthwise. Make sure the foil is at least a few inches longer than the salmon fillet on each side. You will be wrapping the salmon completely in the foil, so if the foil isn't wide enough to cover the fish, add a few more sheets of foil crosswise. If the salmon has been skinned, lightly spray the foil with cooking oil so it won't stick.

Place the salmon in the middle of the foil, and evenly coat the top of the fish with the dill aioli. Sprinkle the onions on top. Layer the top with overlapping lemon rounds.

Fold the foil around the fish like you're wrapping a gift, making sure it's completely encased. First, fold the ends up and over the fish, then pull the sides up. Fold the foil over itself and crimp. If there are holes, juices will escape, and you'll be left with a mess to clean.

Put the salmon package on a large baking sheet and put it on the middle rack of the oven. Bake until the fish is firm and flaky but still slightly pink. The cooking time depends on the thickness of the fish, but it should take between 25 and 45 minutes. You'll be able to smell when it's done. Suddenly your kitchen will be filled with the delicious scent of onions and dill.

Variation: Grill the salmon on the barbecue (on foil) over medium heat. Serve with the dill aioli on the side. To keep the fish moist, generously drizzle with olive oil and lemon juice before grilling.

ASIAN ZUCCHINI PANCAKES

Anyone who has ever had a vegetable garden knows how zucchini can pretty much take over your life during the later summer months. This is one of my favorite ways to eat the bounty. It's so good that you might even wish you had more zucchini! And when you eat this dish in the winter, you'll instantly feel transported to the long, hot, and languid days of summer. There's no better way to eat the energy of summer than with Asian Zucchini Pancakes.

DIPPING SAUCE
MAKES 1 CUP

3 Tbsp. sugar

⅓ cup tamari

¼ cup seasoned rice vinegar

1 Tbsp. mirin (Japanese sweet cooking wine)

1 tsp. toasted sesame oil

¼ cup water

2–3 cloves garlic, crushed

1 Tbsp. sesame seeds

1 bunch of green onions, thinly sliced (use only the white part)

1 tsp. red chili flakes (optional)

PANCAKES
MAKES ABOUT 10 PANCAKES

6 cups grated zucchini (from 1½ to 2 lbs. of zucchini)

¾ cup grated sweet yellow onion (from 1 small onion)

2-inch piece of ginger, peeled and grated

5 large eggs, lightly beaten

1 cup sweet rice flour*

vegetable oil for cooking the pancakes

*Sweet rice flour has a fine texture and is often used as a thickener. It can be purchased in Asian markets, natural food stores, or online. You can also use wheat flour, but the pancakes will be denser.

To make the dipping sauce:

In a small bowl, combine the sugar, tamari, rice vinegar, mirin, sesame oil, and water. Mix in the garlic, sesame seeds, sliced green onions, and chili flakes. Set aside.

To make the pancakes:

Using a food processor fitted with a shredding disc, grate the zucchini. To remove the excess liquid from the zucchini, bundle it into a clean dishtowel and squeeze. This is best done in multiple batches. Since this can be messy, do it over the sink. Put the squeezed zucchini in a large bowl.

Grate the onion and ginger in the food processor and toss with the zucchini. Remove any fibrous bits of ginger that don't look like they'll be easy to chew.

Mix the zucchini with the onion and ginger. Crack the eggs into a small bowl and beat lightly. Pour the eggs over the zucchini mixture. Add the sweet rice flour and mix until fully combined.

Heat a generous splash of vegetable oil on medium to medium-high on a griddle (about 400°F on an electric griddle) or skillet. With a large spoon, scoop about ½ cup of batter and flatten into a pancake on the hot griddle. Cook each side until golden brown and crispy (2–3 minutes per side). Add more oil and repeat.

ALL-AMERICAN POTATO SALAD

The great flavor in this potato salad comes from lots of eggs and pickles,
but the real secret is marinating finely diced onions in pickle juice.
What summer picnic would be complete without potato salad!

3 lbs. gold potatoes, boiled and cut into bite-size pieces

6 large eggs, hardboiled and cut into bite-size pieces

½ cup finely diced onion

⅓ cup dill pickle juice

1½ cups chopped dill pickles

a scant ¼ cup mild Dijon mustard (like Grey Poupon)

½ cup mayonnaise (plus a bit more if the potatoes are dry)

salt and freshly ground pepper, to taste

Bring a large pot of water to a boil. Add the potatoes (skin on). Boil the potatoes until tender but not mushy, about 20–30 minutes, depending on size. Drain and rinse with cool water.

In a small pot, boil the eggs until hardboiled. Place all six eggs in a medium saucepan and cover with at least an inch of cool water. Boiling for 10–15 minutes is a good rule of thumb. Immediately plunge the eggs into cool water to stop the cooking.

While the eggs and potatoes are cooking, dice the onion. Combine the onion and the pickle juice in a large bowl and allow the onions to marinate while you chop the pickles. Add the pickles to the onions. When the potatoes are cool, chop them and add them to the bowl. Peel and chop the eggs. Combine the eggs with the onions, pickles, and potatoes. Add the mustard and mayonnaise and stir to combine. Add salt and pepper to taste.

ITALIAN PRUNE CLAFOUTIS

Clafoutis is a traditional French pastry, usually made with cherries. But I've put my own spin on this one, making it with fresh Italian prunes that are only available for a short time at the end of the summer, and it's also dairy- and gluten-free. If you can't find Italian prunes, substitute apricots. As apricots are a bit larger than prunes, you'll only need about eight. This is one of the most delicious ways to expand your horizons and eat the energy of summer!

SERVES 6

1 lb. fresh Italian prune plums (about 12), pitted and halved

⅓ cup sugar

⅓ cup brown rice flour

2 large eggs

¾ cup canned coconut milk (do not use light)

½ tsp. vanilla extract

vegetable shortening (for greasing the pan)

Preheat the oven to 400°F.

Grease a 10-inch pie plate with vegetable shortening. Pull or cut the prunes into two halves and remove the pit. Line the pie plate with the prunes face up, in a single layer.

In a medium bowl, combine the sugar and brown rice flour. In the same bowl, whisk in the eggs and coconut milk. Add the vanilla and mix to combine. Since the brown rice flour does not contain gluten, the batter can be whisked until smooth without worrying about making a tough pastry. The batter should be the consistency of pancake batter.

Pour the batter over the plums, making sure to distribute evenly. Place on the center rack of the preheated oven and bake until golden, about 40–45 minutes.

The clafoutis can be eaten warm or cold. When you take it out of the oven, allow the fruit to cool before digging in so you don't burn your mouth. Hot fruit . . . *ow!*

As a variation, apricots can also be used in this recipe.

AUTUMN HARVEST SALAD

This combination of autumn ingredients is the perfect balance of salty, sweet, sour, and savory. You won't want to stop eating this salad. It's that good!

SERVES 6

SALAD:

1 6-oz. bag of baby spinach

1 cup very thinly sliced red onion (from half an onion)

½ cup dried cranberries

1 cup raw walnut halves

1 apple cored and thinly sliced (such as braeburn, which is sweet-tart and firm)

6 oz. crumbled blue cheese (about one cup)

DRESSING:

Extra-virgin olive oil

Aged balsamic vinegar

Salt and cracked black pepper

Toss the spinach with the red onion, cranberries, and walnuts. Add the apples and blue cheese and toss to combine. Dress with a simple vinaigrette made from extra-virgin olive oil, aged balsamic vinegar, salt, and cracked pepper.

To Harvest Prosperity: Eat Autumn

Throughout the ages, autumn has symbolized prosperity. Autumn is the time to reap the bounty and harvest the fruits of your labor. The cornucopia, the symbol of plenty, is filled with the fruits and vegetables of the fall. With the sun low in the sky, the land glows in shades of gold. This is the season of abundance.

Eat autumn and fill your body with this prosperous energy. With each bite of butternut-squash soup, boiled potato freshly dug from the earth, baked apple, cranberry muffin, or roast turkey with stuffing, affirm that you're even more prosperous. It's not by chance that Thanksgiving is celebrated in the autumn. It's a grand celebration of the harvest and the reward for all the love, attention, and work that made the bounty possible.

To eat autumn is to seize the moment and reap your rewards. A meal dedicated to the energy of this season can be a great way to bring more abundance into your life. Eat "autumn" with the intention that your life will be more prosperous, and so it shall be. To fill your body with the abundant feeling of autumn, choose foods that feel bountiful to you. Consider those that are traditionally associated with the fall, such as apples, squash, grains, and root vegetables.

Affirmation: *As I eat "Autumn," I reap rewards in every area of my life. Prosperity is flowing into my life with greater and greater measure.*

PROSPERITY RICE

In some cultures rice is considered a gift from the gods and is treated with great respect. It's often thrown in wedding ceremonies as a symbol of fertility and prosperity, and as such, eating rice is a wonderful way to internalize the energy of autumn.

Wild rice is grown primarily in the upper Midwest of the U.S. and in southern Canada and typically harvested in the early autumn. It has a wonderful nutty flavor that pairs really well with the cranberries and pecans in this dish. Serve with roasted pork or chicken. Or try it cold, tossed with arugula and crumbled feta and dressed with balsamic vinegar and extra-virgin olive oil for a delicious autumn salad.

SERVES 4 – 6

1½ cups uncooked wild rice

½ cup pecans, toasted and chopped

½ cup chopped green onions

¼ cup dried cranberries

¼ tsp. sea salt

2 Tbsp. extra-virgin olive oil

Bring 6 cups of water to a boil. Add the wild rice, stir, and return to a boil. Cover and reduce heat to low. Simmer until the rice is cooked and soft but still has a bit of a crunch, about 35 minutes. Drain.

Meanwhile, toast the pecans on a small baking dish in the oven at 350°F until they're fragrant, approximately 10 minutes. You'll know when they're done as the kitchen will be perfumed with the delicious scent of pecans. (You can purchase roasted pecans, but there's something so alluring about making them yourself.) When they're cool enough to handle, chop them. In a large bowl, combine the wild rice, green onions, cranberries, and pecans. Dress with salt and olive oil.

VELVETY SPICED
SWEET POTATOES

Sweet potatoes, coconut milk, and ginger are an ambrosial combination.
The first time I served this dish was at a Thanksgiving celebration. Everyone loved it,
especially my friend's 8-month-old baby. She ate huge spoonful after huge spoonful.
There is something both warming and grounding about this dish.

SERVES 6

3 lbs. red-skinned sweet potatoes, peeled and chopped into 1-inch chunks

⅓ cup coconut "cream" from one 15-oz. can of coconut milk (do not use light)

1 tsp. ginger juice from a 2-inch-long piece of peeled ginger, grated and pressed through a garlic press

¾ tsp. Chinese five-spice powder

sea salt (to taste)

To make the coconut "cream," chill a can of coconut milk in the refrigerator for a few hours (overnight is even better) so the creamy solids will rise to the top. Do not shake the can before chilling. Use the remaining coconut milk to make piña coladas or Thai curry. Do not use the coconut cream found in many grocery stores. It contains sweeteners and thickeners and will not work in this recipe.

Bring a large pot of water to a boil. Meanwhile, peel and chop the sweet potatoes. Add the sweet potatoes to the boiling water and boil until soft, about 10–15 minutes. Drain well.

Return the sweet potatoes to the pot and add the coconut cream. Use a potato masher to mash them until smooth. Use a Microplane to grate the ginger and then press the pulp through a garlic press to make ginger juice. Add the ginger juice, Chinese five-spice powder, and salt. Mix to combine. Enjoy!

BAKED APPLES WITH BRANDIED WALNUTS AND RAISINS

Years ago, when I was living in Maine, I went apple picking with a friend on a beautiful autumn morning. The tall grass was dewy, our jeans were soaked from our knees down, and the morning mists hung low in the sky. It was like walking through a fairy tale. Nothing says autumn more than brightly colored leaves and crunchy, juicy apples. Baked, they're an extra-special treat. Your kitchen will be filled with the heady scent of cinnamon, brown sugar, and brandy.

SERVES 6

2 Tbsp. coconut oil or softened unsalted butter

½ cup lightly packed brown sugar

½ tsp. cinnamon

¼ tsp. nutmeg

¼ tsp. salt

1 tsp. lemon zest

2 Tbsp. brandy

1 cup chopped walnuts

½ cup raisins

6 Granny Smith apples (or favorite baking-apple variety), peeled and cored

Preheat oven to 350°F. Line a baking dish with parchment paper.

In a medium bowl, use a fork to cream the oil or butter with the brown sugar, cinnamon, nutmeg, and salt. Add the lemon zest and brandy. Mix in the walnuts and raisins. Set aside.

Peel the apples. To core the apples, use a melon baller to make a good-sized well inside each apple. Approach the apple from both ends until the inner core is completely removed.

Fill the apples with the nut and raisin mixture. If you fill the apple from both the top and the bottom and press firmly, it won't fall out. Place the apples in the parchment-lined baking dish and place on the middle rack of the oven.

Bake for an hour to an hour and a half, depending on the size and variety of apple. To test for doneness, pierce the apple with a fork. If it's soft, then it's done. You may want to baste the apples a couple of times while they're cooking. Use a soupspoon to pick up the delicious syrup that pools on the bottom of the baking dish and drizzle it over the apples. If any raisins on the top have burned, remove them before serving. Serve warm with vanilla ice cream.

CURRIED CARROT AND APPLE SOUP

The flavor and texture of this soup are reminiscent of butternut-squash soup,
but the curry, apples, and coconut milk add many layers of flavors.
A self-proclaimed soup connoisseur once told me this was the best soup she'd ever
had. It's an especially satisfying way to pull more autumn energy into your life.

SERVES 6-8

1 Tbsp. coconut oil
(or butter or olive oil)

1 cup diced onion

1 tsp. fresh ginger, finely
grated

1½ tsp. sea salt

2 tsp. curry powder

2 lbs. carrots, peeled and
chopped

½ lb. apples (approx. 1 large
apple), peeled, cored, and
cut into chunks

1 13.5-oz. can of coconut milk
(about 1⅔ cup)

4 cups water, plus more if
soup is too thick

TO GARNISH:

Chopped cilantro

Plain yogurt

In a large pot over medium-low, melt the coconut oil. Add the onion and sauté with the ginger, salt, and curry powder, stirring frequently, until the onions are soft and translucent, about 5–10 minutes.

Meanwhile, peel and chop the carrots and apple. When the onions are soft, add the carrots and apple, and continue to sauté for a few more minutes. Add the coconut milk and water to the pot and increase the heat. Bring the soup to a boil and then reduce to a simmer.

When the carrots and apples are soft, after 20–30 minutes of simmering, purée the soup until smooth, using either a blender or an immersion blender. If using a blender, only fill the canister halfway and purée in batches to prevent the hot soup from splattering. I also recommend removing the middle part of the blender lid and placing a clean dishtowel or paper towel over the hole while blending. This will allow the steam to escape.

If the soup is too thick, add warm water until you reach your desired consistency. Serve with a dollop of plain yogurt and chopped cilantro. The tartness of the yogurt nicely balances the sweetness of the carrots and apples in the soup.

BRAISED RED CABBAGE WITH APPLE

Braised red cabbage pairs well with roasted poultry. It's a favorite
in our house at Thanksgiving and Christmas. I especially like how easy it is.
Once everything is chopped and in the pot, it needs very little attention, so you'll
be free to make other holiday favorites. This is my go-to winter comfort food.

SERVES 4–6

1 head of red cabbage
(2–3 lbs.), cored and
chopped into 2-inch pieces

1 red onion, sliced (2 cups)

1 apple (½ lb.), such as
braeburn or fuji, peeled,
cored, and thinly sliced

½ cup apple cider vinegar

1 tsp. sea salt

This dish is so easy and delicious. Combine everything in a large pot. Cover and cook on medium-low for as long as you possibly can. The cabbage will be soft after an hour and a half, but if you have more time, 3 hours of cooking will yield sweeter, softer, and more caramelized cabbage. Be sure to stir occasionally to make sure the cabbage doesn't stick to the bottom of the pan, though these bits can be the sweetest.

To Nurture Yourself: Eat Winter

Traditionally, winter has been a time to pull inward. The bear hibernates in its den, and other animals burrow underground. Winter is an opportunity for reflection and solitude. It is the season to soak in the warmth of the fire, read a good book, and cocoon yourself within a soft and luxurious blanket. It's a time to tend to your needs in a quiet and contemplative way.

To nurture yourself, eat winter. Ingest the energy of the season, and allow yourself this quietude. It's easy to get caught up in the go-go-go of modern life but when you can, take time to cherish yourself with the spirit of winter. Eating a meal dedicated to the energy of winter can be an especially useful way to replenish your inner resources when you've been spreading yourself too thin among your many commitments.

To fill your body with the energy of winter, eat warming foods like soups, stews, roasted meats, and whole grains. Root vegetables, winter squash, and pumpkin are also extremely satisfying. Their soft texture is comforting, just like when we were babies and our mothers fed us. Kale, broccoli, Brussels sprouts, cabbage, and cauliflower are other winter foods. Most important, however, is that you choose foods that feel nurturing to you.

Affirmation: *As I eat "Winter," I'm open to being cherished and nurtured by life. My life is guided.*

CARAMELIZED BRUSSELS SPROUTS

I love Brussels sprouts. I always have. I like them boiled, steamed, and sautéed, but roasted in the oven is my favorite way to eat them. There's nothing like warm Brussels sprouts on a cold winter evening. I owe my adoration of this often maligned vegetable to my mom who, when I was little, made "Brussels sprouts trees." Using toothpicks, she inserted cocktail onions and cherry tomatoes into the entire Brussels sprout stalk so that it looked like a miniature Christmas tree.

Roasting the sprouts in a hot oven caramelizes them and makes the outside crisp while the inside is soft and sweet. Prepared this way, I could eat them by the bowlful.

SERVES 4-6

2 lbs. Brussels sprouts, trimmed and cut in half

¼ cup extra-virgin olive oil

1 tsp. coarse sea salt

1 red bell pepper, cut into ½-inch-long julienne strips

zest of one lemon

½ cup roasted pecans, chopped

Preheat the oven to 500°F. Trim the Brussels sprouts and remove any blemished leaves. Cut in half from stem to top. Be sure to keep the leaves that fall off. They're the best part, because they get really crispy in the oven. Place the sprouts on a baking sheet lined with parchment paper. Drizzle the olive oil and sprinkle the salt over the sprouts and toss together. I use my hands and do it right on the baking sheet. Place in the oven on the middle rack and roast for approximately 20 minutes.

While the sprouts are in the oven, slice the red bell pepper and zest the lemon. (If you don't have a zester, use a box grater. A Microplane will make the zest too fine.) After about 10 minutes, when the sprouts are just starting to brown, remove the baking sheet from the oven and add the bell pepper and zest. Stir to combine. Return them to the oven. (The later addition of these ingredients will keep them from burning.)

Roast the sprouts for approximately 10 minutes more. They're done when the outside leaves are brown and caramelized, but the insides are still somewhat firm. Don't overcook! Remove from the oven, stir in the pecans, and enjoy.

WORLD'S BEST PUMPKIN PIE

When I first eliminated gluten and dairy from my diet, I missed having pumpkin pie at the holidays. So I decided to re-create it using ingredients that I could eat. After a number of test batches, I finally came up with this recipe. The filling is flavorful and creamy, and without gluten, the crust remains crisp and flaky even after a few days in the fridge. This is a holiday favorite in our home, but anytime you want to treat yourself to the nurturing qualities of winter, consider making the World's Best Pumpkin Pie.

CRUST:

¾ cup brown rice flour

¼ cup potato starch (not flour)

3 Tbsp. tapioca flour

1 Tbsp. sugar

¼ tsp. salt

⅓ cup coconut oil (in its solid state)

1 large egg

3 tsp. water

FILLING:

2 cups canned pumpkin

¼ cup sugar

¼ cup brown sugar, lightly packed

½ tsp. salt

1 tsp. cinnamon

½ tsp. freshly grated nutmeg

¼ tsp. cloves

1 tsp. freshly grated ginger

3 large eggs, slightly beaten

1½ cups canned coconut milk, (do not use light)

Preheat oven to 425°F.

In the bowl of a standing mixer (you can also do this by hand), combine the brown rice flour, potato starch, tapioca flour, sugar, and salt. (When measuring gluten-free flours, to get the most accurate measurements, it's best to scoop the flour from the bag with a spoon rather than dipping in the measuring cup.) Mix to combine. Add the coconut oil. If it's a hot day and the coconut oil is liquid, put it in the refrigerator until it solidifies. It won't work very well in the recipe if it's not solid. Add the egg and water. Mix on medium-low until fully combined and the dough starts to come together. Turn off the mixer, and gather the dough with your hands into a ball. It's not necessary to chill the dough. It's actually kind of hard to work with when it's cold.

With your palms, press the dough into a flat disc. Place the dough between two pieces of waxed paper, and with a rolling pin, roll it into approximately a 12-inch disc. Remove the top piece of waxed paper. Put the pie plate, open side down, on top of the dough and carefully invert the dough into the pie plate. Remove the waxed paper. Use your fingers to repair any rips. Crimp the dough on the rim of the pie plate with your fingers. Set aside.

In a large bowl, combine the pumpkin with the sugar, brown sugar, salt, cinnamon, nutmeg, cloves, and ginger. Stir until fully combined. Add the eggs and coconut milk, and stir until fully mixed.

Pour the custard mixture into the pie shell and bake on the middle rack of the oven at 425°F for 15 minutes. Reduce the temperature to 325°F and bake for an additional hour. When the crust is golden brown and the filling is fully set, remove the pie from the oven and allow it to cool before slicing.

CHAKRA MEALS:
Align Your Energy Centers

One of the most fun meals I've ever created was a "chakra meal." I was a teenager and cooking for one of my mom's residential seminars. Being my mother's daughter, I'd grown up with the word "chakra" as part of my vernacular, and I think at one point I even had a chakra coloring book. Yet up until that time, I didn't fully understand the significance of the chakras or how eating in alignment with them could bring about harmony and increase general well-being.

We made seven dishes, each a different color to correspond with each chakra. We laid them on the table in order, starting with red and ending with white. Years later, people still remember that meal and not only the fun, whimsical nature of it, but they said they felt amazingly different afterward! It was then that I came to better understand the meaning of chakras and knew that they were something beyond images in my coloring book.

⁓ Meadow

Your body has seven energy centers called *chakras* (a Sanskrit word meaning "vortex"), which are of vital importance to your overall health. Each chakra, represented by a different color, reflects an aspect of your consciousness and is connected to a part of your body. Energy flows from one chakra frequency to another, in spiraling fashion, along your spine to the top of your head. When these energy centers flow smoothly, you feel vital and healthy, but when they're blocked, you can feel off balance. The kind of food you eat, as well as its color, can raise the vibration of your chakras.

There are a number of ways a Mystic Chef can cook up chakra magic in the kitchen. If, for instance, you feel that one particular aspect of your life needs some attention, you could create a meal dedicated to the associated chakra. Alternatively, for general well-being, you could create a lavish feast in which each dish or course is dedicated to a different chakra. Approach such a banquet as a fun and outrageous dinner party idea, or approach it as a spiritual endeavor in which you cook and eat in a meditative state with the intention of opening and balancing your chakras. Both can lead to powerful results. (For more information about color and food, see Chapter 2.)

First Chakra Meal (Red) for Grounding, Abundance, and Strength

Red is the color associated with your first chakra. Mother Earth's energy flows from the ground into your root chakra, which is located at the base of your spine. To feel strong, gain courage, secure abundance, or have balanced sexuality, consider activating the energy of your first chakra. When your root is balanced, you'll feel safe and protected.

For a root chakra meal, choose red foods and/or foods that feel grounding. Also, anything that grows in the earth—such as potatoes, sweet potatoes, beets, turnips, and parsnips—is excellent to include in a first chakra meal. As you consume these foods, do so mindfully and know that with each bite, you're filling your body with the vibrant energy of the first chakra. You may want to consider decorating the table in crimson tones. Toast abundance and passion with a glass of red wine (or red juice), and allow the energy of the first chakra to fill you.

Second Chakra Meal (Orange) to Activate Pleasure, Creativity, and Joy

The color orange represents your second or sacral chakra, which is located slightly below your navel. When this chakra is balanced, you experience emotional pleasure, flexibility, fluidity, joy, and creativity. However, when the sacral chakra is blocked, your zest for life may be dragging. The second chakra inspires and opens you to living life at its fullest.

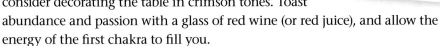

Indulge in your creativity as you immerse yourself in an orange cornucopia of foods. Decorate with colors of burnt orange, rust, peach, copper, and ochre. Also, any foods that gave you emotional joy as a child are excellent to include in a second chakra meal. This would also be a great meal to get creative with the foods you eat, where you eat them, and how you eat them.

Third Chakra Meal (Yellow) to Inspire Confidence, Freedom, Clarity, and Power

Your third chakra glows with the color yellow. Found right in the area of your solar plexus, when this chakra is balanced, you experience decisive action and focus. You feel in control of your life, and you have good "gut reactions" to life's circumstances. You're assertive (without being aggressive), and you have

healthy personal boundaries. As you eat yellow foods, imagine the energy of the third chakra illuminating you.

When you create a third chakra meal, choose your menu plan confidently. Use yellow foods such as corn, pineapple, bananas, or yellow squash. Even if you don't feel particularly assertive, imagine how someone confident would act and then try to approach the shopping, cooking, and eating of this meal in that way. Consider putting a piece of citrine at each table setting or having a bowl of lemons or a large vase of daffodils as your centerpiece.

Fourth Chakra Meal (Green) for Love, Harmony, and Kindness

Your fourth chakra, the heart center, reflects the color green. This chakra is located in the center of your chest and is associated with love, kindness, and connection to others. When this chakra is in balance, your relationships with yourself, others, and the Creator are in harmony. You're open to receive love and support from others, and you radiate love in ever-widening circles. The heart chakra expands when you bless your food and when you're grateful for its gifts and bounty. By sharing food, such as creating a dinner party for your friends, you can increase the flow in your fourth chakra.

Consider eating green foods and decorating your table in shades of green. You may even want to bring in a bit of greenery from the outdoors to complement your fourth chakra table. This meal will make your fourth chakra open with love for the bounty of nature.

Fifth Chakra Meal (Blue) to Encourage Communication, Truth, and Expression

The color blue fuels your fifth chakra, which is the throat chakra. This represents your communication skills and is associated with self-expression. When it's in balance, you communicate your truth with ease and grace. When it's out of balance, you may feel constriction in your throat and feel choked up or repressed.

Blue is the theme for this meal. You may want to consider dining under the bright blue sky or next to the azure ocean. As you eat, spend time noticing how the foods feel in your throat as you swallow, and imagine that with each bite you're centering your throat chakra and releasing any blockages. Using blue glasses for your water also brings this chakra into harmony.

Sixth Chakra Meal (Purple) to Kindle Your Sixth Sense, Imagination, and Intuition

The third eye chakra, the sixth chakra, is located on your forehead between your eyes and is associated with your intuition, insight, psychic abilities, and dreams. It reflects the color purple, which is calming, soothing, and comforting. When it is in balance, you have excellent intuition and are at the right time and right place. By listening to your inner knowledge, you nourish the sixth chakra, but when you allow your thinking or rational mind to continually override your intuition, you stifle it.

In addition to eating purple foods such as grapes, blackberries, or purple cabbage, this would be a great meal to employ the secret alchemy of intuitive cooking. Throw out your recipes and shopping lists, and head to the market empty-handed. Choose the products that seem to jump out to you and make you feel inspired. As you cook, trust your instinct and allow your third eye to open more fully. Set your table in shades of indigo. At the end of the meal, close your eyes and allow your third eye to open. Notice whatever thoughts and images arise.

Seventh Chakra Meal (Violet or White) for Bliss, Serenity, and Spirituality

The crown, the seventh and final chakra, is located at the very top of the head and is often represented by white. When the seventh chakra is balanced, you experience a Divine connection with the Creator, and you're able to tap into a serene state of bliss. If you're feeling alone, cut off, or lost, and feel a yearning for community or feel yourself searching for your life purpose, you may wish to connect, or reconnect, with your crown chakra.

Invite as many people as you wish to help you prepare for this feast. Set your table in shades of white for an opulent mood. In addition to thinking of white foods to serve at this meal, you may also want to consider foods that feel otherworldly. Imagine what you might eat if you were a completely spiritual being. Breaking bread with others has long been considered sacred and Divine. Connect with your food on a deep, spiritual level, and you'll feed your crown chakra.

HAWAIIAN RAINBOW KEBABS

What better way to tap into the energy of the chakras than by eating a Hawaiian Rainbow Kebab! These are especially great for a party. The pound of beef in this recipe is enough for about one piece per skewer. If you want meatier kebabs, double the amount of beef. There should still be enough marinade, but you might want to consider marinating the meat in a reclosable plastic bag for better coverage. To make these kebabs vegetarian, omit the beef and repleace with cubes of firm tofu.

MAKES ABOUT 20 KEBABS

20 bamboo skewers

MARINADE:

3 Tbsp. brown sugar

⅔ cup pineapple juice

6 Tbsp. tamari

8 cloves garlic, crushed

1 tsp. grated fresh ginger

KEBABS:

1 lb. beef, cut into 1½-inch cubes (top sirloin works well)

8 oz. white button mushrooms

1 lb. sweet potatoes (1 large or 2 small), peeled and cut into 1½-inch cubes and parboiled

1 lb. very small gold potatoes, parboiled (if large, cut them into smaller chunks)

2 green bell peppers, cut into 1½-inch squares

1 red onion, cut into 1-inch chunks

1 fresh pineapple, cut into 1½-inch chunks

1 10-oz. pkg. cherry tomatoes

Vegetable or canola oil

If using bamboo skewers (available in most grocery stores), soak them in water for at least 20 minutes to keep them from burning on the grill.

To make the marinade, combine the brown sugar, pineapple juice, tamari, garlic, and ginger in a large bowl.

Cut the beef and wash the mushrooms. Add the beef and mushrooms to the marinade and stir to combine. Cover with plastic wrap and refrigerate while preparing the other ingredients.

Bring two pots of water to a boil, one for the sweet potatoes and one for the gold potatoes. Meanwhile, peel and cut the sweet potato. When the water is boiling, add the gold potatoes to one and the sweet potatoes to the other. Parboil until just barely soft (about 5 minutes for the sweet potato and 10 minutes for the potato). This is a bit tricky. If they're overcooked, they'll fall off the skewer. But if they're undercooked, they won't cook at the same rate as the meat and vegetables on the grill.

Drain and rinse the potatoes with cool water. Pour them back into the pots they cooked in and toss each with 1 Tbsp. vegetable oil. This will keep them from sticking to the grill.

(CONTINUED ON NEXT PAGE)

Wash the tomatoes, and cut the peppers, onions, and pineapple. I find it helpful to put each ingredient in a bowl and line them up on the counter. That way the kebabs can be made assembly-line style.

Fire up the grill. When the grill is hot, carefully oil the grate with a paper towel dipped in vegetable oil.

It can be fun to put the ingredients on the skewer in the order of the rainbow. Depending on how you assemble the kebabs, you may end up with leftovers of some ingredients. In this case, you can either save them for another use or make some haphazard kebabs with whatever vegetables are remaining.

Grill over medium heat, about 5–10 minutes per side, or until the potatoes are cooked through and the meat has reached desired doneness.

If you have leftover marinade, you can gently boil it in a small pan until any uncooked meat juices are well cooked and the sauce has reduced. This makes a tasty glaze to drizzle over the kebabs.

PAST-LIFE MEALS:
Awaken Who You Were

You might not consciously remember your past lives . . . but your taste buds do. When you try new foods, not only can they potentially activate subliminal memories of your previous incarnations as we discussed in the first chapter, but also you can use food to consciously call forth your past lives. For example, if you're drawn to a certain region or country for no apparent reason, it's possible there's a past-life connection. Simply by eating the cuisine of that area (with the intention of discovering a past life), you can open the gateway to distant memories.

A past-life meal can be like a time machine that allows you to travel back and experience the tastes, scents, and flavors of another lifetime. Plus, it's a great dinner party idea! You can create a past-life meal simply to have fun, learn more about your past incarnations, or start working through any challenges that you may be carrying with you from lifetime to lifetime. The food, music, and decor you choose will transport you through time and space, and you'll enter into the inner realms of a past incarnation. Let your imagination flow and allow images, sensations, aromas, and memories to come in unfiltered as you travel through the space-time continuum. Then sit back, savor each bite, and take notes if you feel compelled to do so.

Planning Your Past-Life Meal

As a Mystic Chef, you can create a past-life meal with the intention of either exploring a possible life during a particular time in history or of triggering a specific memory—especially those related to food—to help you make sense of events in this life. As you embark on the planning of this meal, you may want to research the time period of the past life you'd like to activate. Familiarize yourself with the region and its history. What kinds of foods did people eat? How did they prepare them? What were the dwellings like? What type of music and art were popular? Learn as much as you can about the history and culture of this particular time and place in order to make your meal as authentic as possible. You may even find that doing this research will begin to activate emotions, feelings, and deep-seated memories.

Perhaps you don't really know anything about your past lives, but you're curious to see if you had a life as a nomad, for example. As a suggestion, create the kind of meal you think someone who lived that lifestyle may have eaten, and see if you feel any connection. Perhaps you feel an affinity for the French aristocracy and think Bastille Day is a bit of an overblown holiday. Consider

decorating your dining space for the evening to look like a room in a French château. You may even want to adorn your walls with cloth to give the feeling of having tapestries like the ones on the walls of French castles. Consider a meal of roasted poultry and wild mushrooms or other dishes that fit with that time and place, and as you eat, notice if anything feels familiar.

Play music that matches your theme, and if you can't find anything exactly from that particular region or era, choose something that evokes the *feeling* of that period. Scour old cookbooks and the Internet to find authentic recipes or come up with some of your own based on what you think may have been eaten during that time. You need not be completely historically accurate. What's most important is that you create a feeling of being in that time. Even if you don't have immediate results, know that you're opening the gateway into inner realms, and hopefully you'll have entertaining and delicious meals along the way.

Come as You Were Party

A "Come as You Were" party can be a great way to engage with your friends in new ways. Invite your guests to each come dressed as someone they feel they may have been in a past life. Ask them to dress the part and bring a food or beverage from that era. Encourage your guests to spend some time researching what life was like and what foods would've

been eaten. You can even take it a step further and ask your guests to stay in character throughout the evening. Who knows what interesting conversations and powerful breakthroughs may ensue. Your party may well be like turning the pages in a history book. Imagine an ancient Egyptian princess snacking on a fig while chatting with a Japanese warrior who's making eyes at the sharecropper from the American South. Take plenty of pictures, and enjoy this reliving of possible past lives!

Meals to Activate the Wisdom of Your Ancestors

In addition to delving deep into the far past of your soul, there's value in creating meals that tap into the wisdom of your ancestors. Cooking and eating in the way your forefathers did can be fun and exciting. What's more, such a meal enables you to deeply connect to the people you've come from, as well as initiates healing of ancestral wounds that you might carry in your DNA. Who knows, they might even enjoy watching it all unfold from their vantage point in the spirit world!

When choosing a time period or theme for this meal, you can go as near or as far into your personal history as you like. Perhaps you're looking to activate the innate wisdom of your grandmother who came to America in her 20s from Eastern Europe. As a suggestion, ask her if she has any recipes from that time. If she is no longer living, you can research traditional recipes that she would have eaten as a child to create the experience of being with her in those days. You can also ask her spirit to join you as you prepare and dine on the meal. You can even ask her what information she would like to share with you at this time.

Taking a historical and gastronomical tour of your family tree can be an eye-opening way to connect with your ancestral roots. This can be a powerful experience to do alone; however, it can also be especially rewarding to invite as many members of your family as possible to partake in this meal. Imagine your grandfather's face or your great-uncle's delight when you share with them a meal that *their* grandparents may have served.

Come as They Were Party

Another fun way to cook up magic is to create a "Come as *They* Were" party. Instead of inviting guests to dress up and bring food from one of their past lives, you could create a party in which everyone dresses up in the clothing of their ancestors. Ask them to bring the foods and drinks that would've been consumed by their forefathers. Just as with the "Come as You Were" party, it can also be fun to ask your guests to act as if they're really from that time period and region and stay in character throughout the evening. Undoubtedly, there will be some interesting conversations. This can be a fun and lighthearted activity, but there can also be great power in spending an evening embodying one of your ancestors. Their life is encoded in your DNA. By welcoming them into your life, you'll be activating their wisdom within you.

SPIRIT MEALS:
Welcome Magic

It's possible to have a delightful, magical evening with your angel friends . . . real angels. It's true. You can indeed share a meal with angels, fairies, spirit guides, or possibly even a deceased loved one. The Spirit realm is simply a thought away, and it's completely possible to have spiritual beings join you around your dining table. These meals may be some of the most magical evenings you'll ever enjoy, and the Mystic Chef is always ready for celestial guests!

Invite the Angels for Dinner

What could be more enchanting than dining with angels? Angels are messengers from Spirit, allowing us a greater understanding and connection to the Divine. Planning a meal for angelic friends can be a transcendental experience. When you decide to invite angels to dine with you, the call goes out to them. You can even say these words: "We invite you, dear Angel Protectors, to join us tonight for our meal." Even a simple statement like this can be heard on high, and angels will be attracted to the call. Make sure to leave a place at the table for your angelic visitor!

Most angels aren't seen but *felt*. There are different ways to tell if you're in the presence of an angel. Often the scent of flowers accompanies their presence. Sometimes an angel will announce itself with a slight breeze, even if all the windows are closed. Other times, you'll hear the faint sound of bells, chimes, or trumpets. An angelic presence can also be seen as a flash of light, but the most common way of knowing they're there is by the warm wave of love that washes over you. If you feel like an angel is standing behind you or beside you—it most likely is.

Let your creativity soar as you decorate your dining space for this angelic meal. Consider using billowy layers of white chiffon, tulle, organza, or anything that feels ethereal. White feathers and white flowers, such as baby's breath, angelica, chiming bells, or angel's trumpet, will be especially appreciated. To set the table, think light, airy, angelic, and beautiful. Scatter tea lights up and down the table. You may even want to sprinkle the following stones on the table to further enhance the mood: angelite, blue celestite, selenite (an especially potent angelic connection), amethyst, blue calcite, and quartz.

Additionally, you may wish to create a space-clearing spray to use throughout the room to freshen, cleanse, and ready the room for your visitors. The following scents and essential oils can help call the angels: angelica seed, jasmine, lavender, neroli, rose, sandalwood, geranium, and rosewood. Use a blend of the ones that appeal to you mixed in water to spritz the room.

Light, natural, heavenly foods will delight your guests, both human and angelic. Of course, the angels won't actually partake in the food, but they'll truly appreciate the intention. You might also consider angel hair pasta, angel food cake, or cookies cut in the shape of angels. During the meal, make sure to include the angels in your conversations and when you give grace. Act as if they're there, and they most certainly will be. At the end of the meal, thank the angels for attending.

Invite the Fairy Folk for Dinner

The betwixt and between times have long been considered the domain of fairies, so you may wish to plan your fairy party for dusk or dawn. Create beautiful invitations that bring to mind times of enchantment. Don't forget to mail an invitation to the Fairy Folk, or simply put out the call by saying, "We invite you fairies, near and far, to share a meal with us."

As you would for any ceremony, prepare yourself and dress in clothing worthy of celebration. A leisurely salt bath is best, as the purity of the salt will align your energies to the otherworldliness of the fairy people. If unable to take a bath or shower, scrub yourself with a bit of sea salt.

As you decorate, incorporate natural, fairy-related items, such as acorns, bits of moss, crystals, flowers, or feathers. A valuable addition to any fairy meal is to spritz everything with carefully chosen flower essences. The highly calibrated vibration of flower essences will most certainly be inviting to those in the fairy realm. You may wish to have a bowl of fairy dust with a big brush in it for your guests to brush on themselves upon arrival. It has been said that primroses allow you to see the fairies, so some potted primroses may be appropriate.

The seat of honor belongs to the fairies, so make sure their glass is full and their plate is beautifully arranged. When planning the menu, choose foods that feel fun and spritely. Fairies frolic in nature and enjoy natural products, but they also enjoy honey, fruit, and other sweet treats. You may even wish to have this be a Fairy Nibbles party and serve little bites of everything. Think fresh berries, nuts and seeds, and petit fours. Mead is traditional, but if there's no mead at your local wine store, substitute sparkling water, champagne, or elderflower liqueur.

After you've eaten and drunk and laughed and danced as the fairies would, thank them for honoring you with a visit to your home. Join hands and have each guest thank the fairies and share a few words or even a poem. The fairies do so love poetry!

To "see" fairies in nature:

* Eat lightly before you go out in nature—lettuce or raw vegetables is much better than fast food. If possible, nibble on edible flowers such as nasturtiums or rose petals.

* Drink natural spring water.

* Your clothes shouldn't be washed in perfumed detergent; natural unscented is best.

* Dab yourself with essential oils, and spritz yourself with flower essences. Rose is best, but flowers or plants from the area are excellent as well.

* Go outdoors someplace in nature or a park where you suspect fairies might reside.

* Mentally ask permission to enter. Approach slowly once you feel that permission has been granted.

* If there is anything in that area that is edible, put a tiny bit of it in your mouth, as this attunes you to the area. For example, put a tiny bit of rosemary, a wild blackberry, a rose petal, or a pine needle into your mouth.

* Sit still and allow your eyes to become non-focused, and be open to unusual movements of light or color. Chances are you've seen a fairy.

Invite Spirit Guides for Dinner

Whether you choose to eat alone with your spirit guides or decide to share the experience with others, this meal can be powerful and meaningful. Each of us has guides, and inviting them to dinner can be a good way to get to know them better. Guides have spent time on Earth, unlike angels, and can be helpful understanding earthly issues.

Set a place at the table for you and your guides. Sit across from them, and imagine you're having a conversation. A silent dinner with a journal is a great idea here, soft ambient music playing in the background. If you've chosen to share this experience with others, you may choose to meditate and to share what wisdom you've each gained from the guides.

Spirit guides are with us, some from birth and many others along the way, to help us achieve our soul's purpose and will guide us *only when asked,* so get to know your team and how they communicate with you. Get a sense of their gender or ask for a name or who's there for what purpose. You may want to dine often with these guides to build your relationship. Connecting at the same time and place builds a relationship you can trust, daily is best, so why not a share a bagel or cup of coffee with a wise one before work?

Invite Loved Ones That Have Passed Over for Dinner

Inviting a loved one who's passed on, or even an ancestor, to share a meal is traditional in many cultures and can be a powerful experience. They're never really gone from our life; they've just moved on to another realm, another time, place, and dimension. It's simply a matter of asking if they'd like to join you. Don't expect an immediate connection, as some departed beings are busy on the other side, but keep trying, and when they're ready, they'll come to you. You may feel their presence in an emotional response, or you will just have a feeling that they're there. You might also feel a sense of relief or an inner peace you hadn't felt for a while, or you may even see something move just out of the corner of your eye. Watch for the signs.

If you shared a favorite spot, like a special park bench, you might want to grab a sandwich and invite the spirit of your loved one to join you. Or if you had a favorite restaurant, you could reserve a table for two . . . and call forth their spirit to accompany you. Alternatively, invite them to your home, put their photo at their table setting, pour them a favorite beverage, and you might even want to consider serving some of their special foods.

DELICIOUS DREAMS:
Messages from Beyond

Your dreams are trying to tell you something . . . and your dreams about food are no exception. Believe it or not, you can use your dreams to help you cook up magic during your waking hours. Since the dawn of time, dream travelers have slipped through the crack between the two worlds in their night hours to touch the reaches of inner space and hear the secret messages from Spirit. Dreams were so revered that the destiny of the tribe, clan, or culture often pivoted as the result of a dream, but in our culture, for the most part, dreams are considered unimportant. However, just a small amount of time spent on dream exploration can deepen your spiritual journey and spice up your culinary adventures. You can even use dreams to get recipes from Spirit!

Recipes from Spirit

Dreams can be used in a multitude of ways to spice up your cooking. You can find that missing ingredient, gain inspiration for meals, or even call upon your inner Mystic Chef. All of this can be achieved simply by learning to program your dreams. This idea isn't uncommon. We tell someone who's stuck in a problem to "sleep on it." Then in the morning, as if by miracle, there's the answer that was needed.

A problem presented during waking hours can be resolved during sleep simply by making a *conscious* choice to do so. Perhaps you'd like some guidance about a special meal. You might say before bed, "Dreams, please give me inspiration for the holiday dinner." Or, "Dreams, show me how I can best create a magical and welcoming environment for my guests."

This worked remarkably well for Janet, who had been trying to re-create a favorite potato recipe of her grandmother's she remembered from childhood. Her grandmother had never written down the recipe, and now that Janet was a grandmother herself, she wanted her grandkids to taste this family recipe. But no matter how many ingredients she tried, it just didn't taste the same. Then one night before Thanksgiving, after asking her dreams for guidance, she dreamed she was in a log cabin with her grandmother (who had passed on). When she looked at the logs, however, she saw that each one was really a large cinnamon stick. When she awoke, she raced to the kitchen to create the potato dish but this time added a dash of cinnamon, and when she tasted it, she knew she'd found the missing ingredient.

Dream Incubation

The idea of programming your dreams (also called "dream incubation") originated in ancient Greece. Dreamers would go to sacred dream temples for the purpose of receiving a useful dream. They believed that by sleeping in holy places and appealing to the gods, they could obtain profound answers to their inner questions. To participate in dream incubation now, it isn't necessary to sleep in a sacred place or to appeal to a specific god. If you honor your place of sleep as an inner temple and if you appeal to Spirit, both the vivid clarity and the contents of your incubated dreams will be enhanced.

When you use dream incubation, anticipate that all your dream expectations will be met. However, the manner in which you phrase your request is important. Instead of, "I hope that tonight my cooking abilities are activated," say, "Tonight, I activate my mystical cooking abilities." Or instead of, "I hope I can get some clarity about what food my body needs now," say, "Tonight my dreams reveal my dietary needs easily and effortlessly." Your dreams will respond with clarity proportionate to your intention.

You may want to keep a dream journal near your bed so you can begin to enter your questions before you go to bed and set the intention that those questions will be answered. Set time set aside in the morning to process the messages from Spirit before you get out of bed. Ask yourself, *What answers did I receive during my dreamtime?* Record them in your dream journal, and if at first they're not clear, keep at it. Perhaps you begin simply with a couple words, a drawing, or a *feeling,* but over time, you'll learn how to make sense of it all. And eventually, your dreams will become a useful ally in your mystical kitchen. (See Denise's book *Hidden Power of Dreams* for more information about dreams.)

∽∾ ∾∽

Now that you've had a chance to cook up some magic and eat in alignment with the elements, the seasons, and your energy centers, as well as explore your dreams and your past lives, and even dine with fairies and angels, you're ready to embark on what might be the most exciting and powerful of all . . . Legendary Meals.

LEGENDARY MEALS TO EXPAND SPIRITUAL CONSCIOUSNESS

A Legendary Meal is more than simply good food. It's a profound experience that ignites all the senses and expands consciousness by increasing your awareness of other realms, cultures, and times in history. This is the kind of meal people will talk about for decades. A Legendary Meal combines the knowledge and skills you've gained throughout these pages to catapult your dining experience into an even higher dimension. This is the culmination of your Mystic Chef odyssey.

These epic feasts will awaken your spirituality and invite magic and mystery into your life. They take you beyond the confines of your home, and sometimes even beyond the confines of the earthly dimension. Bringing about transformation at your dining table, however, need not be extravagant, expensive, or time-consuming. All you need is a bit of imagination and a willingness to experiment. By engaging the senses and creating mysterious, sensual, mythical, and mystical meals, you'll open the portal into otherworldly realms to expand your spiritual consciousness in a fun and whimsical way. Legendary Meals are powerful when eaten alone, but they're transcendent when shared with others. Invite a group of friends to your home, and embark on a journey to the center of your soul.

Hop on the magic carpet . . . and away we go!

TIME TRAVELER MEALS:
Activate Your Inner Mysteries

A Time Traveler Meal can be an exhilarating way to activate your inner mysteries and understand yourself even more deeply. Dining on authentic foods and decorating your home in the style of whatever period in history you choose can open the gateway to mystical experiences from that era.

You may want to consider taking yourself and/or your guests on a guided meditation before the meal to set the scene and aid in the activation of inner mysteries. Before even bringing out the first dish, ask your guests to close their eyes and picture themselves in the destination of your choosing. Describe the scene. After you've spent a few minutes creating a sensory picture for them, allow some time for them to explore in their mind's eye on their own.

You may also want to play period music, dress in traditional clothing, use dishes that emulate those of the time period, and serve foods true to the experience you're creating. Photographs and images of your destination can be helpful in setting the scene as are scents, such as incense, flowers, and cooking aromas. Consider enlisting your guests' help in the kitchen or doing some sort of activity—like belly dancing, mulling wine, or language lessons—that engages the mind and spirit beyond simply filling the stomach.

Arabian Dreams

Soak in the world of Scheherazade and picture yourself in *One Thousand and One Nights*. Close your eyes and inhale deeply. Imagine yourself in a world where herbs and spices permeate the air and hand-shaped loaves of bread are fed into stone ovens heated by blazing fires. Snake charmers and vegetable vendors line the streets, and hand-painted pottery, intensely sweet dates, and herb-scented olives are available in every corner store. Take a deep breath. What do you smell? Maybe it's the heady scent of a chicken and lemon stew simmering in an earthen pot or perhaps cinnamon, cardamom, and coriander. Does the aroma of mint and cilantro dance on your tongue? What do you hear? Perhaps it's the sizzle of spicy meats cooking over an open flame or shouts of joy and laughter as children play in a neighboring square. What are you touching?

Is there a luscious carpet beneath your bare feet or a warm cup of sweet mint tea cradled between your hands? Are you listening to the wise words of Rumi? Can you taste the air scented with orange blossoms and jasmine in the land of the

ancient Sufis? What do you see? Are there rows of date palms, miles and miles of vast golden sand, snow-covered peaks, long stretches of beach and azure water, or narrow and sinuous streets in the medina?

Now open your eyes and examine how this journey made you feel. What thoughts, feelings, and emotions flood your being in this moment? Perhaps you have a sudden urge to dance with your whole being and jangle bells as you sway your hips from side to side, or maybe you feel deeply connected to all humanity, as it's believed that humankind originated in the Middle East.

Turning Your Vision into a Legendary Arabian Dreams Meal

To turn the feeling you had on your inner journey into an Arabian meal, you'll want to consider music, lighting, decorations, table settings, scents, clothing, and of course, the food. How would you decorate the table if you were in a Saharan oasis, North African Kasbah, or Persian palace? If you want to go all out, you could hire a belly-dancing instructor to give a short lesson before your meal, or you could rent a belly-dancing DVD and practice the moves with your guests using bells and colorful scarves. Perhaps someone could read Rumi poems or teach Sufi dances.

You'll also want to consider how you can use this experience to expand your spiritual consciousness. By transforming your dining room into a riad in Marrakesh or an outpost in Giza, how can you create the feeling of traveling through time and

space? You may want to think about invoking the mysteries of the Egyptian pyramids or indulging in the secrets of the *Arabian Nights*. Try to make it feel as magical and mystical as possible.

Traditionally, food in the Middle East is eaten with the hands. Before sitting down to eat, consider washing your guests' hands in the traditional way. Fill a teakettle with warm water perfumed with rose water, and pour it over their hands into a large basin. Not only is this a fun way to wash hands before embarking on a meal full of sensuous delights, but also it's thought that the scented rose water can aid in symbolic purification. It's common in the Middle East to sit on the floor on large overstuffed cushions and eat at a low table.

Additionally, you could print out images of the Sahara, a Kasbah, the snow-covered Atlas mountains, or a bustling marketplace and pass them around during the meal to help your guests imagine where they're dining and connect more deeply with the spirit of the land and its people. Download traditional music from the Internet, and play it in the background to set the scene. Fill the air with the scents of Arabia, such as frankincense and myrrh, which are thought to have Divine properties.

MOROCCAN SPICED KEFTA

(Meatballs with Cinnamon)

Lamb is more traditional in Moroccan cooking; however, I prefer turkey. Experiment to see which you like better. I've also had good success making this dish vegetarian by substituting crumbled firm tofu. You may need to add an additional egg to make it stick together, and you'll need to squeeze firmly to form the vegetarian "meatballs." Serve with raita.

MAKES 12 LARGE MEATBALLS; SERVES 4–6

2 cups cooked white basmati rice (¾ cup dried rice will yield just over 2 cups cooked)

1 cup raw walnuts, toasted and chopped

½ cup golden raisins, chopped

½ cup minced fresh mint

1 Tbsp. ground cinnamon

1 tsp. salt

5 cloves of garlic, crushed

1 22-oz. pkg. ground turkey (do not use ground breast meat because it will be too dry)

3 large eggs, slightly beaten

¼ cup olive oil

Preheat the oven to 350ºF.

If not using leftover rice, measure ¾ cup rice and rinse thoroughly. Combine rice with 1 cup of water in a saucepan. Bring to a boil and then cover, reduce to low, and cook for about 15 minutes. The rice should be on the firmer side. (This will yield a tad bit more than you need.)

While the rice is cooking, put the walnuts on a baking sheet and bake in the oven on the middle rack for approximately 10 minutes. They should be golden and aromatic. Remove from the oven, and when they're cool, chop. Keep the oven at 350ºF.

Meanwhile, chop the raisins and mint.

Line a baking dish with parchment paper and set aside.

In a large bowl, combine the walnuts, raisins, mint, cinnamon, salt, and garlic. When the rice is done cooking, measure 2 cups and combine it with the walnuts, raisins, and spices. Mix in the ground turkey, eggs, and olive oil.

Using your hands (be sure to remove jewelry, since this can get kind of messy), form 12 large meatballs. They will be sticky because of the egg, but that's okay; they're meant to be that way.

Put the kefta in the baking dish and cover with foil. Bake until cooked through and starting to brown, about 1 hour. I love the ease of putting them in the oven and forgetting them for an hour. Although keeping the kefta covered means they won't be very browned, they'll stay moister and juicier this way.

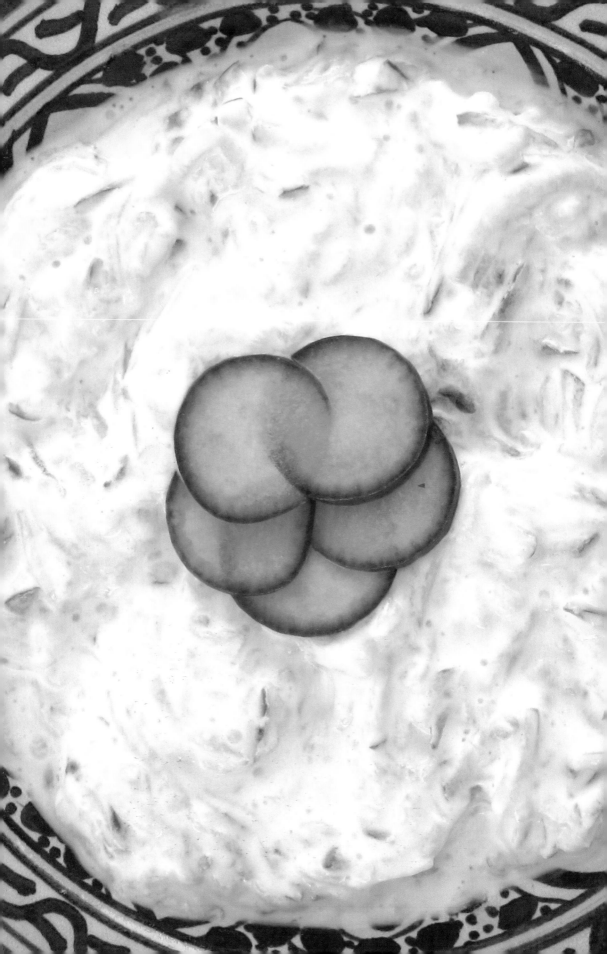

RAITA

(Yogurt and Cucumber Sauce)

Raita (called *tzatziki* in Greece) is a great addition
to Indian, Middle Eastern, and North African dishes
and is an essential component of Moroccan Spiced Kefta.

SERVES 4–6

1 English (hothouse)
cucumber

1–2 cloves of garlic, crushed

1 cup whole, lowfat, or
Greek plain yogurt (nonfat
will be too watery)

½ tsp. salt

Grate the cucumber using a box grater or food
processor fitted with a grating disc. To remove
the excess liquid from the grated cucumber, place
it on a clean dishtowel (or sturdy paper towel),
fold the sides of the dishtowel up around it, and
squeeze out the liquid. Be sure to do this over a
sink. It can be messy. Cucumber water is cooling
and nutritious. Rather than squeezing it down the
drain, consider saving it and mixing it with cool
water for a refreshing tonic.

In a medium bowl, combine the cucumber, garlic,
yogurt, and salt.

TUNISIAN GARBANZO BEANS WITH HARISSA

A number of years ago, we were having some special dinner guests, and my mom asked me to prepare a memorable feast. We decided to theme our dinner "Night at the Kasbah." My mom turned our patio into a luxurious Saharan tent, and we were transported to another time and place. With the first bite, our guests could not only taste North Africa, but also they could feel, sense, and smell it. I created this dish for that special dinner.

You can purchase harissa (Tunisian chili paste), but I prefer to make my own. Not only is it fun to make, but also you can control how spicy it is by the types of chilies you use. Traditional harissa can be mouth-searingly hot, but this recipe makes a mild one. Although I love the ease of canned garbanzo beans, for this salad, I prefer the texture of home-cooked ones. If you do use canned beans, drain and rinse them well.

SERVES 6

2 cups dried garbanzo beans (chickpeas), soaked overnight or 6 cups cooked

1 cup finely diced onion

1 cup diced tomato

½ cup minced cilantro

½ a lemon, minced (peel included)

1 Tbsp. lemon juice (from ½ a lemon)

¼ cup harissa paste*

2 tsp. salt

*If using store-bought harissa, adjust this amount to suit your taste, since it will most likely be quite spicy.

Soak 2 cups of dried garbanzo beans overnight. If you can, change the water periodically. Drain and rinse.

To cook the garbanzo beans, place them in a large pot and cover with approximately 3 quarts of water. Do not salt the water. This will make them tough. Cook at a low boil uncovered for approximately 45 minutes. If foam appears on the top, skim it off with a large spoon. The garbanzo beans should be soft but still have a bit of texture (not mushy). Drain and rinse with cool water.

While the garbanzos are cooking, dice the onion and tomato and toss in a large bowl. Wash and chop the cilantro and add to the bowl. Since you will be eating the lemon peel, wash the lemon really well. Cut the lemon in half and reserve one half for juice and mince the other half, including the peel. The little surprise of sour-bitter lemon peel balanced with the sweet-spicy harissa is so delicious.

When the garbanzo beans are cooked, drained, and rinsed, add them to the bowl with the vegetables, and toss with the juice of the other half of the lemon. Stir in the harissa paste and salt. Allow the salad to sit for at least 30 minutes to give the flavors time to marry. The salad can be served chilled or at room temperature.

HARISSA

This Tunisian chili paste is a delicious accompaniment to any Arabian Dreams meal. Just as the United States has ketchup, Mexico has hot sauce, and Germany has mustard, North Africa has harissa. It's the essential flavoring in the Tunisian Garbanzo Beans dish, but it's also delicious with grilled meats, vegetable stews, and couscous. Whatever you don't eat can be covered in olive oil and kept in the refrigerator for up to a month.

MAKES ABOUT 1 CUP

3 oz. dried mild red chilies (such as "New Mexico" or "California")*

1½ tsp. coriander seeds

1½ tsp. caraway seeds

½ tsp. cumin seeds (optional)

5 cloves of garlic, crushed

1 tsp. salt

¼ cup olive oil

*Any moderately spiced red chili will work. Experiment to see which you prefer.

Remove the stems from the chilies. Open the chilies and remove the seeds and ribs (the majority of the spice is found in the seeds and the ribs). In a medium bowl, soak the chilies for 15–30 minutes in warm water until they're soft and tender. Immediately wash your hands to avoid inadvertently wiping your eye . . . boy does that hurt! Luckily, these are pretty mild, but it's better to be on the safe side.

While the chilies soak, toast the coriander, caraway, and cumin seeds in a dry skillet over medium heat. Stir constantly, as the seeds can burn very quickly. Remove from the heat as soon as the spices are golden and aromatic. This takes just a few minutes. Using a spice grinder or a coffee grinder, pulverize the spices to a fine powder.

Once the chilies are soft, drain them. In the bowl of a food processor fitted with a steel blade, combine the soaked chilies, ground spices, crushed garlic, and salt. Process until a paste begins to form, scraping down the sides as necessary. With the motor running, slowly pour the olive oil through the feed tube, and process until a smooth paste is formed. Depending on the type of chilies you use, you may need to slightly adjust the amount of olive oil.

ARABIAN CHOPPED SALAD

The cuisines of North Africa and the Middle East rely heavily on the use
of fresh herbs. This salad is light and refreshing on a hot summer night.
It's also a wonderful accompaniment to Moroccan Spiced Kefta,
Tunisian Garbanzo Beans, Aladdin's Quinoa Tabbouleh, or grilled meats.
It's especially delicious when made with heirloom tomatoes.

SERVES 4 – 6

1 cup onion, diced
(from 1 small onion)

3 Tbsp. lemon juice
(from 1–2 lemons)

1½ tsp. salt

1 English (hothouse)
cucumber, chopped

4 cups chopped tomato
(from 3–4 large tomatoes)

½ cup chopped cilantro

¼ cup chopped mint

¼ cup extra-virgin olive oil

1 clove of garlic, crushed

In a large bowl, combine the onion, lemon juice, and salt. The lemon and salt will "pickle" the onion while you prepare the other ingredients, so it won't be quite so piquant. Chop the cucumber, tomato, and herbs; and put them in the bowl on top of the onions. Whisk the olive oil with the garlic in a small bowl. Drizzle the garlic-infused oil over the vegetables and toss everything together. This salad has a tendency to be very juicy. Serve with a slotted spoon.

Mayan Mysteries

The ancient Mayan culture is steeped in mystery. By traveling back in time and creating a Mayan Mystery Time Traveler Meal, you can ignite your own personal mysteries.

The Maya were an advanced and vast civilization whose empire covered much of what is now Southern Mexico and Central America. Their history dates back approximately 3,000 years. This thriving civilization built impressive monuments, temples, and pyramids. They had an advanced mathematical system, an accurate calendar, an understanding of astronomy, and a detailed form of hieroglyphics, as well as a complex social and political system. Their spiritual and religious beliefs are shrouded in mystery and magic, and a Mayan Meal can help you explore mystical avenues within yourself.

Turning Your Vision into a Legendary Mayan Mystery Meal

Before embarking on your Mayan Meal, you may want to go on an inner journey to explore this period and connect more deeply with the Mayan mysteries. Close your eyes and spend some time exploring the sights, sounds, smells, tastes, and feelings you associate with this time in history.

To turn this vision into a Legendary Meal, try to re-create the feeling you had on your inner journey. Think about the ways you can incorporate the unknown and the mysterious into your feast. One way you can do this is with storytelling. The Maya have a rich history of mythology. Maybe you choose to dine outdoors around a campfire and roast chilies and crush them into cocoa powder and imagine that you're taking part in an ancient and powerful ceremony. Corn was a staple of the Mayan diet, and it was believed that the gods created humans from ground corn. Perhaps you imagine you're a Mayan god, and see what beings you can create from ground corn mixed with water. Beans, fruits, vegetables, fish and seafood, and

other wild game, including turkey, featured predominantly in the Mayan diet. You can also serve modern Mexican dishes to activate your inner Mayan mysteries and travel through time to visit the temples and pyramids in the dense, humid Central American jungle.

FRIJOLES BORRACHOS

(Drunken Beans)

There's nothing quite like being in the wilderness to connect more deeply
with the energy of Mayan Mysteries. When I go camping, I love making fajitas with
flank steak grilled over the campfire and serving Frijoles Borrachos. I usually make
up a batch at home and then heat them at the campsite. They're filling and
so flavorful. I absolutely love beans, and these are some of the best I've had.

SERVES 8

1 lb. dried pinto beans,
soaked overnight

1 Tbsp. vegetable or canola oil

1 cup chopped onion

4 cloves garlic, chopped

3 bay leaves

1 Tbsp. Mexican oregano*

2 sprigs fresh thyme

2 canned chipotles
(canned in adobo sauce)

2 tsp. adobo sauce

1 12-oz. bottle Mexican beer
(you can substitute water)

1 28-oz. can diced tomatoes
4 cups water

1½ tsp. salt (or to taste)

*Although you can substitute
Italian oregano (generally labeled
"oregano" in the stores), it's worth
seeking out Mexican oregano—
which has delicious citrus
undertones—for this dish.

Soak the beans overnight in a large bowl filled
with water.

Drain and rinse the beans. Set aside.

Chop the onions and garlic. In a large pot over
medium heat, sauté the onions and garlic in the
vegetable oil. Add the bay leaves, oregano, and
thyme. (Do not add salt at this time. This will
make the beans tough.)

When the onions are soft and translucent, about
5 minutes, add the chipotle peppers, adobo sauce,
beer, tomatoes, beans, and water. (The leftover
chipotles can be frozen for a later use.) Turn up
the heat and bring to a boil, then reduce the
temperature to maintain a gentle boil. Continue
to simmer, uncovered, for approximately 2 hours
until the beans are soft and tender and most of
the water has been absorbed, stirring occasionally.
However, you may need to stir more often as the
water level decreases. Add the salt once the beans
are mostly cooked. Before serving, remove the bay
leaves and stems from the sprigs of thyme.

PESCADO VERACRUZ

(Fish with Tomatoes and Chilies)

I love Mexican food. In the States, we're mostly familiar with tacos, burritos, and enchiladas, but traditional Mexican cuisine is so much more than that. This dish originated in Veracruz, a port city on the Gulf of Mexico. Although the Veracruz region was not directly connected to the Mayan civilization, by building your repertoire of Mexican cuisine and sampling and savoring dishes from multiple regions, you'll find you begin to connect more deeply with the land and the mysteries of these enigmatic people.

Serve with warm corn tortillas and a side of Frijoles Borrachos, and you'll be sure to have a delicious feast.

SERVES 6

1 Tbsp. vegetable or canola oil

1 cup sliced onion (from ½ large onion)

8 cloves of garlic, chopped

¼ tsp. sea salt

1 28-oz. can of diced tomatoes in tomato juice

⅓ cup canned, sliced jalapeños in escabeche* (or to taste)

1 Tbsp. jalapeño juice (escabeche)*

½ cup pitted green olives

2 Tbsp. lime juice (from 1 or 2 limes)

2 lbs. white fish, such as tilapia

TO SERVE:

Chopped cilantro

Sour cream

*"Escabeche" in Mexican cuisine describes the pickling liquid often found in cans of jalapeños.

Slice the onions and chop the garlic. In a medium pot or large sauté pan over medium heat, warm the oil and then add the onion, garlic, and salt. Sauté until the onions are soft and translucent, about 10 minutes.

Add the canned tomatoes, jalapeños, jalapeño juice (escabeche), and olives. Squeeze in the lime juice and stir. Bring to a rapid simmer, and cook for 10 minutes to allow the flavors to marry.

While the Veracruz sauce simmers, preheat the oven to 350°F.

Line a large baking dish (15x10x2) with parchment paper. Place the fish in the baking dish in a single layer.

Cover the fish with the hot Veracruz sauce and bake in the oven until the fish is just cooked through, approximately 20–30 minutes (depending on the thickness of the fish). Top with chopped cilantro, and drizzle with sour cream. Don't skimp on the cilantro. It adds flavor and freshness.

CALDO de POLLO al LIMÓN

(Chicken Soup with Lime)

This recipe is based on a chicken and lime soup I ate while traveling
in the Yucatán (the Land of the Maya). This soup is an especially quick and easy
weeknight meal if you have leftover roasted or grilled chicken, but it can also
be a delicious first course in an elaborate Mayan Mystery meal.

SERVES 4-6

8 cups (2 qt.) chicken broth,
preferably homemade

¼ cup lime juice
(from 2 limes)

⅓ cup uncooked white rice

3 cloves garlic, minced

3 Roma tomatoes, chopped

½ cup very finely diced onion

2 cups diced cooked chicken

½ cup chopped cilantro

salt (to taste)

TO SERVE:

1 avocado, cut into bite-sized
pieces

8 oz. Monterey jack cheese,
grated

tortilla chips

Mexican hot sauce

To make most soups, you start by sautéing the vegetables before adding the liquid. This recipe, however, turns convention on its head. Start with the broth and then add the vegetables. This way the onions will still have a teeny bit of a crunch to them.

Pour the broth into a soup pot and bring to a gentle boil over medium-high. Add the lime juice and reduce to a simmer. Add the rice and garlic, and stir to keep the rice from sticking. Meanwhile, chop the tomatoes and onions and add them to the pot. Chop the chicken and cilantro, and add those to the pot. Stir. Add salt to taste. Simmer the soup for about 20–30 minutes, until the rice and vegetables are cooked and the flavors have had a chance to blend.

To serve, put avocado, grated cheese, and crumbled tortilla chips in the bottom of each bowl, and ladle the soup on top. If you like to spice things up a bit, sprinkle some Mexican hot sauce on top. Buen provecho!

MAYAN MYSTERY
GUACAMOLE

To this day, this is my very favorite guacamole, despite numerous
trips to Mexico and even a cooking class in Puebla.
I hope this will become your favorite as well.

With each dip of your tortilla chip into the bowl of guacamole, you're igniting
Mayan legends and connecting more and more deeply
with your own inner mysteries.

MAKES ABOUT 2 CUPS

1 Roma tomato, seeded and diced

¼ cup white onion, diced

¼ cup chopped cilantro

2 Tbsp. fresh lime juice

½ tsp. sea salt

3 ripe avocados

Chop the tomato, onion, and cilantro and combine in a medium-sized bowl. The easiest way to chop the tomatoes is to cut them in half lengthwise and then either squeeze or scrape out the seeds with your fingers (this only works with Roma tomatoes, which tend to have a firm texture). To have similarly sized tomato pieces, slice the tomato halves into long, thin strips. Then line up the strips and chop them. Toss with the lime and salt. Cut the avocados in half, remove the pit, and scoop out the fruit with a large spoon. Add the avocado to the bowl, and mash all the ingredients together with a potato masher. Enjoy with tortilla chips.

MANGO SALSA

If I were told I could only make one thing for the rest of my life, it would probably be salsa. Finding the right combination of salty, sweet, sour, and spicy makes me feel like an alchemist. Chilies, tomatoes, onions, fruit, and lime juice . . . oh my! There are so many delicious things that can be combined to make salsa.

This is not a traditional Mayan salsa; however, the act of using kitchen alchemy to create it will open the gateway into a deeper understanding of your own mysteries. Mango Salsa is so tasty I often eat it with a spoon like soup. It's great with tortilla chips, but where it really shines is with fish or shrimp tacos.

MAKES ABOUT 4 CUPS

2 cups diced mango
(from 1 or 2 mangoes)

2 cups diced Roma tomatoes, seeds removed (from about 5 tomatoes)

1 cup diced white onion
(from ½ a large onion)

¾ cup finely diced cilantro
(from one bunch)

1 serrano pepper, ribs and seeds removed, and then minced (optional)

3 Tbsp. fresh lime juice
(from about 2 limes)

1 tsp. sea salt

Mangoes are tricky to cut because of the large pit in the middle. To cut the mango, stand it on end and slice off one side, avoiding the pit. Then slice off the other side, once again avoiding the pit. Use a large spoon to scoop out the fruit. Once the fruit is separated from the skin, cut it into long, thin slices and then cut the slices into bite-size pieces. Dice the tomato, onion, cilantro, and serrano pepper.

In a medium bowl, combine the mango, tomato, onion, cilantro, and pepper. Serrano peppers are spicy. Add the pepper bit by bit until you reach your desired spiciness. I like spice, so I usually add the whole pepper, which is about 1 tablespoon. Toss with the lime juice and salt, and enjoy!

THE MYSTIC COOKBOOK

The Soul of the Etruscans: Tuscan Vineyard Picnic

Tuscany and Umbria have captivated our imagination for decades. From the cathedral and chapels in Assisi and the bell towers of San Gimignano, to the horse races in Siena and the expanse of vineyards, sunflower fields, and warm Italian sun, this is a magical land. Tuscany and Umbria are a feast for the senses. Nature's bounty in this Mediterranean hill country is colorful, flavorful, and full of life-force energy. Salamis curing in store windows, laundry strung from ancient buildings, and homemade olive oil, wine, and cheese wherever you turn.

Tuscany was home to the Etruscans, a mysterious ancient people. Little is known about their origin or their demise. Not much Etruscan literature has been left behind, and their language, unlike any other, has taken years to decipher. What is known, scholars have gleaned from remaining dwellings, pottery, monuments, and other artifacts, but it's still unclear what people they came from and what happened to them. Some say they had mystical healing abilities; however, their existence is steeped in mystery. Delve into a legendary meal in a Tuscan vineyard, and you may very well tap into the soul of the mystical Etruscans and ignite your own innate healing abilities.

Planning Your Tuscan Vineyard Meal

When planning your vineyard feast in the land of the mysterious Etruscans, think about the many ways you can create a full body, sensory experience for yourself and your guests. What scents, sounds, textures, and sights most represent the Northern Italian hill country? You may want to spend some time tuning in and activating your inner Etruscan by doing an inner journey into this time and place.

You may want to think of ways to encourage your guests to be active participants in the creation of this memorable meal. Maybe you buy an assortment of Italian wine varietals and have a competition to see who can make the best tasting blend, or perhaps you provide your guests with herbs and flavored vinegars to flavor olives. Or you could take the idea a bit further and throw a pizza party. Pizza is originally from the southern town of Naples, but who cares! Everyone loves a pizza party. Start with the dough; give your guests the opportunity to knead it and feel its silky texture between their palms. But maybe you want to travel back to the age of the Etruscans. Dress in period clothing, serve common foods from that era, and take your guests on a guided meditation to the time when these ancient people inhabited modern-day Tuscany.

INSALATA DI FRUTTI DI MARE AL LIMONE

(Seafood Salad with Lemon)

When I was backpacking through Europe in my early 20s, one
Sunday afternoon my friend and I found a small trattoria in Tuscany situated
across from a beautiful park. We dined on a delectable assortment of seafood dishes.
One of my favorites was a salad made of shellfish marinated in lemon juice.
We even imagined the ancient Etruscans eating a similar meal.

SERVES 4

1 lb. fresh mixed seafood,
such as shrimp, scallops,
and calamari

1 shallot, minced

1 red bell pepper, diced

1 cucumber, peeled, seeded,
and diced

½ cup chopped Italian
flat-leafed parsley

2 Tbsp. capers

DRESSING:

1 tsp. sugar

½ tsp. sea salt

¼ tsp. fresh ground pepper

1 tsp. Dijon mustard

3 Tbsp. fresh-squeezed lemon
juice (from 2 medium-sized
lemons)

2 Tbsp. extra-virgin olive oil

Bring a medium pot of salted water to a boil.

While you're waiting for the water to boil, make the
dressing. In a large bowl, combine the sugar, salt,
pepper, and mustard. Mix in the lemon juice. Slowly
whisk in the olive oil until fully combined. Set aside.

Blanch the seafood in the boiling water until just
cooked, about 1–3 minutes, but this will depend on
the type and size of the seafood you use. Drain the
seafood and run under cool water or dunk in an ice
bath to preserve color and stop the cooking.

If the pieces of seafood are large, you may want to
chop them into smaller, bite-size pieces. Add the
seafood to the bowl with the dressing and toss
to combine. Cover and put in the refrigerator to
marinate while chopping the vegetables for the salad.

Mince the shallot. Dice the bell pepper. Peel and seed
the cucumber. The easiest way to remove the seeds
from a cucumber is to cut it in half lengthwise, and
then scrape out the seeds with a small spoon. Dice
the cucumber. Chop the parsley.

Remove the seafood from the refrigerator, toss with
the vegetables, and mix in the capers. Serve on a bed
of greens and eat with crostini (thinly sliced Italian
bread spread with olive oil and toasted).

ITALIAN WEDDING SOUP

The name of this soup is most likely a mistranslation of the Neapolitan soup, *minestra maritata* or "married soup," which means the ingredients are well married together. Although not something traditionally served at weddings in Italy, the name has stuck, and apparently over time, the soup has become a fixture at many Italian–American weddings.

As you slurp this soup, imagine you're eating outdoors at a long wooden table on a warm Tuscan evening and gazing at the stars. What secrets does the soil beneath your feet reveal to you?

SERVES 4 – 6

1 Tbsp. olive oil

1 cup diced onions

4 cloves garlic, minced

8 cups chicken broth

¾ cup dry white wine

1 14.5-oz. can diced tomatoes

1 bunch Tuscan kale (also called dinosaur kale, lacinato, and cavalo nero), stalks removed and leaves roughly chopped or torn (you can substitute curly-leaf kale)

1 15-oz. can cannellini beans, rinsed and drained

½ lb. mild Italian sausage (approx. 2 sausages), squeezed from the casing into small meatballs

salt and pepper to taste

In a large pot over medium heat, sauté the onions and garlic with the olive oil and a pinch of salt. When the onions are soft and translucent, about 5–10 minutes, pour in the broth and wine. Add the tomatoes. Turn up the heat and bring the soup to a boil, then reduce to a simmer.

Pull the kale from its central stalk with your thumb and forefinger (somewhat like husking corn or peeling a banana), tear it into bite-size pieces, and drop it right into the soup pot. It may seem like a lot of kale at first, but it cooks down.

Rinse and drain the beans; pour them into the pot. Add the sausage to the simmering soup by squeezing the meat out of the casing to make little meatballs.

When the sausage is cooked through, taste the soup and add salt and pepper as needed. To create layers of flavor, it's best if the salt is added bit by bit throughout the cooking process.

Although the soup can be eaten as soon as the sausage is cooked and the kale is soft, I prefer to simmer it for at least an hour and a half to allow the flavors time to marry. (It's a wedding soup after all!) Plus, I especially like the kale when it's really soft and tender. This soup is even better reheated the second day. Serve with freshly grated Parmesan cheese and red chili flakes, and eat with crusty Italian bread.

TUSCAN WHITE BEANS
WITH SAGE

For a romantic dinner for two, serve this with roast chicken and kale sautéed with sliced garlic, olive oil, and lemon juice. Eat by candlelight, drink a good bottle of Chianti, and whisper a few words of Italian to one another. Tuscan White Beans are also great for a crowd. Or if it's just you, treat yourself as though you're the most treasured and desired dinner companion around. Plus, these beans are so tasty that you might not actually want to share them. I ate half a pot by myself the other day!

This can be made with soaked and boiled cannellini beans (white kidney beans), but I like the ease of using canned beans for this particular dish.

SERVES 4

4 Tbsp. olive oil

4 cloves of garlic, minced

8 fresh sage leaves, thinly sliced (chiffonade)

pinch of sea salt

pinch of cracked black pepper

2 15-oz. cans (about 3½ cups) cannellini beans, drained and rinsed

Heat the olive oil, garlic, sage, salt, and pepper in a sauté pan over medium-low heat. Stirring frequently, cook until the oil is infused with the flavor of the garlic and sage, and the garlic is soft and slightly translucent (3–5 minutes). Add the beans. Increase the heat to medium. Cook until the beans are warm and creamy, stirring occasionally. If they become too dry, add a bit of water or more olive oil. Buon appetito!

Land of Mysteries: Lunch in Provence

One of the most captivating mysteries—that of Jesus and the Holy Grail, Mary Magdalene, the Da Vinci Code, the Knights Templar, the Cathars, the Free Masons, and the Priory of Sion—is thought to have its roots in the South of France. It's unlikely that we'll ever know the truth, but ideas, theories, and stories abound. What is the Holy Grail and where is it kept? Who was Mary Magdalene, and what was her role in the life of Jesus? Who is the keeper of these mysteries, and who knows the truth? Are there secrets about the life of Jesus ignored by the Bible, and what mysticism might these offshoots of the Christian Church reveal?

A Southern French meal could be the most legendary of all. What mysteries might this Time Traveler Meal uncover? Provence, the land of sunshine and lavender, captures the essence of the good life. Long and lazy afternoons are spent enjoying good food and conversation. Every meal in France is occasion to celebrate, and no one knows better than the people of Provence how to reap the most from each meal and savor each and every day.

Turning Your Vision into a Legendary Lunch in Provence

When planning your lunch in Provence, first think about the theme and mood you want to set. You might want to go on an inner journey to see what feelings are activated within you. As a suggestion, consider how you can re-create a meal that will elicit some of the same emotions and sensations. What inner mysteries do you want to activate? Do you want to tap into the ancient mysteries of the Cathars and Knights Templar, or do you want to ignite your ability to enjoy life bite by bite and savor each and every moment as it comes? This legendary lunch could include tomatoes, olive oil, goat cheese, and Mediterranean herbs, which are an essential part of any Provençal meal. Fish and seafood as well as poultry, beef, and wild boar are common. Wild mushrooms, truffles, and olives are also popular. Provence is colorful. When decorating, use bright colors. Sunflowers and lavender are emblematic of Provence. Ratatouille, bouillabaisse, and salade niçoise are among some of the most popular dishes of this region. Before eating this meal, take a moment to imagine that the ancient mysteries of the Grail are seeping into you and into your food. Imagine that with each bite, these sacred wonders are trickling deep into the wellspring of your soul.

CROSTINI WITH CHÈVRE AND OLIVE TAPENADE

The year I lived in Provence, I loved buying my fresh bread and goat cheese at the market around the corner from my apartment. Sometimes I just couldn't resist buying a jar of local olive tapenade as well. The combination of the three is heavenly.

These crostini are a party favorite.
No matter how many you make, there probably won't be enough.

MAKES ABOUT 3 DOZEN

1 baguette, cut into ¼-inch slices (cut at an angle to increase surface area)

¼ cup olive oil

1 8-oz. package of chèvre (soft goat cheese)

2 Tbsp. water

2–3 cloves of garlic, cut in half

1 small jar olive tapenade (you may not need the whole jar)

chives for garnish

Preheat oven to 350°F.

Using a sharp bread knife, slice the bread at an angle into ¼-inch thick slices.

To prepare the crostini, put the bread slices into a large bowl and drizzle the olive oil over them. Toss the bread with the olive oil until evenly coated. If you want to be more precise about this, you could "paint" the olive oil on each side of the bread with a pastry brush. I find, however, that although tossing the bread and oil in a bowl isn't refined or precise, it gets the job done, and fast.

Distribute the bread between two baking sheets and toast in the oven until golden brown, about 10–15 minutes. Halfway through, rotate the baking sheets from top to bottom, and using tongs, turn over each slice of bread. Remove from the oven and allow to cool slightly.

Meanwhile, in a small bowl, combine the chèvre with the water. This will make it more spreadable.

When the crostini are cool enough to handle, cut the garlic in half and rub the top of the crostini with the cut side of the garlic. One swipe is sufficient. You want a hint of garlic, but you don't want to overpower the other flavors with it.

Use a knife or spatula to spread the chèvre in a thin layer on each crostini. Put a small dollop of tapenade in the center of the crostini. Using kitchen shears, snip the chives into little pieces right over the tapenade. Not only does this add a burst of color, but also it brings all the flavors together and adds a bright note.

SALADE NIÇOISE PLATTER

For an elegant presentation, place each ingredient individually on a large platter
with the tuna at the center, and invite your guests to construct their own salad.
This is a great dish for a midsummer luncheon. Although I've made this salad with
different kinds of tuna, including seared fresh albacore, chunk light is my favorite
because it absorbs the dressing better than anything else. It may seem like a lot of
dressing at first, but it's so tasty you'll catch your guests sneaking extra spoonfuls.
It's the dressing that makes this dish so spectacular.

SERVES 6

½ lb. blanched haricots verts*

1½ lbs. red potatoes
(6–8 potatoes)

6 eggs, hardboiled, peeled,
and quartered

1 lb. small tomatoes (such as
pearl or campari), cut into
wedges

1½ cups good black olives
(such as pitted kalamata)

3 5-oz. cans of chunk light
tuna, drained

arugula or mâche (lamb's lettuce)

*Haricots verts are thin French green
beans. If not available, you can
substitute ordinary green beans.

TARRAGON VINAIGRETTE
MAKES 2 CUPS

1½ tsp. sea salt

1 tsp. coarsely ground pepper

2 tsp. sugar

1 tsp. Dijon mustard

4 cloves garlic, crushed

2 Tbsp. chopped fresh French
tarragon

½ cup white balsamic vinegar

1⅓ cup extra-virgin olive oil

Bring a large pot of water to a boil. (To save on water
and cleanup, I recommend using the same pot of water
for the haricots verts and the potatoes.) When the
water reaches a boil, toss in the haricots verts, and cook
until slightly pliable, about 3 minutes. Fish out with a
strainer or tongs, and immediately shock them in an
ice-water bath (this will keep them green and crisp).

Add the potatoes to the boiling water and cook until
cooked through, about 20 minutes, depending on the
size of the potatoes. Drain and run cold water over
the potatoes.

Meanwhile, hardboil the eggs in a small pan. Place
all six eggs in a medium saucepan and cover with
at least an inch of cool water. Boiling for 10–15
minutes is a good rule of thumb. Immediately
plunge the eggs into cool water to stop the cooking.

Wash and cut the tomatoes. Cut the potatoes. Peel
and cut the eggs. Drain the tuna. Drain the haricots
verts from the ice bath. Assemble the potatoes,
haricots verts, eggs, tomatoes, olives, and tuna on
a large platter. Serve with mâche or arugula and a
bowl of Tarragon Vinaigrette on the side.

TARRAGON VINAIGRETTE

In a medium bowl, combine the salt, pepper,
sugar, mustard, garlic, and tarragon. Mix in the
vinegar. Slowly whisk in the olive oil to make an
emulsion. Serve in a bowl alongside the Salade
Niçoise Platter. This dressing is so delicious, you
may want to make extra just to have on hand.

FRENCH COUNTRY
POTATO SALAD

I first developed this recipe as a way to use leftovers from the Salade Niçoise Platter, but it ended up being so tasty that now I often make it even when I don't have leftover Salade Niçoise. (It's so good that this could be the Holy Grail of potato salads!) The almonds and lemon zest are my favorite part. They're unexpected and add a great depth of flavor to the dish.

SERVES 6

2 lbs. boiled red potatoes, cut into quarters

½ lb. blanched haricots verts, trimmed and cut into 2-inch pieces (you can substitute green beans)

½ cup toasted almonds, roughly chopped

1 red bell pepper, cut into thin 2-inch strips

⅓ cup diced red onion

1 tsp. zest from one lemon (use a zester, not a Microplane)

VINAIGRETTE

2 tsp. whole-grain mustard

½ tsp. sea salt

2 cloves garlic, crushed

2 Tbsp. balsamic vinegar

⅓ cup extra-virgin olive oil

Preheat the oven to 350°F.

Bring a large pot of water to a boil. (To save on water and cleanup, I recommend using the same pot for the haricots verts and potatoes.) When the water reaches a boil, toss in the trimmed haricots verts and cook until slightly pliable, about 3 minutes. Fish out with a strainer or tongs, and immediately shock them in an ice-water bath (this will keep them green and crisp).

Add the potatoes to the boiling water and cook until cooked through, about 20 minutes, depending on their size. Drain and run cold water over the potatoes.

While the potatoes cook, place the almonds on a baking sheet and toast in the oven until fragrant, about 10 minutes. Remove the almonds from the oven, and when cool enough to touch, chop them. The nuts will get crunchier as they cool.

Meanwhile, slice the bell pepper, dice the onion, and zest the lemon. When the potatoes are cooked and cooled, chop them into bite-sized pieces. Drain the haricots verts from the ice bath and cut into 2-inch pieces.

In a large bowl, combine everything together and toss with the vinaigrette.

VINAIGRETTE

In a small bowl, mix the mustard, salt, and garlic together. Add the vinegar and combine. Slowly whisk in the olive oil to make an emulsion.

In addition to these suggestions, you may also want to consider other Time Traveler Meals, such as a Medieval Feast, Chinese Temple, Native American Harvest, African Safari, High Tea on the Thames, India under the Stars, Mexican Aztec Fiesta, or even travel to an Alien Planet. The sky's the limit. Where do you want to go? What inner mysteries do you want to tap into?

SENSUOUS MEALS:
Ignite the Senses

Eating with the senses is soulful and spiritual. The aroma of chocolate-chip cookies in the oven on a cold and blustery day, the vibrant crimson juice of a ripe cherry, the crunch of a crisp apple plucked from the tree on a misty autumn morning, or the smooth and elastic feeling of yeasty bread dough against your palms as you knead it. These are food experiences that go far beyond simply putting something into your mouth to fulfill a base need for nourishment.

The most pleasurable meals are often ones in which the senses are tantalized by an array of colors, sounds, textures, smells, and feelings. If you think back to some of your most powerful food memories, it's likely that these experiences have stayed with you over the years because your senses were treated to intoxicating music and conversation, unforgettable flavors and textures, or unparalleled beauty both on the plate and around you.

As a Mystic Chef, you can ignite all the senses during a meal to make it a powerful and spiritual experience. When you're fully engaged with your senses, you're in the present moment; nothing else exists but the here-and-now, which can lead to spiritual transcendence.

In the film version of *Eat, Pray, Love*, Julia Roberts as Elizabeth Gilbert sits alone at a café in an Italian piazza and devours a bowl of spaghetti with basil. Who doesn't want to lick the screen when she takes her first bite? What makes the pasta so tantalizing isn't just what's in the bowl—the pasta is, in fact, rather simple—but instead it's all that goes into creating the moment. The opera music in the background, the lovers kissing nearby, and the way she slurps and chews the spaghetti with absolute abandon.

In preparation for your Legendary Meal of Sensuous Delight, you may want to spend some time activating each of your senses. Your food will taste ten times better if you do this. The following exercises are intended to help get you started. When your senses are awakened, you'll be ready to embark on preparing a meal that will be an all-encompassing odyssey to titillate taste, smell, sight, hearing, and touch . . . and open your heart to the secret messages within your food.

Taste: Eating with the Mouth

This perhaps sounds self-evident, but taste is one of our most powerful senses when it comes to food. In one bite, we know whether or not something is fresh or old, salty or sweet, bitter or sour, hot or cold, spicy or cooling. But dig a little deeper, and your taste buds may discover that underneath the ordinary is something extraordinary—a realm filled with complexity, depth, and gradations of flavor.

Unfortunately, we don't always taste our food. It's gulped down to feed hunger or eaten mindlessly to fill time. We don't often really concentrate on what we're eating and exact the subtle nuances. Every food is made up of a myriad of flavors that layer on top of one another to create a complete experience.

Do you know what your food really tastes like? What's the predominant flavor? What are the secondary and tertiary tastes that appear on your tongue? We take it for granted that we know the flavors of certain foods, but if you had to explain the overtones to someone who had never had a cucumber, plum, or papaya, for example, how would you describe them? Based on your description, would they be able to identify the fruit or vegetable?

Exercise

Take five minutes and describe a food to a friend. It's probably best if you start with a fruit, vegetable, meat, or grain rather than a complete dish. Don't reveal what food you're describing, and see if your friend can guess. Assume he or she has never tasted anything like it before. Remember this is an exercise based on taste. Color, shape, size, texture, and other physical and auditory traits don't count. What words would you use? What flavors most represent this food? Salty, sweet, sour, bitter, or perhaps it's what the Japanese call *umami* or savoriness? Is your friend able to guess the food you described? Now switch and have your friend tell you about a particular food. Can you guess what it is?

Exercise

Place a raisin on your tongue and suck on it for as long as you feel comfortable. Really concentrate on the flavor. What does it taste like? How is a raisin different from other dried fruit? Does it taste like a grape? How does the flavor change over time? Be still and be present with the experience. You may even want to take notes. Try this with a few different foods. Is your experience different from what you thought it would be?

Smell: Eating with Your Nose

Warm peaches, ripe melon, baking bread, sizzling meat on an open fire . . . just these words alone can ignite our olfactory system and moisten our salivary glands. Inhaling deeply and imagining the perfume of warm peaches in late summer can feel so real that it's as though there really is a basket of peaches nestled in your arms. Our scent memory is that strong.

Have you ever noticed your stomach growling even when you know you're not hungry? There are probably delicious food smells in the air that are stimulating your appetite. Garlic and onions sautéing at a nearby restaurant, your neighbor's barbecue, or coffee brewing in the early morning hours are all scents that can throw us into a fit of desire.

Taste and smell are intertwined. One cannot taste properly if one cannot smell properly. Much of what we think of as taste is actually related more closely to smell. Remarkably, researchers say that 90 to 95 percent of what we perceive as taste is actually aroma (what we smell while chewing). Imagine eating a passion fruit—known for its intoxicating perfume—if you couldn't smell it!

Exercise

Blindfold yourself and have a friend give you a morsel to eat while holding the scent of something else under your nose. Can you guess what you're eating? Perhaps he gives you a raw potato while holding a sliced apple under your nose. Try this with a few different foods. What do you notice? What is the experience of eating with your nose?

Exercise

The next time you make dinner, take a few minutes to inhale the different cooking smells. Breathe deeply and smell each ingredient as it cooks. How do the scents change? Which ingredients are the most potent? What are the undertones? Then before eating the meal, hold the plate to your nose and take in the aroma of the entire dish. Can you pick out individual herbs, spices, or other ingredients? How does the whole differ from its components?

Sight: Eating with the Eyes

Much of the way we experience food comes from how it looks visually. Color, texture, shape, and size all play pivotal roles in our appreciation of the foods we consume (or choose not to). Presentation also greatly affects how we perceive a meal. Oysters on the half-shell can be an elegant delicacy, yet imagine eating the same oysters out of a Styrofoam bowl. The flavor is technically the same, but it's likely that they wouldn't taste exactly the same. There was a study done in the University of Illinois student cafeteria where the same brownies were offered for sale on napkins and on plates. The brownies were identical; yet more students opted for the ones on plates—even though the price was much higher—because the plates made them look like better brownies.

Exercise

Have you ever really looked at your food? Cut a strawberry in half lengthwise, and spend a few minutes examining all aspects of it. Notice the color. Is it bright red or pink? Does the red fade into white? Where? Notice how the seeds make dimples on the outside. What is the shape of the berry? Is it large and robust or small and delicate? Is there a hull? What texture is it? The next time you eat a strawberry, you may find that your appreciation is that much greater. Try this with other foods. What do you discover that you hadn't noticed before?

Exercise

Practice using different colors, textures, and shapes when you cook. Spend an afternoon pretending you're an artist. How would you arrange the food on the plate if it were your canvas and the food your paint? Think about the balance of color. Would you put similar hues together, or would you fan them out like a rainbow? How would you layer assorted textures? Would you use different shapes, or would you make everything the same size and shape?

Hearing: Eating with Your Ears

It's unlikely that sound is the first thing that pops into your head when you think about food. Sound, however, plays an integral role in the sensual experience of eating. Research done in the United Kingdom showed that the loud engine noise on an airplane actually diminishes our sense of taste and makes it harder to taste salty and sweet flavors; yet, it enhances our awareness of crunchiness. Advertisers have long understood the power sound has over our eating habits. Have you ever noticed how much attention is placed in television commercials on the noise foods make? Kellogg's Rice Krispies are touted as having "snap, crackle, and pop," and spokespeople for Vlasic Pickles gush, "That's the tastiest crunch I ever heard."

Have you ever been lying in bed in that sleep state just before waking and heard the sound of someone frying bacon in the kitchen? Without even opening your eyes, you know what it is. And chances are you'd know the sound of popcorn popping even if you couldn't see or smell it. What would it be like to eat a potato chip if there were no crunch? Or what if noodles and soup didn't slurp?

Music and conversation also greatly affect our dining experience. Have you ever gotten so involved in a conversation or a program on television that you were surprised to discover you'd finished your meal unknowingly? On the flip side, some conversations can actually enhance the food and the experience. Sometimes engrossing mealtime banter can make us slow down and appreciate what we're eating.

Music can be an integral part of our sensory experience of food. Imagine sitting in a bright and colorful courtyard in Mexico. While you sip frosty beer and savor a bite of enchilada, you hear mariachi music in the background. How would this experience be different if the music were heavy metal or Edith Piaf singing wartime French songs? How would a meal of Italian thin-crust pizza be different if you were listening to the mariachi music instead of Verdi?

Exercise

* **Silence:** Dine in silence. No music. No conversation. Listen to your food. What sounds does each ingredient or dish make? Now put in earplugs and continue the meal. What is the experience of eating without any sound at all? Are the flavors of your meal enhanced, or does the lack of sound detract from them?

* **Music:** Play music while you eat. Play jazz, samba, rock, classical, opera, and whatever else strikes your fancy. Pay close attention to how each style of music affects you and your experience of the food.

* **Conversation:** Watch television while you eat. Have a heated debate while dining. Discuss the food you're eating with a group of friends. Describe the flavors, the textures, the colors, and the sounds. In what ways do these different sounds affect the dining experience?

Touch: Eating with Your Tactile Senses

When picky eaters are asked why they don't like a particular food, often it's because of the texture. Yet the way food feels on the tongue is also the very thing that makes it so delicious and so much fun. Would we eat as much Jell-O if it weren't for the texture? What would yogurt be like if it were chewy? Or how would pudding taste if it were crispy?

Much of the pleasure that's derived from food is due to the way it feels on your fork, in your hands, and on your tongue. Soft and creamy foods often remind us of being fed as babies. These foods feel warm and nurturing, whereas crispy and crunchy foods are satisfying and can take us back to those times in our ancient history when we gnawed and chomped on our food.

In many world cultures, food is primarily eaten with the hands. In some parts of India, people believe food can actually be tasted through the fingers. Many cultures throughout the world—including India, Ethiopia, Morocco, and Mexico, among others—have a long tradition of rolling stewed meats, vegetables, and sauces in flatbreads and eating these foods with one's fingers. Some say this brings them closer to their food because the sensory experience of eating is heightened as the food is felt both by the fingers and the tongue. Imagine eating a hamburger, corn on the cob, fried chicken, or ribs with a knife and fork. Not only is it easier to pick up these foods, but also it adds to the entire sensory experience. Barbecued ribs just wouldn't be the same if the sauce didn't stick to your face and work its way under your fingernails.

Exercise

Eat an entire meal with your fingers (make sure they're clean). What's the texture of the food? How does it feel between your fingers? How does the experience of dining change when you ditch your fork and knife?

Exercise

Feed someone. What does it feel like to feed food to someone else? Then have that person feed you. How does the food taste in your mouth when you don't put it there yourself? Are you surprised by the texture and shape?

Now that you've activated your senses and heightened your awareness of your food, it's time to start planning your Legendary Meal of Sensuous Delight. In what ways do you want to ignite your senses? Do you want to devote each of five courses to a different sense, or do you want to integrate all of the senses into every dish? The planning of a sensual meal can be just as fun as taking part in one. Alternatively, you may even want to include the sixth sense, and if you're having a dinner party, involve your guests in testing their powers of intuition. For example, put different colors, symbols or photos under their plates and have them use their sixth sense to guess what is there.

A meal of Sensuous Delight might be a meal in which you engage all of the senses in the foods you serve, or you could plan a lavish dinner party and incorporate a number of activities to connect more deeply with your many senses. The possibilities are endless!

BLIND MEALS:
Deepen Perception

To further your journey as a Mystic Chef and heighten your senses, imagine you're enveloped in darkness. You're seated at a long dining table, and you feel the softness of the cushion on the seat of your chair, the smooth textures of the wooden table beneath your elbows, and the weight of the crisp linen napkin in your lap. You hear the clinking of glasses, the sound of forks and knifes tapping porcelain plates, and the witty banter of your dining companions. The intoxicating aroma of meats, vegetables, and fresh baked bread waft around you and arouse your sense of smell.

You pick up your spoon and gingerly dip it into what you presume to be a bowl of soup. You bring it to your lips and ever so carefully slurp its contents. In this absolute darkness, unable to see what you've just tasted, your tongue is overwhelmed with sweet, salty, sour, creamy, rich, spicy tastes. Each flavor sensation is unique, yet they seem to blend harmoniously into one delicious and cohesive soup. You've never before experienced soup in this way.

Dining in the Dark

Wanting to introduce people to the experience of eating with senses other than sight, Reverend Jorge Spielmann, a blind clergyman from Zurich, Switzerland, and three others opened the world's first blind restaurant in 1999.

They called it Blindekuh (which means "Blind Cow," the Swiss name for the children's game Blind Man's Bluff.)

Blindekuh provided much-needed jobs for blind and sight-impaired servers, but also it quickly became popular with diners who relished the experience of dining in complete darkness and allowing their senses to taste food in new ways. Since then, "dining in the dark" restaurants have sprouted up in Europe, Asia, and the United States. Most of these restaurants are completely dark, and the servers are either blind or fitted with night vision goggles, but there are some in which diners are given blindfolds.

A few people say food doesn't taste as flavorful when they don't have visual cues to tell them what to expect; however, many others contend that when vision is removed from the dining experience, their sense of taste and smell are much more acute. By dining in the dark, not only are you tapping into your inner resources and giving rise to your other senses, but also you're sharing in the experience of the sight-impaired, which will expand your understanding and solidarity with people of different abilities. Additionally, it activates your sixth sense and your psychic perception to be able to tune in to the meal without use of your sight.

How to Create a "Blind Meal"

Dining-in-the-dark restaurants can be found in many major cities, but it's also possible to create a similar experience at home.

The most ideal location for a blind meal at home is in a completely darkened room. If you have such a place in your home—without any windows—that would be the easiest, but with a bit of ingenuity, you can block off light filtering through windows, doorways, and from electronics. You may also want to plan your dinner during the new moon, when there will be the least amount of moonlight illuminating your dinner plate. Alternatively, you can ask your dinner guests to wear blindfolds. This also has the added benefit of making it light enough in the room that you'll be able to see while serving your dining companions.

You may want to serve a combination of simple foods, such as sliced fruits and vegetables, as well as more complicated dishes that have multiple layers of flavor. It's interesting to see how the experience changes based on the kinds of dishes you serve. Will you tell everyone the menu in advance or keep it a secret? Both ways can have powerful results. As a suggestion, choose whatever foods you think would be flavorful and fun. Some people recommend shying away from messy foods like spaghetti or hard to cut foods like meat; however, part of the experience of eating a blind meal is learning how to eat when you're unable to see. You might also want to consider foods that you can pick up in order to have the tactile experience of eating with your fingers.

When planning your blind meal, you'll want to come up with a strategy for seating and serving your guests. Some other things you'll want to consider when creating your blind meal: Although most of us are pretty good at feeding ourselves—even in the absence of light—there's a chance things could get messy, so be sure to choose a location that can handle some spills and splatters. Also, it's a good idea to remove any potential obstacles or hazards to prevent anyone from needlessly bumping into something, breaking a precious heirloom, or getting hurt.

It can be enjoyable to host a blind meal for friends, but it's also possible to have a blind dinner for just yourself. Prepare yourself a nice dinner, and find a dark and quiet place to sit and enjoy your meal. The added quiet will no doubt heighten your senses that much further. Your senses will be so alert that you may find flavors explode in your mouth, and textures are different from how you usually perceive them visually.

How to Eat a Blind Meal

Although you may worry that using a knife and fork in the dark will be tricky, the truth is most of us have been eating for many years and don't need to be able to see to find our mouth. You may be surprised to discover how adept our muscle memory is. Of course, you may not want to serve something like steak that would require a sharp knife, just in case someone's fingers slip in the dark.

In the restaurants where diners eat in the dark, the servers generally give suggestions on how to eat certain dishes, such as, "This you'll want to eat with a spoon." Alternatively, depending on how tactile you want to make the experience, you could suggest to your guests that they poke and touch their food to decide how best to consume it. It's probably a good idea to have a lot of napkins on hand.

A blind meal can be fun. You may find that you and your dining companions laugh a lot. Chances are there will be a few mishaps, jokes, and awkward moments. To get the most out of the experience, however, you'll also want to eat mindfully and spend time reflecting on what you're doing. Be fully present with what and how you're eating. How do you find the food on your plate when you can't see it? How does the fork feel on your tongue in the dark? If you use your hands, how does the food feel between your fingers, and how does this translate into taste? Do familiar foods taste different when you can't see them? Do they smell different? Are you able to parse out individual flavors, including herbs and spices? What do you gain by not seeing your food? What is lost? Are some senses more heightened than others?

As a suggestion, spend time with your dinner companions discussing what you taste, smell, and feel. If the menu has been kept a secret, perhaps you'll want to try to guess what you're eating. You may also want to talk about the most practical ways you've found to get the food from your plate to your mouth. As another suggestion, consider spending the first five minutes of the meal eating in silence in order to become fully absorbed in the moment as well as intensify the taste of your food.

A blind meal offers an opportunity to experience a myriad of sensations, tastes, and even emotions. It's an opportunity to gain a better understanding of what it's like to navigate the world without sight, but also have a heightened sense of taste. It can even be a spiritual awakening. You may find food tastes completely different when you can't see it. You may taste things you've never tasted before and revel in the subtle flavors and the gentle nuances of everyday food that you'd never noticed before. Your perception of food and dining may forever be changed as a result of this experience.

ZEN MEALS:
Practice Mindfulness

In my very early 20s I spent over two years living in a Zen Buddhist zendo (monastery). It was one of the most peaceful times of my life. Sometimes we meditated up to 16 hours a day. (In Zen this is called "sitting" rather than meditation.) We learned to still our minds and be present in each moment. I wasn't a particularly stellar Zen student . . . my mind wandered, and I got bored and tired. However, in Zen it's believed that enlightenment can occur in a moment, and that moment most often happens when you're being mindful and present . . . and what better way to practice being mindful and present than by cooking and eating. In this way, a meal can indeed be an enlightening experience.

 Denise

Zen meditation is a way of obtaining deep inner peace or nirvana. Since the primary focus of Zen meditation is being still and clearing your mind, meals tend to be quite simple. In traditional Zen monasteries, breakfast may consist of rice gruel and a salt pickle. Lunch might be the same, and dinner might be rice, miso soup, and a cooked vegetable. Meals are often eaten silently to allow for focus and deep appreciation. Food is treated ceremoniously and considered to be a gift. During *sesshen* (extended time of meditation), monks continue to sit in a meditative pose, and meals are brought to them. The server bows to each monk, and each monk in turn bows back. With careful movements and grace, each individual is served. Chants (Zen meal sutras) are said, and the eating of the meal is done in a very stylized and ceremonial way, with everyone ending at the exact same time.

This is an English translation of a part of the meal sutra. It is a reminder to the monk that each bite is dedicated to a higher purpose:

The first taste is to cut off all evil,

The second is to practice all good,

The third is to save all beings;

May we all attain the Way of the Buddha.

In Zen tradition, often a tiny bit of food, even a few grains of rice, is left in the bowl to symbolize feeding the "hungry ghost." The hungry ghost in some Chinese traditions means the spirit of those that have passed on but are still attached to the earth plane; however, in Zen, "ghosts" means not being aware, sleeping through life, and not appreciating the fullness of the moment. So feeding the hungry ghosts means dedicating one's Zen practice to the betterment of others.

The term "Zen meal" has been expanded in Western culture to mean any kind of simple meal, but a true Zen meal, in addition to being simple and elegant, should include an element of reflection and mindfulness.

A Zen meal is one in which not only the meal is simple and prepared in a mindful way, but also every aspect of the preparation, from shopping and cooking to setting the table and eating, is done slowly, methodically, and with consciousness. In our modern world, it can be difficult to slow down and eat in a precise and mindful way, being aware of each bite. And it can also seem strange to eat in community yet in silence. But this might be all the more reason to try. Sometimes what you want and need to do after a long day of work is put your feet up, watch television, and eat a delivery pizza and totally zone out. But when you can, consider eating a meal in the Zen way. There's great value in taking time to savor every moment of your meal.

To create a Zen meal, you might want to consider playing soft, slow Zen shakuhachi flute music to help you slow way down.

Preparation for Your Zen-sational Meal

* **Cherish:** Take time to honor every ingredient. Think about where it came from and all the people that were responsible for the long trip to your kitchen.

* **Do Not Compare:** In a Zen kitchen, you do not compare or judge one apple as better than another. Every piece of food is unique unto itself, and every item of food is to be cherished without comparison.

* **Be Present:** Every movement within a Zen kitchen is done with consciousness. In the *zendo,* most monks desire to chop vegetables because they hear stories about people who become enlightened while chopping. The Zen master explains that when you're one with the vegetable and one with the knife, a gateway could open to enlightenment.

* **Be Sincere:** When preparing the food, use your humility, your sincerity, and your dedication without losing your attention or concentration. Be conscious of what every moment calls for, and go in that direction.

* **Appreciate:** Take a moment to appreciate the colors, aromas, and most of all, the time and energy that the chef took preparing the meal.

* **Be Conscious of Others:** If you're eating with others, take a moment to be aware of each person, even if you're eating in silence. Beneath conversation, there's a deeper and more profound connection—soul to soul. Find and feel that connection.

* **Bow:** Bow in honor of the others who are there and in honor of those who are not. Bow with the intent that the entire meal is dedicated to the welfare of others (all sentient beings), no matter where they are.

* **Focus:** Eat slowly with attention on each bite. Become aware of the richness of flavor and texture, the way the food feels as it enters into your body, and the way your body is responding.

* **Completion:** At the completion of the meal, bow in honor of the meal and in honor of everyone who enjoyed it with you. You might even want to take time to have folks share their perceptions and what thoughts, memories, and emotions emerged for them during the meal.

NATIVE AMERICAN MEALS:
Honor Spirit

To the ancient Native American, all life was sacred. A gathering to share a meal was considered a way to honor Spirit. This Legendary Meal honors this hallowed tradition and allows the qualities of nobility, grace, and wisdom to expand within you. Giving thanks for the gift of life was essential to the Native American philosophy. Even among the gatherers and farmers, the Native American diet was meat-heavy. They ate buffalo, elk, deer, rabbit, salmon, goose, duck, turkey, and shellfish. However, anytime a life was taken for food, it was done with profound gratitude for the animal that gifted its life so that the two-leggeds (humans) could live. A hunter would go into the forest and pray to the Creator for a good hunt, and then he'd pray to the Spirit of the Elk with a depth of gratitude for his "giveaway." (They also believed that the emotions of the animal, at the time of its death, affected the meat. An animal that was feeling fear put fear into the meat. An animal that was feeling strong put strength into the meat. So the Native Americans strived to take a life in a compassionate way, so the meat would be filled with vitality.)

In native cultures, the giveaway was a very precious gift. It meant giving gifts for the benefit of others. There's great honor in giving your best food, your best blanket, and the best of yourself to another. In this spirit, it's believed that when an animal is killed, it's given its life as a giveaway for the good of the people. Because of this, immediately after an animal dies, the hunter takes time to give thanks, say a prayer, and in many cases, do a ceremony of thankfulness.

Even when plants were taken for food, an honoring of the plant occurred. Native people believed that just as there was great power in honoring the gift of the animal, the plant, too, gives its life so that others may live. So even if you're a vegetarian or vegan, as a suggestion, in the Native American tradition, give thanks for the life of the plants you consume. Additionally, one of the guiding tenets of Native Americans and their food was that they never wasted anything. Try to find ways to use every part of the meat and vegetables in your Legendary Meal. If you have bones left, consider putting them into a soup. If you have the tops of celery or stalks of kale left, you might use them in a vegetable broth.

Creating a Native American Legendary Meal

A Native American Legendary Meal can be as simple as spending time before your meal honoring the spirit within each of the foods you consume, or it can be an elaborate affair in which you feast on traditional Native American foods and even practice the ancient art of the giveaway. Consider spending the day leading up to your meal donating your time at a local charity, helping a friend move, or spending quality time with your children. Another form of giveaway is putting your heart and soul into creating a meal filled with love. As a result of your giveaway, hearts will open and magic will unfold.

This would be a good meal to eat in the wilderness under the vast canopy of the heavens. But perhaps you prefer staying inside. Consider sitting around the fireplace (like the campfires of yore) or at a dining table decorated with natural items, drums, clay pots, or Native American blankets. Burn some white sage or cedar, and invite Great Spirit to your table. Invoke the deep mystery within all things, and a powerful, reverent energy will grace your meal.

Additionally, you might consider the Native American practice of eating simply. Meats were roasted on an open fire, and fish was baked or smoked. Maize (corn) was eaten in many ways, including on the cob, popped into popcorn, and as a rustic bread cooked in clay ovens. And berries of all kinds were always cherished. We're now blessed with a surfeit of spices and sauces, but sometimes condiments can dilute the actual taste of the primary ingredient, and we lose its subtle vibrational energy. It can be a valuable exercise to take time to ingest the subtle flavors and sense the deeper energy in the food, as our Native Americans forefathers did. When you first do this, the food most likely will taste very bland and even unappealing, but after a while, it's like walking outdoors in the dark . . . at first you can't see anything, but then a magical, shadowy universe opens for you.

Native American Prayer

May the Creator within all things bring blessings and peace.
You have gifted your spirit and provided for our hunger,
and we give thanks. May your gift help us to better help others.
With thanks to the Great Spirit who made this meal possible,
for the Mother Earth who provided the bounty, and for our ancestors
for showing us the way of living in right relation with all life.

NATURE MEALS:
Connect to Mother Earth

There's a spiritual reason why food tastes better outdoors . . . the vibrational, rhythmic energy of the earth radiates up through your body and into your food. No matter what kind of scrambled or chaotic energy your food may have because of things such as overprocessing or long-term refrigeration, when you stand or sit on the earth, you become a conductor of its vibrant life force. Mother Earth's energy flows through you and into your food, which then almost mystically aligns the vibration of the food with your body's vibrational needs. Eating outdoors can have a deeply harmonizing effect on your body, mind, and soul.

Additionally, there's something about the air and the scenery that enhances the dining experience and the flavor of your food. Your body relaxes as you breathe deeply and absorb negative ions, and you'll also start to feel a deeper connection to Mother Earth. When you finish your outdoor meal—be it a sandwich or a lavish banquet—offer a quiet thanks to Mother Earth. It's important to recognize all that she provides for us.

Sacred Feasts: Calling Heaven and Earth to Your Gathering

Although we tend to think of eating outdoors as something casual like an afternoon picnic or a backyard barbecue, it can also be a sacred feast. Temples, synagogues, churches, mosques, and cathedrals were built to welcome Spirit; however, for many people, being in nature can feel as holy as a house of worship. A gentle breeze on your cheek, the warmth of a sunbeam, or the feeling of soft moss beneath your feet can invite Spirit in magical ways that can only be felt when you allow yourself to be in tune with the elements and in harmony with nature's bounty.

Eating in nature is deeply rooted in our cultural psyche. Although the reasons for eating outside vary from place to place and from person to person, dining on Mother Earth's table connects us to our ancient ancestors who built community while eating together in nature. It can also be a way to connect to the energy of the land.

When planning the menu for this feast, you may want to consider choosing foods that invoke the complementary energies of Mother Earth and Father Sky. As a suggestion, prepare a meal that represents both the energies of heaven and earth. What foods seem "heavenly" to you? What foods seem to have the power of the earth in them? Or if you want to think of it differently, look for dishes that are a balance of the energy of Yin and Yang (harmonizing masculine and feminine energies). Perhaps some aspects of your divine Sacred Feast are light and airy and others are dark and dense, or perhaps some are soft and smooth whereas others are crisp and crunchy. The balance of colors, textures, patterns, flavors, and tastes will help to bring the balance of these sacred energies in harmony at your table and in your life.

A Prayer for Mother Nature and Father Sky

To set the tone for your sacred picnic at Mother Nature's Table, you may want to begin with a prayer to invite magic and mystery to join you in this hallowed space and call forth the powerful energies of land and sky. Place your feet on the earth, preferably barefoot, and ask that the energy of the earth flow from its greatest depths, up through your feet, and into your food. With your eyes closed, throw your hands up toward the sky. Invite the powers of the heavens to your meal, and ask that this powerful energy cascade through you and into the meal.

CHICKEN CURRY SALAD

This is a great dish for a sacred picnic.
It's delicious in a sandwich or on a bed of greens.
Typically, I use leftover roasted chicken, but you can also use
poached chicken or purchase a pre-roasted chicken.
I love walnuts, but raw cashews, pecans, or sliced almonds can also be used.
Additionally, strained Greek yogurt can be substituted for the mayonnaise.

SERVES 4 - 6

1 cup sliced celery

½ cup diced red onion

1 cup chopped raw walnuts

⅓ cup golden raisins

2½ cups diced cooked chicken

4 tsp. curry powder

½ tsp. sea salt (or to taste)

¾ cup mayonnaise

Slice the celery, dice the red onion, and chop the walnuts. Combine the celery, onion, and walnuts with the raisins in a large bowl. Chop the chicken and add to the bowl. Toss everything with the curry powder and salt, and then mix with the mayonnaise. Allow the chicken salad to sit in the refrigerator for about 15 minutes to give the flavors time to mellow and marry with one another. Enjoy with a green salad or on a French baguette.

FRENCH LENTIL SALAD

For some reason, a number of years ago, I got it in my head that I really wanted to take French lentil salad to a sacred picnic, even though it was something I'd never eaten or made before. I spent an evening teaching myself how to make it, and the results were so delicious I've been making it the same way ever since. What I especially enjoy is that eating it makes you feel like you're picnicking in the French countryside and the combination of lentils and vegetables feels simultaneously earthy and heavenly.

SERVES 6

1 cup French lentils

1 cup diced carrots
(about 4)

1 cup diced celery
(about 4 stalks)

½ cup diced red onion

½ cup chopped Italian parsley

VINAIGRETTE

3 Tbsp. red wine vinegar

¾ tsp. sea salt

½ tsp. Dijon mustard

1 clove garlic, crushed

⅓ cup extra-virgin olive oil

Bring about 6 cups of salted water to a boil in a large pot. Wash and pick through the lentils. Add the lentils to the boiling water. Cook at a gentle boil until the lentils are cooked through but not mushy, about 15–20 minutes.

While the lentils cook, peel and chop the carrots, and chop the celery, onion, and parsley. The easiest way to get uniform pieces of carrot is to take a peeled carrot and cut it in half lengthwise. Place the cut side down and then slice the carrot into long, thin slices. Gather these slices together and chop them from right to left—this would be reversed for a lefty—in a gentle, rocking motion. Cut the celery into long, thin strips and then dice them like the carrots. Combine the carrot and celery in a large bowl. Dice the onion and parsley and add to the bowl.

When the lentils are cooked, drain and rinse with cold water. Combine the cooked lentils with the carrots, celery, onion, and parsley. Toss with the vinaigrette and enjoy.

VINAIGRETTE

In a small bowl, mix the vinegar, salt, mustard, and garlic. Whisk in the olive oil.

Eating by the Light of the Moon

Since the beginning of time, we've been beguiled by the moon. Legends of men transforming into werewolves, anecdotes of unusual psychic activity, and stories of strange cases arriving in hospital emergency rooms when the moon is the brightest abound. The moon's gravitational pull has a powerful effect on the waters of the ocean and as a result, is responsible for the ebbing and flowing of tides. Her pull is so strong that not only large bodies of water are affected, but also the water in all living things is influenced—including the water in our bodies and the foods we eat.

Moonbeams can even cleanse people and objects of lackluster energy, while at the same time infusing them with powerful life force. As a suggestion, before you begin to eat, hold your plate or bowl up to the moon to infuse your food with the shimmering moonlight magic. Food that's eaten under the light of the moon absorbs the lunar inner mysteries contained in the silvery light, which you'll absorb as you eat. This will have a positive effect on your dreams and will also support you in becoming more receptive to the gifts from the Universe.

Additionally, you can use the cycles of the moon to create culinary moon magic. If you want to begin a new project or start a new cycle in your life, consider making a meal that contains foods that symbolize new beginnings, such as eggs, sprouts, or baby greens. Dedicate this meal to your new life, and then eat it during the new moon, just as it's beginning to wax. If, however, you want to bring forth expansion and abundance into your life, consider eating a plentiful meal of foods at their peak, such as ripe fruit, bulbous artichoke, rotund squash, or large zucchini. Focus on what you want to expand in your life, and then eat this meal during the full moon. (See Denise's book *Secrets and Mysteries* for more information about how to use the cycles of the moon for spiritual purposes.)

You might also consider embarking on the mystical practice of "Eating the Moon." To do this, have your meal outdoors and position your food so that moonlight touches it. Then raise your head to the heavens, open your mouth, and imagine that you're actually swallowing the moon. And in doing so, you're ingesting the celestial energy of the moon into your life, which will deepen even further when you eat your moon-blessed meal. This ceremony can do this same practice by "Eating the Stars" or the clouds, wind, sun, or sea. Each of these aspects of nature has incredible vitality and can each infuse your meal with the qualities they possess.

MYTHIC MEALS:
Expand Your Vistas

Have you ever wondered what it would be like to have lunch with Zeus, tea with Merlin, or perhaps even toasted marshmallows from the fiery breath of a dragon? Create a mythic meal, and the veil between these realities will thin, and you'll step into a mythic dimension where dragons, wizards, gods, and goddesses roam. Who knows what inner vistas you'll activate! By connecting more deeply with this mythic world, you'll be expanding your spiritual awareness of the magic that's around and within you, even though you can't always see it.

Just as Harry Potter's Wizarding World at Universal Studios can make you feel as though you're actually strolling the streets of Hogsmeade, roaming the hallways of Hogwarts, and talking face-to-face with wizards and dragons, you can create a mythic meal at home that can be equally transformative and perhaps even more powerful, because as a Mystic Chef, you know how to activate inner experience as well as outer experience. Allow your imagination free rein to create a mythic meal of *epic proportion*. Here are some ideas to start with, but indeed the sky's the limit with this kind of meal.

Dragons and Wizards for Dinner

Dragons and wizards dwell in hidden dimensions, waiting for an invitation to the table. To invite a dragon or a wise old wizard for dinner, all you have to do is ask. Put out the call and create a space for them at your table, and they will come. If children are going to help you welcome these special guests, you might want to ask them what they think would be the most inviting foods and decor for a wizard or dragon. For instance, at a friend's Dragon Meal, a child said, "Dragons like moss!" so all the children went outdoors to gather up all the moss they could find to decorate the table. Another child said, "Dragons like gold!" so a gold tablecloth was carefully arranged on the table by little hands.

What foods feel the most magical and mythical to you? Perhaps a medieval banquet with large roasts and mead, or consider serving "fire-roasted" foods, as if the dragon helped cook the meal with his flames. For a wizarding meal, every component might have some inner magic. For example, the dessert might have been dusted with "make your life sweeter" powdered sugar or the pepper you sprinkle on your mashed potatoes is "add spice to your life" dust. And a spear of broccoli could be a magical miniature tree that allows your roots to go deep and your spirit to reach high. You get the idea. These kinds of meals are easy to create and can bring even more sparkle and magic into your life.

At Hogwarts School of Wizardry there's an expression: *Draco dormiens nunquam titillandus.* That's Latin for, "Never tickle a sleeping dragon." You could give each guest a feather for "dragon tickling." You might also want to create a wishing well or serve "wishing water" in large goblets. With each sip, your wishes come true. You can be as silly or as serious as you desire. You could even suggest your guests come in costume. Have fun with this. May your inner vistas be expanded even further as you invite more magic and mystery into your life!

Dine with Greek Gods

Transport yourself to Mount Olympus to share a meal with the Olympians. In Greek mythology, the major Gods all met on Mount Olympus, with the exception of Hades, who preferred to stay in the underworld. Creating a meal that honors this rich tradition can be fun and rewarding. Place grape vines and bunches of grapes, real or imitation, in the center of the table. Have lots of flickering candles on flowing white tablecloths. Drink from beautiful crystal chalices. Make it feel heavenly. The decor for this meal can be as simple or as elaborate as you choose. Make your dining space feel welcoming for Zeus, Athena, Apollo, Aphrodite, Demeter, Ares, and Poseidon, as well as others.

A delicious red wine is an added plus to this meal. If you don't drink alcohol, serve grape or pomegranate juice. Ancient Greek food was much simpler than it is today. Tomatoes, peppers, and potatoes didn't arrive in Greece until the 16th century. Some of their main staples were fish, boar, chicken, deer, goat, rabbit, cabbage, carrots, cucumbers, squash, lettuce, beans, apples, figs, grapes, olives, pomegranates, plums, and, of course, wine. However, Gods can eat anything they like.

As a suggestion, have your guests "adopt" a God or Goddess and come dressed as that divinity. They can even do a bit of research and come "in

character." What would Aphrodite say to Ares? And what sweet nothings might Zeus whisper to Hera? Alternatively, everyone can come dressed in togas, and the meal can be so good that it elevates everything to the status of the Gods. And of course, you can eat with your hands . . . or you can even feed each other.

Dine with God and Goddess

Choose a God or a celestial deity and dedicate a meal to him or her. Simply invoking the God or Goddess for the meal will help bring those qualities to the table.

If you decide to invite Ganesh, the Indian God who's the Remover of Obstacles, for example, you might want to have an Indian theme. Make a feast of curries, paneer, chapatti, chutneys, and dal . . . and create a feast for the eyes, nose, and mouth with spicy Indian food. If an Indian God really were coming for dinner, what food would you serve? How would you serve it?

Consider decorating with bright madras or paisley prints, or maybe even use a sari as a runner down the center of the table with a statue or photograph of Ganesh. Light some incense. Use vibrant colors like hot pinks, reds, oranges, and greens. Don't be afraid to go over the top. Ganesh is the elephant God and not afraid of living large. You might want to play Indian music or ragas, and have your guests dress in saris. After dinner, everyone could write down any blockages they desire to overcome, and these could be burned in the fireplace. Alternatively, dance around the fire with the idea that Ganesh will help you overcome that obstacle.

When creating mythic meals, think bold. Your friends will love the experience. This is a great way to try new foods, share recipes, stretch your imagination, and even bring some Hollywood or Bollywood into your dining room.

There are many Gods and Goddesses from traditions as varied as that of Scandinavia and Egypt. Consider doing a bit of research to discover what energy you'd like to invite to dinner. Perhaps you're seeking the power and protection of Thor or maybe the motherly energy of Isis. The possibilities are endless.

TANDOORI CHICKEN

What better way to welcome Ganesh, Krishna, or any number of other Hindu gods to your table than with an Indian meal! They won't be able to stay away once they smell the captivating aroma of your Tandoori Chicken. Traditionally, this dish is made in a very hot clay oven called a "tandoor." Since most of us don't have access to such an oven, I've approximated by using a gas barbecue grill. As the chicken cooks, there will be lots of flare-ups and lots of smoke, but this is what gives it delicious flavor. However, it's very important that you start with a clean grill and that when you're finished, you clean the grill well and empty out grease or charred bits that may have accumulated. This will prevent any unwanted fires and flare-ups the next time you use the grill. Alternatively, you can sear the chicken under the broiler and then bake it in a hot oven. It will be good but will lack the flavor that comes from the smoke of the grill. To get the traditional red color, add food coloring to the marinade.

SERVES 4–6

2 Tbsp. tandoori spice blend*

1½ tsp. salt

10 cloves garlic, crushed

2 cups lowfat plain yogurt

1 whole chicken, cut into pieces, with skin on

TO SERVE:

Chopped cilantro

Plain yogurt

Mango chutney

*Tandoori spice blends are available in well-stocked grocery stores, natural food stores, and in some ethnic markets.

To make the marinade, in a large bowl, combine the tandoori spices with the salt and garlic to make a paste. Mix in the yogurt. Add the chicken and mix (I find that using my hands works best) until the chicken is completely coated. Cover with plastic wrap and marinate in the refrigerator overnight.

Heat your grill to high/medium-high. When the grill is hot, put the chicken pieces on the grate and sear each side about 5–10 minutes. You'll know when it's time to turn the chicken because it will no longer stick to the grill. Reduce the heat to medium-low, and cook the chicken covered for an additional 30–45 minutes. Keep an eye on it, and turn the pieces from time to time for even cooking. Generally, the breast meat will cook faster than the dark meat. Most likely, the skin will burn and maybe even stick to the grill, but that's okay. It's protecting the moist and tender meat inside, and the smoke from the burning skin is adding flavor to the meat as well.

Remove from the grill and serve sprinkled with chopped cilantro. Enjoy with plain yogurt and chutney.

INDIAN SPICED
ROASTED VEGETABLES

With most recipes I remember the thought process that led to their creation; this one, however, is a bit of a mystery. I don't remember ever cooking with whole cumin seeds before, and then one day, I tossed them with potatoes, cauliflower, and coconut oil, and this delicious dish was born. Perhaps, Spirit guided me . . .

This is an especially handy recipe for a large group, since the preparation is relatively quick and easy and then you get to stick it in the oven and practically forget about it for an hour. Your dinner guests, both human and gods, will enjoy the intoxicating spices.

SERVES 6

1 cauliflower, cut or broken into small bite-size pieces

1½ lb. gold potatoes (6–8 smallish), chopped into ½-inch cubes (skin on)

1 lb. sweet potato (1 large or 2 small), peeled and chopped into ½-inch cubes

¼ cup coconut oil

2 Tbsp. whole cumin seeds

1 tsp. sea salt

Preheat the oven to 450°F. Line two baking sheets with parchment paper.

Chop the cauliflower and gold potatoes. Peel and chop the sweet potato. Combine the vegetables and divide evenly between the two baking sheets.

Unless it's a very hot day, coconut oil is generally solid. I usually spoon it into a measuring cup and then pinch off bits to distribute among the vegetables. With clean hands, I massage the oil into the vegetables. Sprinkle the cumin seeds and salt over the vegetables and mix (with hands).

Roast until the vegetables are caramelized on the outside and soft and delicious on the inside, about 1 hour. Halfway through, stir them with a metal spatula, and rotate the sheets from top to bottom.

DIVINE DAL

(Curried Lentils)

Dal is a staple in most Indian households, and gods and goddesses are no exception.
They'll appreciate being welcomed to your home to enjoy some Indian comfort food.
A few years ago, I was preparing an Indian feast for a retreat, and just as I was starting my
dinner preparations, I discovered there weren't enough green lentils. I scoured the cupboards
and eventually found a bag of black beluga lentils, which I tossed into the pot. The result
was the best dal I'd ever made. One of the women dining with us that night had just spent
seven weeks traveling in India, and she said she preferred this to the ones she'd had on her trip.

If you don't have exactly the right ingredients for a recipe or the right tools,
go for it anyway! Use your intuition to find substitutes.
You may find that you create something even better than the original.

This dal is delicious served with brown basmati rice and Indian Spiced Roasted Vegetables
or Tandoori Chicken and is a welcome addition at any heavenly feast.

SERVES 6

1 cup black beluga lentils
(if you can't find them,
substitute French lentils)

2 cups green lentils (also
labeled simply as "lentils")

10 cups water

1 Tbsp. grated, peeled,
fresh ginger

2 Tbsp. curry powder

2 tsp. sea salt

2 cups frozen chopped
spinach

Wash and pick through the lentils. In a large pot, combine the lentils with the water, ginger, curry, and salt. Stir to combine. Bring to a boil. Reduce the temperature to maintain a gentle boil. Add the frozen spinach and continue to simmer until the water is completely absorbed, the lentils are soft, and all the ingredients have melded into a cohesive, thick stew, about 1 hour. Stir frequently. Garnish with chopped cilantro and enjoy with plain yogurt and chutney.

MYSTICAL MEALS:
Reveal Your Inner Magic

Magic is in the air, and a Mystical Meal can invite that energy into your home. Simply by dedicating your meal to opening etheric doors, you can transverse from this reality into another.

In our Western culture, we must see something before we believe in it. But what if you must first believe in something to truly experience it? The realm of Avalon, Shambala, and even Atlantis must first be believed in and then—and only then—can you touch the magical. A mystical meal will allow you to gain entrance into these realms. Whether you believe there are otherworldly realms or not, you can still create their innate energy at your dining table. In the same way that people travel long distances to theme parks and the world's seven wonders to experience life out of the ordinary, you can do this simply with a little creative imagination.

Entering Avalon

You might believe the Arthurian stories are just legends with no truth to them. Or you might believe, as many do, that these stories are based on a very real dimension that can be accessed through an etheric gateway. If you believe there's indeed a magical Isle of Avalon, where fairies live and where the sacred sword Excalibur was forged, and where the land—of its own accord—produces bountiful harvests . . . then you're not alone. To invite this sparkling energy into your life, no matter your beliefs, create a mystical Avalon evening.

What mystical foods might have been eaten in Avalon? Choose foods that somehow feel magical or choose the foods that were eaten in ancient times in

the British Isles, such as smoked fish, roasted meats, mead, beer, peasant bread, or a hearty soup made of things such as cabbage, onions, leeks, parsley, and spinach. Of course, if you're having a mystical Avalon meal, make any kind of food you desire and name it in alignment with the Avalon energy. For example, the soup might have been stirred by the horn of a unicorn and might be named Horn Swirled Stew.

If you have a round table, you might decorate in a manner that ignites a feeling of the Knights of the Round Table. Place large, flickering pillar candles everywhere. You can either go for a castle-like feeling of King Arthur and his knights, or you can go for the feeling of the Isle of Avalon, hidden in the mists, and use gauze to drape around

the table to give it a mysterious feeling. You can even rent a fog machine or use dry ice to give the dining area the feeling of ethereal mists.

Play music such a Gregorian chants or soft, ambient flute music that elicits images of fairies, knights, Merlin, and Excalibur. The table in the Arthurian legend was said to be round because it represented equality and the fact that no one was above another. The knights adhered to a code of honor and embraced the qualities of honor, courage, valor, truth, and loyalty. This would be an excellent meal to make sure each person's opinion was given equal weight in the conversation. (This is great for a family with young children, because it reinforces the idea that all opinions are valid.) It can sometimes feel strange to act a part, but after the initial discomfort, usually people rise to the occasion and have fun. Consider having your guests arrive at your meal dressed as knights or ladies of the court, or dressed as people who live on the mystical Island of Avalon.

Entering Shambala

Ancient Tibetan texts speak of a mystical kingdom that guards the secret wisdom of the Universe. It's hidden high in the Himalayas, beyond the reach of ordinary beings. It can appear and disappear and can only be seen by those with a pure heart. Some say there's an ancient text that says, "When the barbarians who might devastate the planet think that no one can conquer them, the icy mists of Shambala will appear." The Dalai Lama says that "It is not a physical place that you can find anywhere on earth." In ancient writings, both Tibetan and Indian, with deep reverence it's mentioned as a place that exists and can be entered while in a profound, meditative state. Like Avalon (and other mystical realms), Shambala exists in another dimension, and yet with deep stillness (or with magical meals), you can touch the energy of these sacred places.

It's said that in Shambala there's an abundance of fruits, and everything grows with great vibrancy. The energy of Shambala is rarefied, so this might be an excellent time to have light fare, perhaps even raw food. Fresh greens and vegetables might be a good starting point for this meal. This would be a great meal to decorate your table with lavish bowls of fruit and an abundance of flowers. You may also want to consider statues or photos of Buddha to pull forth this powerful energy. Aim for a dining space that feels holy and mystical but also alive and vibrant.

As Shambala is a place that cannot be entered without deep meditation, you might consider meditating before this special meal with the intent of opening the gateway to this hallowed realm. You might also want to consider meditating after the meal, maybe in front of a warm fire or candle, and writing about your experience of the meal and the messages you received. The depth of the wisdom that comes may surprise you.

Since the time of Plato, we've been regaled with stories about the lost continent of Atlantis, a mystical realm where arcane skills were highly developed, and the people knew how to harness energy fields and use crystals for transportation and materializations. To activate this powerful energy in your life, consider having a meal dedicated to the energy of Atlantis.

Atlantis is believed to be a mythical island that sank into the ocean. Water was very important to the Atlantians, and anything that speaks of the sea is an excellent way to harness some of this magic. Both your food and decor can evoke the feeling of the powerful and mysterious sea. Imagine a buffet of scallops served in shells and sumptuous bowls of seaweed salad. Or perhaps grilled snapper or other fish served on a bed of spinach (that could resemble seaweed) or peeled tiny potatoes that could look like large pearls.

To design your space to welcome the energy of Atlantis, consider a cascade

of seashells in the center of the table or a blue tablecloth that tumbles to the floor like crashing waves. If you have any crystals, you can use them to energize the plates, or you can use them in the table setting. Include music that's light and uplifting, such as flute music or even a recording of crystal singing bowls. Have fun with the sea theme, and at the same time, know that you're indeed inviting the articulate, crystalline magic of Atlantis into your home.

STORYBOOK MEALS:
Spark Your Imagination

Make-believe, fairy tales, and magical realms are not just for children. Life is full of magic and mystery. A storybook-themed meal can be a great way to call forth this joyful energy.

In past times, long before printed books and, of course, before radio, television, or the Internet, people told stories around the fire while they ate. While friends and family dined, the storyteller regaled them with tales of morality or adventure and heroism. Some were based on real events, such as a retelling of a great hunt, and some were wild stories of fantasy. But the binding weave between all these yarns through history was that these stories made mealtimes an adventure and brought families together. In many ways, we've replaced the flickering light of the tribal fire with the flickering light of television as the place where the family gathers to eat and be entertained, but there is less engagement with each other. However, you can change that. Bring glee and delight to your dining experience with a storybook meal, and activate your imagination in the process.

Breakfast with Goldilocks and the Three Bears

Children love making mealtimes an adventure. Storybook meals can be especially fun and helpful if you have a picky eater. Consider creating a *Goldilocks and the Three Bears* Breakfast. And what will you serve? Porridge, of course! You could first serve a bowlful of cold porridge, and, of course, the kids will yell, "Too cold!" And then some hot (of course, not too hot) porridge, and the kids yell, "Too hot!" And finally you can serve a bowl of "just right" porridge, and the kids yell, "Just right!" These kinds of meals will create memories that last a lifetime. Creating such a meal need not take a lot of time to be fun and meaningful. All you need is an ounce of imagination.

Aladdin's Feast

Aladdin and his magic lamp have ignited enchantment for years. To create Aladdin's feast, consider dining on Middle Eastern food while listening to Arabian music. Sit on the floor while you eat, and imagine the carpet you're sitting on is magic, and it will fly you and your dinner companions wherever you'd like to go. Alternatively, you could drape fabric on the walls to give the feeling of eating in a Saharan desert tent. Play around with this, and have fun activating your childlike sense of wonder. Maybe your guests come dressed as their favorite character from the Aladdin story. Think flowing robes and belly-dancing outfits. Perhaps during the meal, someone might read *Aladdin* or some of the other stories from the book of popular Arabian tales *One Thousand and One Nights*.

ALADDIN'S
QUINOA TABBOULEH

In the Middle East, tabbouleh is typically made with bulgur, which is a form of wheat. However, I prefer quinoa's lighter texture. Quinoa (pronounced "keen-wa") is an ancient grain from South America, grown primarily in Peru and Bolivia. This tiny grain is a powerhouse among grains. It's naturally gluten-free, and it's high in fiber and has all eight essential amino acids. When combined with the cucumber, tomato, and herbs in this salad, it's a knockout and a delicious accompaniment to an Aladdin-themed gathering.

SERVES 4-6

1 cup uncooked quinoa

2 Roma tomatoes, seeded and diced

1 cucumber, peeled, seeded, and diced

1 cup chopped parsley (flat-leaf or curly, though I prefer flat-leaf)

¼ cup chopped fresh mint

2 Tbsp. lemon juice (from one lemon)

¼ cup extra-virgin olive oil

2 cloves garlic, crushed

1 tsp. sea salt

To cook the quinoa, bring a medium-sized pot of salted water to a boil. Add the quinoa and boil for 10–12 minutes. The quinoa is done when it's soft but still has a little white dot in the middle. Cook the quinoa in the same way that you'd cook pasta, and you'll always have delicious results.

When the quinoa is cooked, strain it into a fine mesh colander. Rinse with cool water and drain completely.

While the quinoa is cooking, you can prepare the rest of the salad. Dice the tomato and put it in a medium-sized bowl. Peel the cucumber. Cut it in half lengthwise, and scrape out the seeds with a small spoon. Dice the cucumber and add it to the bowl. Chop the mint and parsley, and combine with the vegetables. Dress with lemon juice, olive oil, garlic, and salt. Toss with the cooked quinoa.

Allow the tabbouleh to sit for 30 minutes before serving to allow the flavors time to marry.

Romeo and Juliet's Tryst

Imagine a romantic, candlelit meal in which you and your love pretend you're meeting surreptitiously. Perhaps you pass secret notes to one another by hiding them under the dishes or read passages from Shakespeare's play to each other.

Romeo and Juliet is set during the Renaissance in northern Italy. This was an opulent era of elegance and manners, and the arts were held in high esteem. Consider decorating your dining room as though it were a banquet room found in the home of the Montagues or Capulets, or maybe you prefer to imagine your tryst taking place in a quiet and secluded part of town or even somewhere in nature.

You can make this meal as elaborate or as simple as you wish. The meal could consist of modern Italian food, or you could take it a step further and research traditional dishes found in northern Italy during the Renaissance. You may also want to consider playing period music during the meal. Enjoy the process of activating your imagination and taking yourself on a trip through time.

In addition to these themes, you may also want to consider storybook meals, such as *The Little Mermaid, Snow White and the Seven Dwarfs, Sleeping Beauty, Rapunzel, Alice's Adventures in Wonderland, Peter Pan, Pinocchio, The Frog Prince,* and many more.

As we've seen in this chapter, it's possible to travel through time and space to experience other cultures, time periods, and even magical worlds from the comfort of your own dining room. By engaging all of the senses and creating mysterious, sensual, mythical, and mystical meals, you can create experiences that will not only be remembered for a lifetime but also will open the portal into mystical realms, which will in no small way expand your spiritual consciousness by connecting you more deeply with all life, great and small, near and far, past and present.

A good meal that expands consciousness and opens the gateway to transformative life experience can be as simple or as outrageous as you desire. As you've seen, lasting memories and powerful results need not take inordinate amounts of time or effort. The stronger your intention, the more potent the experience. Legendary Meals are created with love and passion; however, it never hurts to start with ingredients that were grown, raised, and prepared with care and attention. The following chapter provides an overview of some of the issues and questions you might be faced with at the grocery store as you shop for your epic feasts. May your Legendary Meals be delicious, transformative, and healthy!

MORE THAN MEETS THE EYE

ORGANIC, FREE RANGE,
LOCAL, SUSTAINABLE . . .
OH MY!

Legendary and transformative meals are created
by the love and intention you put into making them,
but as a Mystic Chef, you also understand the deeper
energy of your food and the importance of choosing
well. We're at a pivotal time in history. There's more
choice and diversity of food than ever before. History's
healthiest, tastiest, and highest quality foods are
available to us today, but at the same time, we also
have some of the unhealthiest, most nutrient-poor,
and lowest quality foods of all time lining the shelves
of our grocery stores.

Every day we're faced with decisions about the food we consume. Despite our best intentions, many of us can feel a bit overwhelmed when grocery shopping or eating out, since it takes such an effort to read labels, understand what's really in our food, and cut through all the conflicting opinions about healthy eating. Before the 1950s, food was food, and most of it was grown locally on family farms. Since the advent of the factory-farm system and prepackaged and processed foods, it's harder to know where our food comes from and what's really in it. Nearly everyone has a theory about what's the healthiest and tastiest way to live, but hardly anyone agrees.

Despite the best of intentions, it's possible to become somewhat evangelical once we've bought into a certain belief system about food. There can be a tendency to think about our food choices so much that we forget what's at the heart of a good meal. It's about breaking bread with others, nourishing our body and spirit, and enjoying the sensuous pleasures of being human. To eat well is to eat good food—food that is grown, raised, and prepared with love and care—and enjoy the experience one bite at a time.

This section provides an overview of some of the most common food issues today and includes a brief discussion of some of the pros and cons of such choices. This is intended as an introduction and quick reference; however, for a more in-depth discussion, it's recommended that you consider reading literature devoted to these individual issues.

SUPERMARKET SWEEP

Take a tour of a supermarket, and what do you find? The aisles are jam-packed with eye-catching products, colorful boxes, and a host of other things meant to lure you in with their bright logos and slogans, filled with supposed health benefits. Processed foods are some of the worst culprits. Even the unhealthiest treats are often sold with the promise of vitamins and minerals. A recent study of breakfast cereals by the Environmental Working Group discovered that many of the most popular cereals have 40 percent and 50 percent sugar by weight, and a few have *as much sugar as a Hostess Twinkie*. Yet we feed these to our children daily and believe we're feeding them well because they're enriched with vitamins and minerals.

Healthy food advocates suggest shopping the perimeter of a grocery store. Generally, fresh fruits and vegetables are found against one wall and the meats, fish, and dairy are found against the others. The middle of the store tends to be reserved for more processed foods. Who doesn't enjoy these treats from time to time? We certainly do! They are, however, designed to make us want them, and they tantalize us with their colors, flavors, and nifty packaging. Additionally, many of these "foods" have excitotoxins, such as monosodium glutamate

(sometimes a hidden ingredient in so-called natural flavors), hydrolyzed protein, and aspartic acid. These are substances added to food and beverages to supposedly enhance flavor, but unfortunately, they can overstimulate neurons and in severe cases, even cause varying degrees of brain damage.

In addition to lacking substance, processed foods are also often devoid of soul. These foods are created in large factories, primarily by machine. They lack the care that a farmer on a small piece of land puts into the things he raises or the love that your grandmother puts into her pies. Of course, a Mystic Chef can enhance the vibratory rate of any food; however, the fresher and more natural it is to begin with, the more vitality and life force it will have.

WHOLE FOODS

Many people today hear the words *whole foods* and immediately think of the chain of grocery stores, Whole Foods. While the grocery chain does sell whole foods, their products are not limited to them. Whole foods are edibles—fruits, vegetables, grains, and animal products—that are in their most natural state. Sometimes "whole foods" and "organic" are used interchangeably; however, not all whole foods are organic, and not all organic foods are whole foods. (Ideally, you should consider eating whole foods that are also organic.) Whole foods are unprocessed, unrefined, and whole in every possible way. For instance, grains that contain the bran, endosperm, and germ are whole foods. Whole milk, unless it's been homogenized, is a whole food, as is most anything you'll find in the produce aisle or meat and fish section of your local grocery.

To eat whole foods is to eat the way your ancestors ate. Eating foods as they were intended by nature connects you more closely with Mother Earth and with the Divine creation of living things. Plus, whole foods are the healthiest and most nutrient-rich foods available. When it comes to fueling your body, you get the most "bang for your buck" when eating whole foods because the

calories they contain are ones that your body can most easily turn into energy. Nature is pretty remarkable. She creates these little packages of goodness that contain the exact nutrients we need to get the most out of that food.

NATURE'S PACKAGE

Consider an apple for a moment. A delicious, crisp, and juicy apple eaten as an afternoon snack can tide you over until mealtime. It contains a little jolt of natural sugar, juice to quench your thirst, and a number of vitamins and minerals. The fiber—that's what gives it shape and texture—fills you up, in addition to being healthful and disease fighting. Now imagine drying that apple. It's still, in many ways, a whole food; however, you don't get full nearly as quickly. This is what happens with many processed foods. They're full of calories (and other undesirables), but just don't fill us up as quickly as a whole food would. Nature, in her Divine wisdom, creates whole foods so that every part works together to help us get the most out of that food and keep us from overeating. One nutrient helps break down another, while another nutrient makes assimilation of another that much easier.

Our modern lives are busy and full of hustle and bustle. It's not always practical to grow your own food or shop exclusively at farmers' markets to get the freshest and most wholesome foods available; however, whole foods are some of the easiest "health foods" to find. Most grocery stores and even some convenience stores offer fresh fruits and vegetables, and some even have whole grains, nuts, meats, and dairy. They might not be organic or sustainably raised, but it's a great way to start. When you have a choice, choosing whole foods is almost always a healthy option.

OUR CHANGING FOOD VOCABULARY

*Try organic food . . .
or as your grandparents called it,
"Food."*

— FROM A MAGNET ON
MEADOW'S REFRIGERATOR

Organic, free range, local, and *sustainable* are fairly new words in our collective food vocabulary. Up until a few generations ago, the majority of food available was all of these things. It wasn't until the advent of mechanized farm machinery, refrigerated trucking, and large corporations taking over small family-run farms that these words entered the vernacular and came to be understood as something new, different, expensive, and in many instances, reserved for the elite. There's a lot to think about at the grocery store these days. Even those who are well versed in food issues can have a difficult time, for instance, choosing which eggs to buy. It can be overwhelming to figure out whether you want organic, free range, cage-free, pastured, or some combination of these.

There was an agricultural boom when chemical fertilizers, pesticides, and herbicides hit the market. Crops grew to Herculean proportions, and the markets were flooded with large, beautiful products. A few years later, however, we started to see the toll that this so-called green revolution was taking not just on the health of farms and wildlife but also on ourselves. Bigger, brighter, and blemish-free fruits and vegetables doesn't necessarily mean tastier and healthier. As a result of overuse, fields would be barren if it weren't for the continual addition of increased amounts of chemical fertilizers. We've learned to take from the land, but we've forgotten how to give back. A farmer who works on a small scale in harmony with nature's natural cycles knows that the healthier and more loved the soil is, the healthier the plants. Many believe, including us, the way to do this is not with chemicals but with age-old, time-tested farming practices that are sustainable and more spiritually fulfilling as well.

What Does Organic Mean?

The term *organic* for fruits and vegetables means that they were grown without the use of chemical fertilizers, herbicides, or pesticides. For meat,

organic generally means that the animal's feed was grown organically and not supplemented with prophylactic antibiotics and other pharmaceuticals. In order to yield good crops, an organic farmer must constantly add nutrients back into the soil. Much of what an organic farmer uses to fertilize his fields is repurposed from other parts of the farm, such as compost, manure, bone meal, and blood meal. Many organic farmers also practice something called "crop rotation." By not planting the same things in the same fields year after year, they're not depleting the soil of nutrients, which makes this system more sustainable. Cover crops are also used extensively to fix the soil with nutrients and keep the ground moister, which means less water is wasted. A small-scale organic farm strives to be in harmonious balance, in tune with the seasons and the cycle of life, death, and rebirth.

The farming industry and our food systems are growing and changing rapidly, and so is their marketing. While there are many guidelines and rules to follow to be a certified organic farm, there is much less standardization when it comes to some of the other terms. *Free range, cage-free, grass fed,* and *natural* are just a few of the words used to described poultry, beef, and eggs. Meat and poultry labeled free range or grass fed are the best options both for flavor and health, as well as for the welfare of the animal, but this varies from farm to farm. Cage-free means that poultry are not confined to cages; unfortunately, they're often still tightly packed together in large warehouses. At this time, there aren't clear standards on the term *natural,* and it's used at will to market products to consumers.

Wild vs. Farm-Raised Fish

There are similar considerations on the fish aisle, too. Wild or farm-raised? We're told fish is healthy, but how do you know what to choose? Commercial fishing can be potentially devastating to sea habitats, and much of what is caught by dragging football field–sized nets along the sea floor is immediately discarded, resulting in waste and unnecessary destruction. Additionally, widespread pollution of our watersheds and oceans has resulted in harmful toxins, like mercury, dioxins, and PCBs (polychlorinated biphenyls) in our wild

fish supply. However, there's a growing movement to adopt more sustainable fishing practices, and many groups are working to clean up the oceans, so there's hope that we can again find harmony and balance.

You may think that fish farming would be a more environmentally friendly alternative, but there are also challenges with this system. Fish farms can actually add to sea-life depletion: It can take about three kilograms

(6.6 pounds) of wild-caught fish to produce one kilogram (2.2 pounds) of farm-raised. This is because they're often fed fishmeal made from wild fish. Additionally, they're given antibiotics and dyes to make them grow big and add color that they'd normally derive from their native diet. Added to that, farmed fish, despite being fattier, usually have lower quantities of omega-3 fatty acids that make fish a recommended food in the first place.

Feeling a bit overwhelmed? We are, too! To learn which are the best fish to consume, the Monterey Bay Aquarium publishes an invaluable reference called *Seafood Watch* that lists the most sustainable choices for fish and shellfish.

Meat-Free: Vegetarian, Vegan, and Raw

There's a great line in the movie *My Big Fat Greek Wedding* that illustrates some of the confusion, especially in traditional meat-eating cultures, about vegetarianism. The main character, a young Greek woman, brings her vegetarian, non-Greek boyfriend to a family dinner. At first, the aunt is perplexed that the boyfriend doesn't eat meat, but then she responds, "That's okay. He can have lamb."

People choose to eliminate meat from their diet for various reasons, ranging from health, animal welfare, environmental concerns, and even taste. There's research and scientific data that support both eating animal products and not eating them. The evidence of plant-based diets curing disease and helping the planet is pretty staggering; however, there are also doctors and nutritionists who have sound evidence that a return to traditional food systems, which include eating meat, whole dairy products, and fermented foods can be equally good for us.

In addition to vegetarian (no meat, poultry, or fish) and vegan (no animal products of any kind), raw is an increasingly popular diet, which consists of plant-based foods not heated beyond 115°F. There are some forms of raw diets that consist of eating raw meats, dairy, and eggs, but this is less common. Contrary to popular belief, "raw foodists" don't nibble on carrots and graze on celery all day. It's actually a complex cuisine that relies on fermentation and dehydration for many of its dishes. Nuts, seeds, and grains are soaked and sprouted before consumption in order to activate the life force within them and make them easier to digest. There has been significant research and empirical evidence to support that a raw diet can potentially cure ailments and ward off some diseases.

Whether you're a vegetarian, a vegan, a raw foodist, or an omnivore, enjoy what you eat, and believe in your choices. There's a lot to be said for faith and belief. If you've chosen a plant-based diet because you believe it's the best choice for you and your path toward optimal health, then go for it and have faith in what you're doing. If, on the other hand, you choose to eat meat because you enjoy the taste and believe your body thrives on it, then sally forth with the intention that you're nourishing your body the best way you know how.

Animal rights issues and the environmental impact of the large-scale farming of crops and food animals are important issues to think about when making your food choices; however, they're beyond the scope of this book. If you seek to explore these topics further, there are many interesting documentaries and books on these subjects to consider.

The Local Food Movement

One of the best ways to ensure you're getting wholesome, sustainably raised produce and meat is to procure it locally. When you eat food grown, raised, or prepared locally, you're absorbing the life-force energy of your community, and you're supporting your neighbors. As an added bonus, eating locally lessens your carbon footprint. Many foods are flown and trucked long distances, which means not only that many fossil fuels are being burned to get that steak, broccoli, or banana to your plate, but also it means that foods are picked and harvested before they reach their peak to make them travel better. And, unfortunately, they lack vitality and life force as a result.

Generally, to buy local is to shop for what's in season. Additionally, local products are most easily obtained at farmers' markets, which means you're most likely buying directly from the farmers and can spend time tuning in to their energy. Many small farms can't afford to go through the lengthy organic certification process even if they use many organic and sustainable practices, so when you can, talk to the vendors to learn more about how they grow their produce.

It's also likely that these local, small-scale farmers are using heirloom seeds rather than hybrids or genetically modified seeds (GMOs). Heirloom varieties of fruits and vegetables and heritage breeds of livestock are those that have been around for generations, which have been bred for flavor and nutrition rather than shelf life or in the case of animals, rapid growth. Unfortunately, with the consolidation of our food systems, much of this knowledge and biodiversity is being lost. The best way to help save our plant and animal species is, believe it or not, to eat. It seems counterintuitive to save the heritage Bourbon Red turkey, for instance, by eating it; however, the more consumer demand there is, the more they'll continue to be raised.

Organic and local foods tend to have a higher vibratory rate and are more nourishing. As a caveat, however, junk foods that are labeled as organic are still junk food. Organic cookies, though made with higher-quality products, are still cookies. It can be easy to fall into the trap that organic means healthy. It can, but not always.

Frankenfoods: Genetically Modified Foods

Ever since people started raising food, farmers have selected seeds from the best plants and bred animals from their best stock. Selection for desirable characteristics is not a new idea; however, the scientific modification of plant genes in modern times is new, and it's potentially scary. It may have started with good intentions—to find ways to more easily feed our rapidly growing population and make foods more presentable and less perishable in the marketplace. And from a financial standpoint, businesses found they could make more money: they sold seeds that resist weed killer so they could sell more herbicides, and hormones that could make cows grow fast and produce more milk, fruits, and vegetables that traveled well so there was less waste and, therefore, more profit.

The problem is that once we start altering the genetic makeup of organisms, *we potentially irrevocably change all living things on this planet.* Genetically modified organisms (GMOs) are plants whose genetic makeup has been changed in order to give them certain characteristics. Genes are either deleted or inserted to create certain traits. For instance, there was a type of genetically modified (GM) tomato called FlavrSavr, in which the enzyme involved in ripening was suppressed so that the tomato would ripen without softening. This meant that it could be more easily transported to market, and fewer tomatoes would spoil. It also means that consumers are buying scientific experiments rather than one of nature's creations. What's natural and delicious about that? Additionally, pesticides are now being engineered directly into crops, so there will be less need for using overhead sprays. However, it also means there's a high probability we're consuming increased levels of these chemicals. And it makes you wonder what all this does to us on a spiritual level. Because though it may look like a tomato, for instance, genetically it's something different.

The topic of GMOs is hotly debated. At this point, there aren't regulations on labeling in the United States, which means that unless you grow your own fruits and vegetables, purchase organic foods, or buy your produce at your local farmers' market, you're most likely eating GMOs. What's especially frightening is that even if you do grow your own, you're still not guaranteed that you're getting seeds free of genetic modifications. Sadly, it's becoming increasingly difficult to protect stocks of pure organic and GM-free seeds. Once these mutations reach all corners of our food supply, there will be no turning back.

THE FUTURE?

We're at a crossroads. The environmental, ecological, and nutritional toll of GMOs is yet to be fully written. If we act now and refuse to purchase anything that's been genetically modified, require GM products to be labeled, and lobby our senators and representatives, perhaps we have a chance of protecting our children from an unknown and precarious future. When GMOs were first created, most developed nations around the world refused to provide these products to their citizens until proven safe. The United States, however, took a different approach and decided to market these products until proven *not* safe. Although GMOs are being created in the U.S. and being sold to unsuspecting American consumers, this is a global issue. As a result of our changing food systems and GM foods, biodiversity is dwindling daily. Once we lose the seeds and animal breeds of our ancestors, they will be gone forever.

The full extent of the toll that GMOs will take on our health and well-being has yet to be discovered, though the current statistics on the role they're playing in our epidemic of food allergies is pretty staggering. A complete examination of this issue is beyond the scope of this book, but if you're interested in your own health and well-being and that of the planet, we urge you to do what you can to stop GMOs before it's too late. As the saying goes, Rome wasn't built in a day. No step is too small.

FOOD ALLERGIES AND INTOLERANCES AND GMOS

As we discussed in the first chapter, many food allergies have their root in past lives, but others are the direct result of our physical environment and changing food systems. In recent years, food allergies and intolerances have become rampant. A food allergy is when the body's immune system recognizes a food protein as something foreign and goes on the attack (often resulting in a rash or anaphylaxis, which is the restriction of the airway). An intolerance or sensitivity is when the body has difficulty absorbing or digesting a given food. The most common reactions are often localized to the gut; however, intolerances, like allergies, can impair your autoimmune system and adversely affect your health in multiple ways.

In the past 20 or so years, the instances of allergic reactions to food have dramatically increased. Wheat, soy, eggs, dairy, shellfish, tree nuts, and peanuts are among some of the most common food allergens. This coincides with the introduction of GM foods into our food system, and many researchers believe there's a connection. For instance, soon after GM soy was introduced in the United Kingdom, researchers at the York Laboratory found that soy allergies increased by 50 percent, and peanut allergies skyrocketed by 41 percent, since the allergens in soy are similar to those in peanuts.

Genetic modification of a food often involves adding or mutating the proteins found in a given plant. Since a food allergy is defined by the body's immune system attacking what it sees as a new or foreign protein, it makes sense our bodies would be on high alert. Supporters of GM foods say that though allergic reactions to these new proteins are possible, concerns about widespread allergic reactions are not justified. The U.S., however, has opted not to run human clinical trials, which means that only time will tell how harmful their effects will be, since allergies and intolerances often develop over time.

What Can Be Done?

Though working through past-life issues can help relieve some food allergies and intolerances, eating organic products, which by definition cannot contain GMOs, may help to prevent others from developing.

Recent increase in knowledge about food sensitivities means that doctors are more readily diagnosing them, and grocery stores are now lining their shelves with products that are free of some of the most common culprits. If they're not already, encourage your local market to stock allergy-friendly foods and carry an array of organic products. You might also consider raising awareness about the effects of agribusiness, factoring farming, and processed foods on our health and their possible links to allergies and intolerances. If you think you may have a food allergy or sensitivity, avoid the possible allergens, and consult your health-care professional to devise a diet and regimen suited to your individual needs.

SUPPLEMENTS:
Vitamins, Minerals, and Herbs

As a result of our consolidated food systems, food is not as nutritious today as it was in 1940 or even in 1975. We would have to eat ten tomatoes today in order to get the same amount of copper that our grandparents would have in one tomato. Factory-farm eggs are now so lacking in carotenes—the pigments that make eggs yellow—that laying hens are actually given feed that will dye their yolks. According to a study of roasting chickens at the London Metropolitan University in 2004, today they contain twice as much fat, a third more calories, and a third less protein than in 1940. The United States Department of Agriculture (USDA) recognizes the importance of consuming the recommended daily allowance of vitamins and minerals to improve our health and ward off illness, yet continues to let the overall quality of our food decline.

So what can you do? Unfortunately, organic food is not completely immune to all of this—according to a study in the United Kingdom, organic chickens today are more nutritious than factory-raised chickens, but they're still less nutritious than those raised in 1940. However, by eating organic you avoid GMOs and potential chemicals and toxins. Additionally, you're buying food with more nutrition and vitality. And the best part, it usually tastes better!

Until we succeed in turning back the clock to the point when we can buy food that contains all the nutrition we need, you may want to supplement your diet with vitamins, herbs, and minerals. Talk with your health-care provider to discover which ones most suit your individual needs. Or try experimenting with your cooking to add flavorful fresh herbs to favorite dishes or add ground flax seeds to your daily oatmeal, for example. There are many clever ways to increase the nutrition of standby recipes and boost their restorative and healing powers.

You may also want to consider planting an herb and vegetable garden. There's no such thing as a garden too small. It could be just a basil plant on your kitchen counter, a couple of strawberry plants in a pot on your balcony, or a few tomato plants on your patio, but you'll know that those plants were infused with your love and energy and contain higher levels of vital vitamins and minerals. Or if you have space and live in a rural area or a town or city with ordinances that allow for backyard chicken raising, why not raise a couple of laying hens and enjoy their beautiful, golden-yolked, nutrient-rich eggs. Happy eating!

ENJOY WHAT YOU EAT!

Knowledge of the politics of food and the important issues facing our current food supply can be daunting. It's important to make educated decisions about the foods you buy and the foods you consume, but fear and angst aren't

particularly healthy, nor fun either. Good nutrition is important, but eating well is also about joy and sharing communion with others. It's likely that you won't be able to buy everything organic or avoid GMOs all the time, and who remembers to take vitamins every day? We certainly don't! As a suggestion, consider making a pledge to yourself to do something today to bring more wholesome and vital foods into your kitchen. It could be as small as deciding to buy one organic or local product a week or writing a letter to a politician to ask them to create legislation that would require labeling of GM foods. Or maybe it's eating whole grains or opting for an apple instead of a candy bar. Whatever steps you take, do so with joy and passion. Good food is to be enjoyed.

A F T E R W O R D

Savor Your Life

We've so enjoyed reliving some of our favorite meals and sharing ancient and mystical traditions with you. It's been a delight journeying with you through vegetable gardens, grocery stores, and magical kitchens to create sacred feasts that nourish the mind, body, and soul. We hope that within these pages you've found some new recipes to add to your repertoire and have learned some techniques to raise the energy, vibration, and flavor in the foods you eat.

Whether you create a different legendary feast each week, say a simple grace before your meal, or grow your own food, your inner Mystic Chef has been awakened. The more you savor your food, the more you savor life. Here's to living life deliciously, one bite at a time!

With love,
Denise & Meadow

For more information, visit:

www.TheMysticCookbook.com

INDEX OF RECIPES

METRIC EQUIVALENT CHARTS

The recipes in this book use the standard United States method for measuring liquid and dry or solid ingredients (teaspoons, tablespoons, and cups). The following charts are provided to help cooks outside the U.S. successfully use these recipes. All equivalents are approximate.

Standard Cup	Fine Powder (e.g. flour)	Grain (e.g. rice)	Granular (e.g. sugar)	Liquid Solids (e.g. butter)	Liquid (e.g. milk)
1	140 g	150 g	190 g	200 g	240 ml
¾	105 g	113 g	143 g	150 g	180 ml
⅔	93 g	100 g	125 g	133 g	160 ml
½	70 g	75 g	95 g	100 g	120 ml
⅓	47 g	50 g	63 g	67 g	80 ml
¼	35 g	38 g	48 g	50 g	60 ml
⅛	18 g	19 g	24 g	25 g	30 ml

Useful Equivalents for Liquid Ingredients by Volume				
¼ tsp			1 ml	
½ tsp			2 ml	
1 tsp			5 ml	
3 tsp	1 tbsp		½ fl oz	15 ml	
	2 tbsp	⅛ cup	1 fl oz	30 ml	
	4 tbsp	¼ cup	2 fl oz	60 ml	
	5⅓ tbsp	⅓ cup	3 fl oz	80 ml	
	8 tbsp	½ cup	4 fl oz	120 ml	
	10⅔ tbsp	⅔ cup	5 fl oz	160 ml	
	12 tbsp	¾ cup	6 fl oz	180 ml	
	16 tbsp	1 cup	8 fl oz	240 ml	
	1 pt	2 cups	16 fl oz	480 ml	
	1 qt	4 cups	32 fl oz	960 ml	
			33 fl oz	1000 ml	1 l

Useful Equivalents for Dry Ingredients by Weight

(To convert ounces to grams, multiply the number of ounces by 30.)

1 oz	1/16 lb	30 g
4 oz	1/4 lb	120 g
8 oz	1/2 lb	240 g
12 oz	3/4 lb	360 g
16 oz	1 lb	480 g

Useful Equivalents for Cooking/Oven Temperatures

Process	Fahrenheit	Celsius	Gas Mark
Freeze Water	32° F	0° C	
Room Temperature	68° F	20° C	
Boil Water	212° F	100° C	
Bake	325° F	160° C	3
	350° F	180° C	4
	375° F	190° C	5
	400° F	200° C	6
	425° F	220° C	7
	450° F	230° C	8
Broil			Grill

Useful Equivalents for Length

(To convert inches to centimeters, multiply the number of inches by 2.5.)

1 in			2.5 cm	
6 in	1/2 ft		15 cm	
12 in	1 ft		30 cm	
36 in	3 ft	1 yd	90 cm	
40 in			100 cm	1 m

ACKNOWLEDGMENTS

With gratitude . . . to the amazing people we've shared meals with over the years . . . to David Linn, who fed us nourishing meals during our months of late nights and early mornings . . . to our fabulous editor Lisa Bernier, for her dedication and grace at every moment, even when we deluged her with urgent phone calls and e-mails. Under her adept eye, Lisa helped bring our words alive. We are so profoundly honored that she helped us give birth to this book . . . to the ever-wonderful Kate Olsen . . . to the intrepid Kathy Dannel Vitcak . . . to the splendid Maurica Zimmerman and Louis Zimmerman . . . to Jeff Marcove, trainer and chef extraordinaire . . . to the inspiring Samantha Barnes of Kitchen Kid . . . and to the remarkable Charles McStravick, who designed the cover and interior of this book, we are deeply grateful. He took our vision and made it sing! Just as a painting looks even better with the right frame and a meal sparkles even more with the right table setting, Charles turned our words into a feast for the eyes and created a delicious blending of Spirit and joy!

Thank you all!

Denise Linn, the best-selling author of 17 books, including *Sacred Space* and *Soul Coaching®,* is an international lecturer, a healer, and a popular radio talk-show host. She is the founder of the International Institute of Soul Coaching®, a professional certification course, as well as the founder of Interior Alignment®. Denise holds seminars on five continents and appears on television and radio programs throughout the world.

Website: **www.DeniseLinn.com**

Meadow Linn received her bachelor's degree from Williams College and her master's degree from Columbia University. She is the co-author of *Quest* and writes a food and lifestyle column for a Seattle newspaper.

Website: **www.MeadowLinn.com**

HAY HOUSE TITLES OF RELATED INTEREST

YOU CAN HEAL YOUR LIFE, the movie, starring Louise L. Hay & Friends
(available as a 1-DVD program and an expanded 2-DVD set)
Watch the trailer at: **www.LouiseHayMovie.com**

THE SHIFT, the movie,
starring Dr. Wayne W. Dyer
(available as a 1-DVD program and an expanded 2-DVD set)
Watch the trailer at: **www.DyerMovie.com**

THE ART OF RAW LIVING FOOD:
Heal Yourself and the Planet with Eco-delicious Cuisine, by Doreen Virtue and Jenny Ross

GREEN MADE EASY:
The Everyday Guide for Transitioning to a Green Lifestyle, by Chris Prelitz

LOVE, GOD, AND THE ART OF FRENCH COOKING,
by James F. Twyman

THE MAP:
Finding the Magic and Meaning in the Story of Your Life, by Colette Baron-Reid

MESSAGES FROM WATER AND THE UNIVERSE,
by Masaru Emoto

MINDFUL EATING,
by Miraval

NATURE'S SECRET MESSAGES:
Hidden in Plain Sight, by Elaine Wilkes

RAVENOUS:
A Food Lover's Journey from Obsession to Freedom, by Dayna Macy

All of the above are available at your local bookstore,
or may be ordered by contacting Hay House (see next page).

We hope you enjoyed this Hay House book.
If you'd like to receive our online catalog featuring additional
information on Hay House books and products, or if you'd like to
find out more about the Hay Foundation, please contact:

Hay House, Inc.
P.O. Box 5100, Carlsbad, CA 92018-5100
(760) 431-7695 or (800) 654-5126
(760) 431-6948 (fax) or (800) 650-5115 (fax)
www.hayhouse.com®
www.hayfoundation.org

Published and distributed in Australia by: Hay House Australia Pty. Ltd.,
18/36 Ralph St., Alexandria NSW 2015
Phone: 612-9669-4299 • *Fax:* 612-9669-4144 • www.hayhouse.com.au

Published and distributed in the United Kingdom by: Hay House UK, Ltd.,
292B Kensal Rd., London W10 5BE
Phone: 44-20-8962-1230 • *Fax:* 44-20-8962-1239 • www.hayhouse.co.uk

Published and distributed in the Republic of South Africa by: Hay House SA (Pty), Ltd.,
P.O. Box 990, Witkoppen 2068 • *Phone/Fax:* 27-11-467-8904 • www.hayhouse.co.za

Published in India by: Hay House Publishers India,
Muskaan Complex, Plot No. 3, B-2, Vasant Kunj, New Delhi 110 070
Phone: 91-11-4176-1620 • *Fax:* 91-11-4176-1630 • www.hayhouse.co.in

Distributed in Canada by: Raincoast,
9050 Shaughnessy St., Vancouver, B.C. V6P 6E5
Phone: (604) 323-7100 • *Fax:* (604) 323-2600 • www.raincoast.com

TAKE YOUR SOUL ON A VACATION

Visit **www.HealYourLife.com**® to regroup, recharge, and reconnect
with your own magnificence. Featuring blogs, mind-body-spirit news,
and life-changing wisdom from Louise Hay and friends.

Visit **www.HealYourLife.com** today!